MARS BECKONS

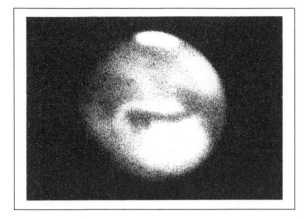

JOHN NOBLE WILFORD

MARS BECKONS

THE MYSTERIES, THE CHALLENGES, THE EXPECTATIONS OF OUR NEXT GREAT ADVENTURE IN SPACE

Alfred A. Knopf   New York   1990

THIS IS A BORZOI BOOK
PUBLISHED BY ALFRED A. KNOPF, INC.

A portion of this work was originally published in *Popular
Science*.

Grateful acknowledgment is made to Penguin Books Ltd. for
permission to reprint an excerpt from "Works and Days" by
Hesiod, from *Hesiod and Theognis*, translated by Dorothea
Wender (Penguin Classics, 1973). Copyright © 1973 by
Dorothea Wender. Reprinted by permission of Penguin
Books Ltd., London.

Library of Congress Cataloging-in-Publication Data
Wilford, John Noble.
Mars beckons : the mysteries, the challenges, the
expectations of our next great adventure in space / by
John Noble Wilford. — 1st ed.
p.   cm.
Includes bibliographical references.
ISBN 0-394-58359-0
1. Mars (Planet) 2. Life on other planets. 3. Mars
(Planet)—Exploration. I. Title.
QB641.W55 1990
523.4'3—dc20   89-43365   CIP

Manufactured in the United States of America
First Edition

To Frank Colella ·

CONTENTS

Color illustrations follow page 86.

MARS BECKONS

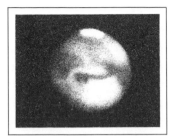

CHAPTER 1

THE ALLURE OF ANOTHER WORLD

A TURNING POINT in mankind's relationship to the universe came in the middle of the twentieth century. We ventured off the surface of Earth and beyond the atmosphere, initially sending only our machines and then accompanying them, creeping out into space in tight little orbits that kept us tied to the planet. We tiptoed to the Moon and hurried back. But the transformation had happened. We were leaving Earth for parts unknown, not merely trying to better understand our place in the cosmos but actually expanding the human presence in the solar system. In the middle of the twentieth century, we became spacefarers.

Only eight years after Yuri A. Gagarin became the first man to fly in space, circling Earth once on April 12, 1961, and seeing two sunrises in less than two hours, there were human footprints on the Moon. Between July 1969 and December 1972, twelve American astronauts tramped the lifeless dust of the Moon and looked back to see Earth as a sphere glistening blue and white in the eternal black void. From a dead world out in space our home planet never shone so beautiful and special.

Our spacecraft surrogates have extended human perception far beyond Earth and the Moon out to the edges of the Sun's family of planets. They have flown by and sent us glimpses of the parched and cratered wasteland of Mercury. They have orbited Venus, plunged through its dense, sulfurous atmosphere, and landed on its hellishly hot surface. They have visited Mars and sent home picture postcards from a world of volcanic peaks, yawning canyons, icy polar caps, and broad russet plains. Traversing the asteroid belt beyond Mars, they have cruised on and passed close to Jupiter, Saturn, Uranus, and Neptune; only Pluto, so distant and odd, has yet to be reconnoitered by spacecraft from Earth. These craft have nosed in for a close look at the celebrated Halley's comet, conducting the first examination into the icy core of that cosmic peacock. They have inspected many of the satellites in the gravitational embrace of the giant outer planets. Some are no more than specks of rock and chunks of ice, while others, like Io and Ganymede and Titan, are revealed as distinctive worlds worthy of further study. Out beyond the most distant planets, one of these durable little machines of human design, Pioneer 10, is approaching the outer boundary of the solar system, heading for interstellar space.

These voyages of exploration and discovery set our age apart from all others. Whatever else may be recorded about our time, we live in what should be known forever as the golden age of planetary exploration. Carl Sagan, the astronomer and writer, has said: "In all the history of mankind, there will be only one generation that will be first to explore the solar system, one generation for which, in childhood, the planets are distant and indistinct discs moving through the night sky, and for which, in old age, the planets are places, diverse new worlds in the course of exploration."

Sometimes the scientists guiding these planetary expeditions are overwhelmed by their good fortune. If he had been born fifty years earlier, Sagan has said, he would have missed out entirely on planetary exploration, which then would have been nothing more than "figments of the speculative imagination." Born fifty years later, alas, the preliminary reconnaissance of the solar system would have been completed before his time, and he would never have known the thrill of being at the beginning.

The excitement of being there, at the Jet Propulsion Laboratory in Pasadena, California, as the first pictures came from the surface of Mars on July 20, 1976, was not to be missed. The first panorama appeared ever so slowly, line by vertical line from the extreme left-hand side of the television monitor. The suspense was palpable. The lines finally added up to a section revealing a rock. A seemingly ordinary rock, a few inches across, but this was a rock on Mars. This was Martian. The laboratory hush was broken by gasps and then rousing cheers from the scientists. Abandoning all pretense of professional reserve—no waiting to analyze all the data, no counseling journalists to refrain from drawing incautious conclusions—these scientists cheered the first sight of a rock that happened to be in front of a man-made camera that had been plunked down on a plain of Mars.

Joy and relief overcame Thomas A. Mutch, a geologist and leader of the photo-interpretation team, as he was describing the Viking 1 spacecraft operations from the mission control room. "It's just incredible to see that Mars is really there!" he exclaimed. Mars was there, of course, but until this moment it had been a planet seen from afar, and now it could be touched, the tactile sense of it reinforcing the visual to excite wonder in the realization that not only was Mars there but we, our spacecraft, were there on Mars, too. Mars is like that: More than any other planet, it evokes an emotional response, even in scientists.

"I don't feel like talking," Mutch said hoarsely. After a while, others spoke, but not in the usual numbers, equations, and abstruse words of science. They spoke of colors, in everyday words. When the first pictures were processed for color, scientists grew excited over the most obvious and least surprising revelation: The soil of Mars really was red—quite red. They also saw that the sky was not blue. Come to think of it, why should all skies be blue? Their surprise betrayed the terrestrial chauvinism that can afflict even the most knowledgeable scientists. No, the sky over Mars and Viking 1 in July 1976 was salmon pink.

Such electric moments of fulfillment and anticipation, the alternating currents of discovery, have been repeated many times in our spacefaring across the expanse of the solar system. A century ago, Thomas Henry Huxley, the eloquent champion of Darwinian natural history, said: "The known is finite, the unknown infinite; intellectually we stand on an islet in the midst of an illimitable ocean of inexplicability. Our business in every generation is to reclaim a little more land." Some of the land reclaimed by this generation, in this golden age of planetary exploration, is extraterrestrial. We are now spacefarers, our fantasy become reality, and our travels have only begun.

AS THE END of the century draws near, flight into space is an almost routine reality. Despite setbacks and tragedies—some of these dealing staggering blows to Americans and their sense of competence in spacefaring—it is no longer an extraordinary achievement just to power a machine to escape velocity, sending it into an orbit of Earth or on a trajectory to the planets. The days of striving to put an object into orbit just to prove it could be done belong to history. The days of choosing destinations simply because they are reachable are also behind us. The challenge now is not to demonstrate the power to go into space, a relatively straightforward exercise in technological prowess, but to make intelligent choices as to how the power will be used. These choices are constrained less by technology than by economics, politics, and our willingness to accept some failures as the price of success. In practical terms, this means that decisions will be dictated more and more by what we feel we can afford to do and by how we define the importance of space in the human future.

Decisions made, or deferred, in the next few years will be critical in determining the pace and direction and participants in this new phase of the space age. We are in the process of choosing future destinations for not only our machines but ourselves. Will we stay close to Earth? Will we build space stations to orbit Earth and serve science and defense, and voyage back and forth to them? Or will we expand on earlier achievements and venture farther out from our home planet? Will we return to the Moon, establishing more or less permanent human outposts? Will we go to Mars?

Perhaps the questions should be rephrased: Not will we but when will humans take longer strides beyond Earth? Nor is there doubt that someday those strides will take human beings to Mars. The two major spacefaring nations, the Soviet Union and the United States, acknowledge that an ultimate goal in the twenty-first century is human flight to Mars. But how soon in the next century? How vigorously should this goal be pursued? Surely it can be only a matter of time and commitment until humans are standing out there on Mars in response to an enduring fascination.

Mars tugs at the human imagination like no other planet. With a force mightier than gravity, it attracts the eye to its shimmering red presence in the clear night sky. It is like a glowing ember in a field of ethereal lights, projecting energy and promise. It inspires visions of an approachable world. The mind vaults to thoughts of what might have been (if Mars were a little closer to the warming Sun) and of what could be (if humans were one day to plant colonies there). Mysterious Mars, alluring Mars, fourth planet out from the Sun: so far away and yet, on a cosmic scale, so very near.

At its closest approach, Mars is less than 35 million miles from Earth—seven months of flying time for small unmanned craft, some seven to eleven months away for vehicles carrying people. The Moon, by contrast, is some 240,000 miles away—a mere three-day jaunt for the Apollo astronauts. Mars, with a diameter of approximately 4,200 miles, is little more than half the size of Earth. Yet Mars has always seemed larger and closer to those who have watched it with wonder and perplexity down through the centuries.

Long ago, presumably before the written word, people became aware of Mars as they first sought to make sense out of the heavens. They somehow assumed a connection, a relatedness, between events on Earth and in the sky. Looking into the sky day and night, season by season, year after year, they perceived a predictable pattern in the movements of the Sun, the Moon, and the stars. In this way, they learned to gauge the passage of time and to anticipate the onset of seasons. With an eye to the sky, they planted and harvested. As Hesiod, the early Greek poet, wrote:

> *When great Orion rises, set your slaves*
> *To winnowing Demeter's holy grain. . . .*
> *But when Orion and the Dog Star move*
> *Into the mid-sky, and Arcturus sees*
> *The rosy-fingered Dawn, then Perseus, pluck*
> *The clustered grapes, and bring your harvest home.*

An appreciation of the mystery and order of the sky marked the beginning of the first science, astronomy, in Mesopotamia more than 3,500 years ago.

Likewise, this was the beginning of the pseudoscience astrology. An enduring preoccupation of these ancient astronomers was a study of the seven most peripatetic objects: the Sun and the Moon, of course, and also those five wandering "stars" that we know today as Mercury, Venus, Mars, Jupiter, and Saturn. Observers noted that these wanderers kept to a narrow band in the sky, which they divided into twelve zones, each containing one distinctive constellation. Thus was conceived the twelve signs of the Zodiac, and to the Babylonians the position of any one of these wandering "stars" along the Zodiac was of vital importance, affecting the affairs of men. Soothsayers thereafter presumed to see in the orderly movements of the heavens omens by which they might predict the future.

These wanderers looked like stars but behaved in a different and seemingly capricious manner. They thus came to be called planets, from the Greek word *planetes*, meaning wanderer. And the movements of Mars seemed to be especially erratic. It moved relatively fast, but in apparent fits and starts. The Greek astronomer Hipparchus, in the second century B.C., recognized that Mars did not always move from west to east when seen against the fixed stars. Sometimes it moved in the opposite direction. This was a peculiar planet that bore watching.

The most alluring aspect of Mars was its distinctive color. The Viking scientists in 1976 were as one with their ancient colleagues in their fascination with the planet's redness. Red evoked imagery of blood and fire, and from the time of the Sumerians, the planet was seen as a symbol of war. In the earliest written records of the Babylonians 3,000 years ago, the planet is called Nergal. It was the abode of Nergal, their god of death and pestilence. "When Nergal is dim, it is lucky; when bright, unlucky," according to a surviving Babylonian cuneiform text, reflecting the early place of Mars in the astrological firmament.

Other cultures also identified the planet with gods of war and warriors. To the Persians it was Pahlavani Siphir, and to the Egyptians, Harmakhis. The Norse called it Tui (the source of the English Tuesday). The ancient Greeks named the planet Ares, for their god of battle. Later, the Romans adopted the equivalent name Mars, by which the Red Planet is known to us today. Even astronomers, acknowledging the planet's traditional repute, employ in their learned papers a symbol for Mars (♂) that represents a shield and a spear, the ancient implements of war.

The sanguinary reputation of Mars flourished in the Middle Ages of Europe, when astrology was ascendant. In a fifteenth-century German manuscript, the astrological properties of Mars are described with authority:

> Mars rules catastrophes and war, it is master of the daylight hours of Tuesday and the hours of darkness on Friday, its element is the fire, its metal is iron, its gems jasper and hematite. Its qualities are warm and dry, it rules the color red, the liver, the blood vessels, the kidneys and the gallbladder as well as the left ear. Being of choleric temper it especially rules males between the ages of 42 and 57.

Two centuries later, in 1609, Johannes Kepler, the great German astronomer, applied the scientific mind to Mars and finally solved the

In the pre-Copernican universe, as illustrated in Peter Apian's Cosmographia *(1539), the earth was at the center.*

riddle of the planet's apparently capricious motions. In so doing, Kepler established the laws of planetary motion, which explain the movement of the planets around the Sun, set the stage for Newton's theory of universal gravitation later that century, and are fundamental to tracking the planets and plotting the course of spacecraft across the solar system.

A man of social ineptitude whose clothes were often food-stained, Kepler had tried to earn a living casting horoscopes. Yet, in time, he would be described by Immanuel Kant as "the most acute thinker ever born." His genius began to emerge in 1600 when he went to work for Tycho Brahe, the greatest observational astronomer of that day. The imperious Tycho had told the young Kepler in so many words: If you are so smart, here, figure out the apparent retrograde motions of Mars. To Tycho, who was not much of a theoretician, this was an impossible problem; to Kepler, it was a challenge. Using Tycho's meticulous observational records, Kepler addressed the problem as a confirmed Copernican and recognized that Mars's backward motion was an illusion.

Nicolaus Copernicus, the sixteenth-century Polish scholar, had demolished the ancient concept of an Earth-centered universe. In the fourth century B.C., the Greek geometer Eudoxus surmised that the firmament was more than an inverted bowl through which the fires of the gods flickered. He imagined instead that the stars and planets were fastened to a series of concentric spheres, with a motionless Earth in the center. But observations simply did not fit the theory. Aristarchus of Samos, 1,700 years before Copernicus, put the Sun at the center, but he was largely ignored. The geocentric concept of Ptolemy, a scholar at Alexandria in the second century after Christ, became conventional wisdom for more than a millennium. In an elaboration of Eudoxus' idea, Ptolemy enmeshed the heavenly bodies in a labyrinth of epicycles, wheels within wheels. Earth stood at the center, surrounded by eight spheres that carried the Moon, the Sun, the stars, and the five planets. The outermost sphere held the so-called fixed stars. Each planet moved on a smaller circle attached to its respective sphere, an arrangement that seemed to account for the complex but predictable motions of the Sun, the Moon, and the planets and still leave Earth where it surely belonged, at the center. The estimated width of Ptolemy's universe, with the stars fixed at the boundary, was no larger than Earth's orbit.

Tycho Brahe, the sixteenth-century Danish astronomer, in his observatory.

So firm was Ptolemy's grip on scholars that they chose to ignore mounting observational evidence disputing the concept, or else invented tortured explanations. Finally, in 1543, Copernicus replaced the decrepit Ptolemaic system with a whole new theory. He argued that the Sun was stationary and the planets, including Earth, revolved around it in what he called the "ballet of the planets." This was a daring concept, putting Copernicus and subsequent astronomers at odds with both the venerated Ptolemy and the Christian Church. But it still left unexplained the strange motions of Mars.

This was where Kepler came in, and the result of his thinking far exceeded an understanding of the Mars problem. Yes, the planets revolve around the Sun, he reasoned, but at different distances and hence different velocities. Mercury, the closest to the Sun, completes an orbit every 88 days; Saturn, the farthest out of the planets known to Kepler, takes 29½ years. Earth completes a solar orbit in 365¼ days, an Earth year. Mars, farther out, takes 687 days to orbit the Sun, a Mars year thus being about six weeks short of two Earth years. As Kepler figured it, the faster-moving Earth overtakes and passes the slower Mars in the course of their separate orbits. To an observer on Earth, though, Mars appears to be slowing down, stopping, and then reversing course.

Kepler had not completely solved the problem. Copernicus had assumed that the orbits of the planets were circular. He might challenge Ptolemy, but not Aristotle. "The shape of the heavens is necessarily spherical," Aristotle affirmed. "The circle is primary among figures." Geometric perfection the circle may be, but in testing seventy possible circular orbits for Mars, Kepler was unable to find a single one that fit the planet's known motions. A Mars in a circular orbit would be showing up in positions somewhat different from those observed by Tycho, and Kepler had no reason to suspect the accuracy of the Danish astronomer on such a matter. At last, his voluminous calculations led him to the solution. Kepler wrote a friend: "The orbit of the planet is a perfect ellipse."

The apparently erratic motions of Mars, Kepler concluded, were a consequence of the relative motions of both Earth and Mars in their elliptical orbits around the Sun. His report in 1609 was entitled *Astronomia nova* and subtitled *De motibus stellae Martis,* or *On the motion of Mars.* So Kepler arrived at his first two laws of planetary motion via

Johannes Kepler, the sixteenth-century astronomer.
(Bettmann Archive)

Mars. The orbit of Mars is an ellipse, an elongated circle, along which
the planet moves with nonuniform but predictable motion, and it
must be the same for the other planets. So Kepler promulgated his
first law: The orbit of each planet is an ellipse with the Sun as one
of the foci, the other being a theoretical point in space. (To support
his contention that planets move in elliptical orbits, it has recently
been revealed, Kepler may have been guilty of fabricating data. He
argued that the motions of Mars served as an independent confirma-
tion of the theory. In fact, he seems to have derived the data by
calculations based on the theory itself—an unscientific approach to a
correct insight.) His second law: All the planets speed up in their
orbits as they approach the Sun and slow down proportionally as they
get farther away. Later, Kepler formulated a third law showing the
mathematical relationship between the cube of a planet's distance

from the Sun and the square of its orbital period. Applying this formula, he was able to calculate the relative distances between the Sun and the individual planets even though the actual distances were not yet known with any accuracy.

Mars thus had a key role in dismantling the Earth-centered conceit of the ancients and in opening the modern era of astronomy. Its allure became scientific as well as mythic. For in the same year, 1609, that Kepler was reporting his findings, Galileo pointed the first telescope into the sky, and Mars came into increasingly sharper focus.

ASTRONOMERS began seeing that Mars was the planet most like Earth, a revelation that would fix forever its place in the human imagination.

Galileo Galilei brought the heavens closer to us when he first peered through an "optick stick" at the Moon and the planets. Focusing on Jupiter, he found it was accompanied by several small satellites that orbited around it. The discovery confirmed Copernican theory. It showed that everything did not orbit around Earth as Ptolemy had assumed. Glimpsing the objects orbiting Jupiter was like gazing upon the larger solar system from some elevated perspective. But Galileo had little luck with Mars. When he looked at the Red Planet through a telescope the next year, 1610, he seemed to learn little more than that it "is not perfectly round." The observations of a Neapolitan named Francesco Fontana were no more enlightening; his drawing, made in 1646, showed one dominant surface feature, a large black dot, which was later attributed to an imperfection in his telescope.

As telescopes improved, astronomers began to glimpse the striking similarities between Earth and Mars. In 1659, the Dutch astronomer Christiaan Huygens, using lenses more finely ground and polished, noticed that a dark marking, roughly triangular in shape, appeared regularly on the disc of Mars. The area was what we now call Syrtis Major, the most conspicuous of the Martian surface features as seen through telescopes. By tracking reappearances of the feature, he determined that Mars, like Earth, rotated on its axis and that the length of the Martian day must be close "to 24 terrestrial hours." The exact value is now known to be 24 hours 37 minutes 22 seconds. (To avoid confusion with a terrestrial day, scientists have taken to calling the slightly longer Mars day a "sol.")

The Italian astronomer Giovanni D. Cassini not only was the first to report sighting white polar caps on Mars but also had a hand in making the first fairly accurate calculation of the planet's distance from Earth. In 1672, Cassini (who the next year would become a French subject and change his name to Jean Dominique Cassini) and Jean Richer first measured the distance to the Sun by means of a clever experiment. At a time when the Sun, Earth, and Mars formed a straight line, Cassini at the Paris Observatory determined the angular position of Mars at its highest point in the sky, while Richer was making the same observations some 4,000 miles away, at Cayenne, on the northeast coast of South America. Lines drawn from both places to Mars made a small angle of about three-thousandths of a degree. With that triangulation information they were able to calculate the distance from Earth to Mars as about 50 million miles. The Earth-Sun distance could then be determined by employing Kepler's third law. Cassini and Richer figured that distance at 87 million miles, which was not far off the correct value, now known to be about 93 million miles.

In the next century, William Herschel, a German émigré in England, turned his attention to Mars. He had discovered the first of the outer planets that had been unknown to the ancients—Uranus. In observing Mars, Herschel made careful studies of the tilt of Mars's axis. Earth is tilted at an angle of 23½ degrees to its axis of rotation, which accounts for the seasons (summer comes to the hemisphere pointing more toward the Sun). Herschel found that the tilt of Mars is almost identical—23.98 degrees. So it was learned that Mars has four seasons, much like Earth. But with a year lasting almost two Earth years, the Martian seasons are twice as long.

Like Cassini and other earlier astronomers, Herschel could make out white patches over the polar regions of Mars. In 1784, he correctly concluded that these were ice caps and he noted that they seemed to change in size and shape with the seasons. He also observed that Mars "has a considerable but moderate atmosphere" and that some of the dark areas on the surface are probably seas. Four seasons, polar ice, open seas, a roughly 24-hour day—Herschel was wrong on only one count (the seas), but he felt justified in concluding that the inhabitants of Mars "probably enjoy a situation in many respects similar to our own."

The idea of Martians was not a radical proposition in the eighteenth century. Ever since early telescopic observations showed the nearby planets to be solid worlds and not simply lights in the sky, many learned people were prepared to believe in the existence of life there. As early as 1686, Bernard de Fontenelle had reasoned: "The earth swarms with inhabitants. Why then should nature, which is fruitful to an excess here, be so very barren in the rest of the planets?"

Huygens sacrificed none of his respectability as an astronomer by writing a book in which he speculated on what inhabitants of the planets would be like. The eminent Kant thought that "those planets that are not inhabited now, will be at some time in the future." He went so far as to categorize the likely physical and moral condition of these beings: "In fact, the two planets Earth and Mars are the middle links of the planetary system, and it may be suspected with fair probability of their inhabitants that they stand in the center between the extremes as regards physiology as well as regards morals." Similarly, Johann Elert Bode, the eighteenth-century astronomer best known for Bode's Law (each planet is roughly twice as far from the Sun as the previous one), contended that the same mathematical proportions held for the spirituality of their inhabitants. By Bode's reckoning, Martians, being on the fourth planet from the Sun, were considerably more spiritual than the people of Earth. Benjamin Franklin, writing in his *Poor Richard's Almanack* of 1749, stated: "It is the opinion of all the modern philosophers and mathematicians, that the planets are habitable worlds." In the early nineteenth century, the German mathematician Karl Friedrich Gauss assumed that the inhabitants of Mars were intelligent. It was said that he proposed growing a vast wheat field in Siberia in the form of a right triangle, surrounded by pine trees, which could be seen from far away. This would demonstrate to the Martians that we on Earth not only existed but also were intelligent enough to understand mathematics.

A century ago, the discovery of Martians seemed imminent. Some astronomers gazed on Mars and professed to see signs of a canal-building civilization fallen on hard times. Before long, belligerent Martians escaping their desiccated planet haunted our literature. In our time, spacecraft with electronic eyes have traveled to Mars and dispelled any lingering fears, or hopes, of Martians. They discovered instead a world more dynamic than the Moon and more hospitable than Venus or any other known planet. They discovered a world beckoning to be explored.

Now, we could be on the eve of a new and more ambitious phase of Mars exploration. The Soviet Union is taking steps to lead the way, with bold plans to reconnoiter the planet's surface with cameras, balloons, and remote-controlled roving vehicles. Soviet space officials hope that by the end of the 1990s one of their craft will rocket back to Earth with a sample of Martian soil. The United States has similar plans, but no firm commitment beyond a modest Mars-orbiting mission to be launched in 1992.

This time, moreover, the long-term objective is not so much to search for life as to carry life to Mars. Human travel to the planet could begin as early as the year 2010. More important than the timing is the question: Will these first travelers to the beckoning world be Russians or Americans—or Russians and Americans, and perhaps Europeans and Japanese?

Mars, though demythologized and investigated from far and near, is once again challenging the human imagination and intelligence.

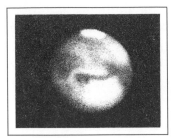

CHAPTER 2

LOWELL'S MARS

ONE MAN, ABOVE all others, is identified with Mars. The planet possessed him. He observed its changing face assiduously and convinced himself that this was an abode of intelligent life. His pronouncements, so authoritative and specific, excited the Mars mania that swept the world at the end of the nineteenth century, and the Martian of the human imagination was, by and large, the creation of his passion. Even today, no scientist can contemplate Mars without acknowledging some debt to this man, or without accepting the burden his legacy has imposed on subsequent Mars studies. He was Percival Lowell.

Lowell was a Boston Brahmin through and through, scion of wealth and privilege. His family was memorialized in Massachusetts town names, Lowell and Lawrence, and was the subject of the wheeze about the Lowells talking only to the Cabots and the Cabots talking only to God. His mother, Katharine Bigelow Lawrence, was the daughter of Abbott Lawrence, a minister to Britain. His father, Augustus Lowell, was descended from early Massachusetts colonists. The families had amassed fortunes in textiles, finance, and landholdings. A first cousin of his father was James Russell Lowell, the abolitionist and man of letters. Percival's younger brother, Abbott

Lawrence Lowell, was president of Harvard University from 1909 to 1933. His youngest sister, Amy, was the cigar-smoking avant-garde poet.

Young Percival did not start out to be an astronomer, but neither was he inclined to settle into a staid Boston-bound life. He graduated from Harvard in 1876 with distinction in mathematics, an interest in the classics, and a facility for languages. After a year traveling through Europe, sampling the continental delights and even trying for a piece of the action in the Serbo-Turkish War, he did what was expected of a young Brahmin: He entered the family business. In a few years, though, even wealthier and feeling he had fulfilled family obligations, he set out for more exotic horizons. He sailed for Japan in 1883 to pursue the life of an Oriental scholar, diplomat, and man of the world.

For a decade in Asia, Lowell was anything but the idle dilettante. He applied himself with enthusiasm and industry to the study of Japan's people, customs, and language. He served on a special diplomatic mission from Korea to Washington and took part in writing a new Japanese constitution. Out of these experiences and studies he wrote four books, the best known of which was *The Soul of the Far East*. Some critics saw in his observations a Westerner's condescension toward Oriental "backwardness." But Lowell could point the finger of irony at his own kind. He was struck by the similarities between the ancestor worship of the Japanese and his own patrician Bostonians. Like the Japanese, he noted, the Brahmins "make themselves objectionable by preferring their immediate relatives to all less connected companions, and cling to their cousins so closely that affection often culminates in matrimony, nature's remonstrances notwithstanding." Moreover, Lafcadio Hearn said the "splendid, godlike" book *The Soul of the Far East* inspired his own travels and masterly writing. An envious Hearn once wrote to a friend: "If I had Lowell's genius and Lowell's independence, how happy I should be. He can go where he likes, see what he likes, write what he likes and make beautiful books."

When Lowell tired of the Far East, he returned to the United States in 1893 and took up a new enthusiasm on an even more exotic horizon. He was responding to the lure of Mars.

With an especially favorable opportunity to view Mars due toward the end of 1894, Lowell resolved to build his own observatory and make the planet the new focus of his energies. Astronomy had been a fascination of his in childhood and at Harvard, and in recent years he seemed to revive that interest. On his previous trip to Japan he had taken along a 6-inch telescope, saying that he planned to write a book on the philosophy of the cosmos. His mind, it seemed, was already taking flight. In one of his books on Japan he had written:

> Gulliver's travels may turn out truer than we think. Could we traverse the inter-planetary ocean of ether, we might eventually find in Jupiter the land of Lilliput or in Ceres some old-time country of the Brobdingnagians. For men constituted muscularly like ourselves would have to be proportionally small in the big planet and big in the small one. Still stranger things may exist around other suns. In those bright particular stars—which the little girl thought pinholes in the dark canopy of the sky to let the glory beyond shine through—we are finding conditions of existence like yet unlike those we already know. To our groping speculations of the night they almost seem, as we gaze on them in their twinkling, to be winking us a sort of comprehension.

At the time, as well, Lowell followed avidly the writings of astronomers concerning discoveries of possible canals on the surface of Mars. The most influential of these astronomers was Giovanni Schiaparelli, whose observations in 1877 generated a rush of excited interest in the planet. Schiaparelli and Lowell—the names would become inextricably linked in the history of Mars studies.

THE SUMMER OF 1877 had been propitious for observing Mars. Every 26 months the slower-moving Mars comes especially close to Earth, creating the most favorable opportunity for observations—or, in the space age, for travel to the planet. Sometimes these opportunities are better than others. Because of the large ellipticity of the Martian orbit, the distance between Mars and Earth at the closest approach of opposition (when Mars is on the opposite side of Earth from the Sun) varies from as near as 35 million miles to as far as 63 million. The closest of these oppositions occurs approximately every 15 years, and 1877 was one of those choice viewing times.

Among the astronomers taking advantage of the opportunity was Giovanni Virginio Schiaparelli, director of the Milan Observatory and a scientist highly esteemed, particularly for his research concerning meteors and comets. (The name may be more familiar outside scientific circles because of its association with high fashion; the astronomer was the uncle of the celebrated Paris couturiere.) While examining Mars with a relatively small 8-inch telescope, Schiaparelli saw faint linear markings across the disc. Earlier observers had glimpsed some such streaks, but nothing as prominent and widespread as those Schiaparelli described seeing. His drawings of Mars showed the dark areas, which some took to be seas, connected by an extensive network of long, straight lines. Schiaparelli called the lines *canali*.

In Italian, the primary meaning of *canali* is "channels" or "grooves," which is presumably what Schiaparelli intended in the initial announcement of his discovery. He said that they "may be designated as *canali* although we do not yet know what they are." But the word can also mean "canals," which is how it usually was

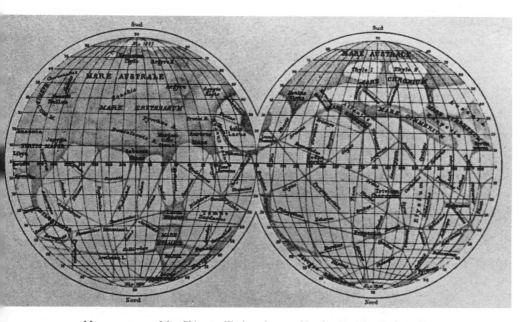

Mars as mapped by Shiaparelli, based upon his observations during six oppositions from 1877 to 1888; he observed canals, shown here as narrow stripes.

translated. The difference in meanings had tremendous theoretical implications.

"The whole hypothesis was right there in the translation," Carl Sagan has said. "Somebody saw canals on Mars. Well, what does that mean? Well, canal—everybody knows what a canal is. How do you get a canal? Somebody builds it. Well, then there are builders of canals on Mars."

It may be no coincidence that the Martian canals inspired extravagant speculation at a time when canal building on Earth was a reigning symbol of the Age of Progress. The Suez Canal was completed in 1869, and the first efforts to breach Central America at Nicaragua or Panama were being promoted. To cut through miles of land and join two seas, to mold imperfect nature to suit man—in the nineteenth-century way of thinking this was surely how intelligent beings met challenges, whether on Earth or on Mars.

Schiaparelli seemed to be of two minds about the markings. Of the canal-builders interpretation he once remarked: "I am very careful not to combat this suggestion, which contains nothing impossible." But he would not encourage speculation. At another time, Schiaparelli elaborated on observations suggesting to him that the snows and ice of the Martian north pole were associated with the canals. When snows are melting with the change of season, the breadth of the canals increases and temporary seas appear, he noted, and in the winter the canals diminish and some of the seas disappear. But he saw a thoroughly natural explanation for the canals. "It is not necessary to suppose them to be the work of intelligent beings," he wrote in 1893, "and notwithstanding the almost geometrical appearance of all of their system, we are now inclined to believe them to be produced by the evolution of the planet, just as on the earth we have the English Channel and the Channel of Mozambique."

His cautionary words had little effect. Those who wanted to believe in a system of water canals on Mars, built by intelligent beings, were not to be discouraged.

Yet most of his colleagues in astronomy, the audience he wanted to impress, were not prepared to believe the canals actually existed until they could duplicate the sightings. No one else seemed to be seeing what Schiaparelli said he saw. But he was unmoved: "I am absolutely certain of what I have observed." His report in 1882 in a French astronomical journal summarized the observations of Mars:

There are on this planet, traversing the continents, long dark lines which may be designated as *canali,* although we do not know what they are. Those lines run from one to another of the somber spots that are regarded as seas, and form, over the lighter, or continental, regions a well-defined network. Their arrangement appears to be invariable and permanent. . . . This is not all. In certain seasons these canals become double. This phenomenon seems to appear at a determinate epoch, and to be produced simultaneously over the entire surface of the planet's continents. . . . There is nothing analogous in terrestrial geography. Everything indicates that here there is an organization special to the planet Mars, probably connected with the course of its seasons.

One of the few prominent astronomers to come to Schiaparelli's support initially was Camille Flammarion, who produced an annual French journal of astronomy. In the 1882 edition, while most astronomers reserved judgment, he endorsed Schiaparelli's drawings of Martian canals. Flammarion went further to revive ideas of an inhabited Mars, declaring with a flourish in 1892:

The considerable variations observed in the network of waterways testify that this planet is the seat of an energetic vitality. These movements seem to us to take place silently because of the great distances separating us; but while we quietly observe these continents and seas slowly carried across our vision by the planet's axial rotation and wonder on which of these shores life would be most pleasant to live, there might be at the same time thunderstorms, volcanoes, tempests, social upheavals and all kinds of struggle for life. . . . Yet we may hope that, because the world of Mars is older than ours, mankind there will be more advanced and wiser.

According to a theory widely accepted at the time, the solar system was created in distinct steps. As the cosmic dust cloud rotated faster and faster, the center grew denser and became the Sun, much larger then than it is now. The Sun's faster rotation at that time created an equatorial bulge, and this mass was eventually thrown out to the distance of Neptune and contracted into the sphere that is that planet. Subsequent solar equatorial bulges were tossed off one by one, forming the other planets in sequence from the outer ones progressing inward. Thus Mars had to be older than Earth, and must represent an advanced state of development. Glimpsing Mars, in this view, was glimpsing some future era of Earth.

It was not until 1886 that two French astronomers at Nice became the first to confirm Schiaparelli's observations. They detected many features that appeared to be double lines, and their positions agreed with the Italian's map. Others still could not make out these features, even with more powerful telescopes, and they remained skeptical.

But no astronomer could be indifferent to Mars. As Flammarion remarked to Schiaparelli: "Your observations have made Mars the most interesting point for us in the entire heavens." Charles A. Young, an astronomer at Princeton University, said: "Probably there is no astronomical subject concerning which opposite opinions are so positively and even passionately held." Professional astronomers, who used to disdain the study of planetary markings as work more fit for amateurs, devoted more and more of their time to trying to find out what was going on on Mars. Reports of canal sightings became more common.

WHILE OTHERS may have had their doubts, Percival Lowell became a true believer. Indeed, the explanation most often advanced for Lowell's return home from the Orient is that he wanted to complete the provocative work of Schiaparelli, whose eyesight was beginning to fail. However, in *The Extraterrestrial Life Debate: The Idea of a Plurality of Worlds from Kant to Lowell,* published in 1986, Michael J. Crowe, a University of Notre Dame scholar, pointed out that this could not have been the case. In 1893, Schiaparelli had not realized, let alone revealed, that his eyesight was impaired. So we may never know exactly what prompted Lowell's decision to make Mars his new life's work. Crowe also noted that a psychoanalytic interpretation has been raised. He cites a proposal by the psychiatrist Charles K. Hofling that Lowell's Martian work was "heavily influenced by unconscious forces, taking the final form of incompletely sublimated voyeuristic impulses [arising from] unresolved oedipal conflicts."

Be that as it may, Lowell plunged into his role as novice astronomer with characteristic vigor. His fortune and Harvard contacts also helped. At the suggestion of William H. Pickering, a Harvard astronomer, Lowell dispatched an assistant to the Arizona Territory to search out a place for the observatory in the clear mountain air. A site was selected on the edge of a mesa near Flagstaff, at an altitude of more than 7,000 feet and, as Lowell said, "far from the smoke of men." Lowell's "most important contribution to astronomy," writes Brian G. Marsden of the Harvard-Smithsonian Astrophysical Observatory, "was his realization that superior observational work can be conducted only where atmospheric conditions are superior." As Lowell himself frequently said, observatories should be situated "where they may see rather than be seen." This was no trivial contribution, as practicing astronomers will attest, but to the public Lowell made his astronomical mark with Mars.

Although Harvard backed off from agreeing to a joint venture with the "egoistic and unreasonable" Lowell, as a university official described him, other accommodations were made. Pickering and his assistant, Andrew Ellicott Douglass, were given leaves to work with him, and one of the Harvard telescopes was leased to him. Construction proceeded swiftly, abetted by Lowell's long purse. Astronomers began gazing into the sky at the Lowell Observatory in April 1894, a few weeks before Mars was to show itself high and clear.

The high mesa near Flagstaff where Lowell established his observatory was, in his romantic way of looking at things, a "fitting portal to communion with another world." There the erstwhile Oriental scholar, working with Pickering and Douglass, studied Mars night after night in the summer and fall of 1894. No one ever looked at a planet through a telescope with more excited anticipation. Lowell described seeing two dazzling lights flash from the Martian polar cap. It was the glint of sunlight reflected off the ice, he concluded, for once resisting the impulse to claim some new evidence for Martians. "But though no intelligence lay behind the action of these lights," he said, "they were none the less startling for being Nature's own flashlights across one hundred millions of miles of space."

The Mars Lowell saw did not fail him. "Over a geography not unakin to the Earth's," he wrote, he viewed "a mesh of lines and dots like a lady's veil." His sketch maps prepared during the opposition showed 184 canals, more than twice as many as Schiaparelli had described. As early as July, according to William Graves Hoyt, in his history *Lowell and Mars*, the Bostonian had proceeded to formalize his

Percival Lowell observing the sky through a 24-inch refractor telescope. (Lowell Observatory)

thinking into "a full-blown scientific theory." The canals were real, and the work of intelligent beings.

Lowell's announcements found an eager popular audience. People seemed to want to believe in Martians. Telescope sales soared, and backyard observers reported detecting light signals from the planet. One newspaper published the claim that certain dark markings on the planet's surface spelled the words "The Almighty" in Hebrew, though another paper reacted to one of Lowell's pronouncements with wry skepticism: "A yen to a kopeck the doctor had a dark brown taste the morning after this happened." In lectures and magazine

articles, Lowell spread the news of his discovery and his interpretation of its meaning. In 1895, after all the sightings from the opposition
were completed, he published a popular book, entitled simply *Mars*.
His writing style had lost none of the vividness that had characterized
his earlier works about the Far East. He was clearly on personal,
sympathetic terms with the planet, writing:

> . . . we have before us the spectacle of a world relatively well on
> in years, a world much older than the earth. To so much about his
> age Mars bears evidence in his face. He shows unmistakable signs
> of being old. Advancing planetary years have left their mark legi-
> bly there. His continents are all smoothed down; his oceans have
> all dried up. . . . If once he had a chaotic youth, it has long since
> passed away. Although called after the most turbulent of the gods,
> he is at the present time, whatever he may have been once, one of
> the most peaceable of the heavenly host. His name is a sad misno-
> mer; indeed the ancients seem to have been singularly unfortunate
> in their choice of planetary cognomens. With Mars so peaceful,
> Jupiter so young, and Venus bashfully draped in cloud, the plan-
> ets' names accord but ill with their temperaments.

Many elements of Lowell's theory were not original, but no one
ever argued them more forcefully, and with each subsequent opposition of Mars and Earth he introduced more evidence seeming to
bolster his interpretation. "The broad physical conditions of the
planet," he wrote, "are not antagonistic to some form of life."

Take the polar caps that glisten white in the telescope. They were
fundamental to the theory. The caps were seen to expand in the
winter on Mars and shrink in the summer. Conversely, the dark areas
elsewhere on the planet, which appear to be green and so perhaps
were vegetation, recede in winter and spread in summer. With its
weak gravity the planet could not have more than a thin atmosphere
and little moisture. But when the polar ice melts in summer, water
is released to produce, in Lowell's phrase, the "wave of darkening"
that suggests the seasonal revival of life across the planet.

Now take those lines that etch the Martian surface, the canals. "It
is by the very presence of uniformity and precision that we suspect
things of artificiality," Lowell contended. "The better we see these

lines the more regular they look." He was certain he saw a pattern. "Instead of running anywhither, they join certain points to certain others, making thus, not a simple network, but one whose meshes connect centers directly with one another," he explained. "The intrinsic improbability of such a state of things arising from purely natural causes becomes evident on a moment's consideration." Since Mars was arid and its only apparent reservoir of water was in the frozen polar regions, it seemed reasonable to Lowell that "if beings of sufficient intelligence inhabited" the place, this was the global irrigation system they had developed for survival on an old and parched planet.

To be visible as far away as Earth, these lines had to be at least thirty miles wide, but Lowell was ready with a sensible explanation. We were not seeing the canals themselves, which would be of considerably less width, but the dark irrigated croplands bordering the waterways. Lowell saw the same circular dark spots at canal intersections that Pickering had interpreted earlier as lakes. Lowell thought they were more likely to be oases, centers of population surrounded by vegetation. They were, he said, "where we should expect to find the lands thus artificially fertilized, and behaving as such constructed oases should."

In his 1895 book, Lowell concluded: "All this, of course, may be a set of coincidences, signifying nothing; but the probability points the other way."

Most astronomers remained unconvinced. One famous scientist of the day is said to have received a message from the newspaper publisher William Randolph Hearst: "Is there life on Mars? Please cable one thousand words." The astronomer's reply to the publisher was: "Nobody knows"—written five hundred times. Most astronomers were not amused by this outsider Lowell and his pronouncements. They found it curious that Edward E. Barnard, one of their most eminent colleagues, had peered at Mars through a more powerful telescope at Mount Hamilton, in California, and could see no such markings that Lowell so confidently said were canals. "To save my soul, I can't believe in the canals as Schiaparelli [or Lowell] draws them," Barnard said. "I see details where some of his canals are but they are not straight lines at all."

How could this be? Canyons and valleys do stretch across the planet's landscape, but in nearly all cases their position and irregular lines rule them out as the canals Lowell thought he saw. His canals, it is now agreed, were optical illusions or products of the imagination. The human eye tends to arrange scattered, barely visible spots into a line, and this could explain why Schiaparelli and then Lowell saw their canals. The British astronomer Edward W. Maunder illustrated this in a simple experiment. On a large white sheet of paper he drew a random arrangement of dots, circles, ovals, straight lines, wavy lines, and irregular smudges. He hung the paper at the front of a classroom and asked students to draw what they saw. He then compared the drawings by students who were closest with those by students who were farther away. Try it. The drawings made from the greater distance are more apt to contain imaginary lines to connect objects that are entirely separate.

A few sightings of canals might be explained in this way. But hundreds of canals seen and meticulously charted over the course of years? Mark Twain, writing in another context, perhaps had the best explanation. "Partialities," he said, "often make people see more than really exists."

Astronomers were quick to suspect as much of Lowell. Edward S. Holden, director of Lick Observatory in California, wrote: "It is a point to be noted that the conclusions reached by Mr. Lowell at the end of his work agree remarkably with the facts he set out to prove before his observatory was established at all." In a review of Lowell's Mars, William Wallace Campbell, a respected astronomer at Lick and future president of the National Academy of Sciences, charged: "Mr. Lowell went direct from the lecture hall to his observatory in Arizona, and how well his observations established his pre-observational views is told in this book."

Simon Newcomb of the United States Naval Observatory was more charitable. While admiring Lowell's "energy and enthusiasm," he felt obliged to remind him "of the fact that the ablest and most experienced observers are liable to error when they attempt to delineate the features of a body 50 to 100 million miles away through such a disturbing medium as our atmosphere."

Lowell left the tumult behind and sailed for Europe at the end of 1895 to find a somewhat more agreeable reception. He dined in Paris with Flammarion, who could be counted on to give him a favorable audience. The French astronomer asserted that it had been "ascertained indubitably" that water from the poles flows through the Martian canals. His visit with Schiaparelli in Milan was also reassuring. The Italian, now showing Lowellian inclinations himself, had just written about the variations in darkening as seasonal vegetation on Mars. That this "may be due to intelligent beings," he wrote, "ought not to be rejected as an absurdity."

"EXTRATERRESTRIAL life," Lowell wrote in *Mars,* "does not necessarily mean extraterrestrial human life. Under changed conditions, life itself must take on other forms."

Except for this proviso, for the rest of his life Lowell made no significant concessions in his advocacy of a belief in intelligent beings on Mars. He acquired more powerful telescopes and expanded facilities on the mesa he now called Mars Hill. But he saw nothing on Mars or heard anything from the critics to make him change his mind. Lowell lived there in his "baronial mansion," a rambling house that commanded a spectacular view of the snowcapped San Francisco Peaks. He lived well but worked so hard, at the telescopes much of the night and writing by day, that he suffered a nervous breakdown in 1897. After taking the wealthy person's cure of foreign travel, in Bermuda and on the Riviera, he was back at the observatory charting Mars at the oppositions of 1901, 1903, and 1905. His ideas and arguments were elaborated with little change in two more books, *Mars and Its Canals* in 1906 and *Mars as the Abode of Life* in 1908. A longtime bachelor, he married in 1908 at the age of fifty-three.

The "changed conditions" that Lowell recognized as affecting life on Mars were the extreme thinness of the atmosphere and its aridity, which precluded the existence of "creatures resembling us." With such a tenuous atmosphere, the Martians would probably not have lungs. On this point Lowell had a ready and witty riposte. "But lungs," he said, "are not wedded to logic, as public speeches show, and there is nothing in the world or beyond it to prevent, so far as we know, a being with gills, for example, from being a most superior person. To argue that life of an order as high as our own, or higher, is impossible because of less air to breathe than that to which we are locally accustomed, is, as Flammarion happily expresses it, to argue not as a philosopher, but as a fish."

Lowell generally declined to be drawn into speculation about what the intelligent Martian beings would look and be like. His explanation for this reluctance had a self-righteous tone. Although in the same context he would assert that life on Mars "is the only rational deduction" from current observations, he added: "For just as it is unscientific to deny observations because we fear the seemingly startling conclusions to which they commit us, so it is not the province of science to speculate where observation is wanting, however interesting and even useful such speculation may be."

But a few supporters managed to outdo Lowell in their characterization of a populated Mars. An extreme view was posited by Samuel Phelps Leland, professor of astronomy at Charles City College in Iowa. He wrote in 1898 that new telescopes were so powerful that it would soon be possible "to see cities on Mars, to detect navies in its harbors and the smoke of great manufacturing cities and towns." Then he concluded: "Is Mars inhabited? There can be little doubt of it. . . . Is it possible to know this of a certainty? Certainly." This supremely confident astronomer's book was entitled *World Making*, and it was published in Chicago by the Women's Temperance Publishing Association.

With rare exceptions, however, professional astronomers still questioned the existence of Lowell's canals and deplored inferences concerning Martian life. James E. Keeler, an astronomer at Lick, feared that once the Martian balloon was eventually burst people would become disillusioned with all science. At the dedication of the Yerkes Observatory in 1897, Keeler said:

> It is to be regretted that the habitability of the planets, a subject of which astronomers profess to know little, has been chosen as a theme for exploitation by the romancer. . . . The result of his ingenuity is that fact and fancy become inextricably tangled in the mind of the layman. . . . When he is made to understand the true state of our knowledge of these subjects, he is much disappointed and feels a certain resentment towards science, as if it had imposed upon him. Science is not responsible for these erroneous ideas, which, having no solid basis, gradually die out and are forgotten.

After the turn of the century, most astronomers became convinced that Lowell's canals were an illusion and that conditions on the planet were, in the opinion of Newcomb, "unfavorable to any form of life unless of the very lowest order." But the most thorough and effective refutation of Lowell's ideas came from an unlikely source: not an astronomer, but a great biologist.

Alfred Russel Wallace had conceived the concept of evolution by natural selection independently of Darwin; indeed, the competition forced Darwin to quit procrastinating and get on with the publication in 1859 of his monumental book, *On the Origin of Species.* Wallace, old now but still intellectually active, was asked to review one of Lowell's books. Warming to the task, he wrote not an ordinary review but a 110-page book, which was entitled *Is Mars Habitable?* and published in 1907.

Wallace proposed a natural origin for the linear features that Lowell called canals. They were actually enormous cracks in the crust created in the cooling following the formation of Mars. But he was uncompromising in his attack on the notion of Martian life. His argument centered on temperatures. "Owing to the distance of Mars from the sun," he said, "it would have a mean temperature of about minus 35 Fahrenheit, even if it had an atmosphere as dense as ours." In analyzing light reflected off Mars, Wallace correctly deduced a mean temperature well below the freezing point of water. He further argued that because of the weak Martian gravity large amounts of water vapor could not remain in the atmosphere; it would mostly escape into space. For the same reason, there could be no liquid water on the surface, in canals or anywhere. As for the polar ice caps, he concluded that they must be composed in part of frozen carbon dioxide—dry ice. "Mars not only is not inhabited by intelligent beings as Mr. Lowell postulates, but is absolutely UNINHABITABLE."

SOON MARS AND Martians receded into the shadows of world war. Schiaparelli died in 1910 still defending his and Lowell's observations of the canals. Lowell was in Flagstaff, near his observatory, when he died in 1916. He is buried on Mars Hill in a mausoleum that looks like a small observatory with a dome of translucent blue glass. To the end he had maintained a staunch belief in a Mars with a global system of canals built by heroic beings struggling to make the best of an aging, arid world.

Percival Lowell was inspired, enthusiastic, eloquent, and, of course, absolutely wrong about Mars. His Mars never was. In time, most people could accept the passing of Lowell's Mars, either with relief (if they were astronomers, who were tired of responding to the latest Martian theory) or perhaps with disappointment, for some human longing after cosmic companionship had been aroused. We would have to look elsewhere, farther away. But James Keeler was mistaken in his conviction that Lowell's Mars, like other erroneous scientific ideas, would gradually die out and be forgotten. Wrong though Lowell surely was, his influence has lived on into the age of space flight.

Lowell cannot be dismissed as merely a misguided amateur and "romancer." His interests in astronomy ranged beyond Mars, sometimes with more fruitful results. He had an idea that the spiral galaxies might be proto-planetary systems around other stars in our Milky Way galaxy. So he had an assistant, Vesto M. Slipher, conduct intensive observations of these spiral features, in the course of which Slipher found they were all receding. This accidental finding was fundamental to the discovery in the 1920s by Edwin P. Hubble that the universe is expanding. The road to a transcending truth can be paved with erroneous ideas.

For the last eight years of his life, Lowell made an exhaustive study of the motions of distant Uranus and Neptune. The two huge planets were behaving erratically for no apparent reason. It was as if some mighty force at the edge of the solar system was tugging at Uranus and Neptune and disturbing their orbits. Lowell proposed that this force was the gravity of a ninth planet, which he designated Planet X. By his calculations, it should be in an orbit some 5.2 billion miles away from the Sun. Planet X eluded Lowell, but the search continued after his death and, in 1930, led to the discovery of Pluto. It was identified by Clyde Tombaugh, an astronomer at Lowell Observatory. The symbol for Pluto (♇) also depicts the initials of Percival Lowell.

It turns out, however, that Pluto is too small to account for the gravitational forces seemingly disturbing the orbits of Uranus and Neptune. Another Lowell idea had led inadvertently to another discovery, a ninth planet, yes, but not the sought-for Planet X. Thus, Lowell's Planet X must still be out there somewhere, undetected, and the search goes on. The evidence remains indirect, though tantalizing.

Besides the still unexplained perturbations of Uranus and Neptune, the possible clues include the orbit of Pluto and the clockwise rotation of Triton, Neptune's large moon. Thomas C. Van Flandern and Robert Harrington of the United States Naval Observatory have shown with computer simulations that a planet a few times larger than Earth and with peculiar orbital characteristics could explain both Pluto's odd orbit, which is inclined to the plane of all the other planets, and the fact that Triton is the only major satellite in the solar system that does not revolve counterclockwise. In the scenario developed by Van Flandern and Harrington, Planet X passed sufficiently close to Neptune in the distant past so that it expelled one of its satellites (Pluto) and reversed the motion of Triton. If this happened, Planet X is now in an orbit of its own with a period of about 800 years and a present distance of about three times Neptune's distance from the Sun. A survey of the sky in that region has found nothing yet. Four spacecraft—Pioneers 10 and 11 and Voyagers 1 and 2—are exploring the outer reaches of the solar system, and their motions are being tracked carefully by radio antennas for any sign of unexpected course deviations that could be attributed to Planet X.

The presence of an unseen giant planet has also been invoked in one of many recent theories to explain the mass extinctions of life, including the dinosaurs, that befell Earth 65 million years ago. What if there is a Planet X and it travels an orbital course that periodically disturbs the cloud of comets at the edge of the solar system and precipitates a rain of comets, some of which crash into Earth and spread death and destruction? Daniel Whitmire and John J. Matese of the University of Southwestern Louisiana proposed the idea in an effort to account for the fossil record indicating that mass extinctions may occur on Earth regularly every 26 million years. Such periodicity suggests a regular natural phenomenon, perhaps extraterrestrial, and not something random like asteroid impacts.

Planet X aside, the legacy of Lowell is viewed with mixed emotions by the astronomy profession. Was Lowell's influence, on the whole, positive or negative?

According to some assessments, any harm done by Lowell to science was outweighed by the stimulus his ideas gave to the study of Mars and planets in general. On the other hand, it is argued that, largely because of Lowell, planetary astronomy fell into disrepute in the early twentieth century. This, coupled with the growing appeal of high-energy physics and cosmology, produced a shortage of scientific talent addressing the study of the planets that has only recently, with the advent of space flight, been partly remedied. Examining the conflicting assessments of Lowell's legacy, Crowe, in his book on extraterrestrial life, concludes: "Many benefits came to astronomy from the canal controversy, but the price paid by the astronomical community in loss of credibility, internal discord, methodological misconceptions, and substantive errors, was far too high."

All this may be true, and certainly is regrettable, but it fails to take into account the lasting impression Lowell's Mars and Martians made on the human mind.

At the beginning of the twentieth century, the young Robert H. Goddard experienced an overpowering vision of a voyage to Mars. He was a boy in Worcester, Massachusetts, in the grip of the Mars fever. He had listened intently, though not uncritically, to Lowell's enchanting lectures and was captivated by the recent outpouring of science fiction about Mars travel, spawned by Lowell's canal theories. So inspired, Goddard went on to propose trajectories for spaceships traveling to Mars and combined theory and practice in his lonely development of liquid-fuel rocketry. His experiments in rocket technology before World War II were so thorough and innovative that Wernher von Braun, the German developer of the V-2 rockets and the Saturn 5 moon rocket, would later exclaim, "Goddard had everything." Give Lowell and the attraction of Lowell's Mars some of the credit.

When rockets began escaping Earth's gravity, there was no gainsaying the appeal of Mars as one of the first targets for space flight. Credit Lowell. Mars was irresistible to rocket engineers, political leaders, and scientists because it had to be seen and visited and compared with the Mars that never was, Lowell's Mars, which has never been altogether erased from human consciousness. As Carl Sagan says, speaking for himself as well as many others, Lowell "turned on all the eight-year-olds who came after him, and who eventually turned into the present generation of astronomers."

Mostly, this influence of Lowell has endured not through his own writings, as perfervid as they were, but in the even more extravagant fiction inspired by his ideas. If our first spacecraft explorations of Mars left us feeling a little cheated, it was because we had been half expecting to find a fictional Mars known as Barsoom.

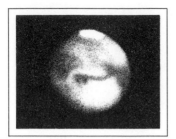

CHAPTER 3

THE MARTIANS
ARE COMING!

ON A SUNDAY evening in 1938, the night before Halloween, the radio announcer in a New York studio opened the 8 p.m. program with these words: "The Columbia Broadcasting System and its affiliated stations present Orson Welles and the Mercury Theatre on the Air in *The War of the Worlds*, by H. G. Wells." At twenty-two years of age, Orson Welles was the wunderkind of drama, brilliant and daring as an actor and director. He signaled the studio orchestra to play the show's theme music from Tchaikovsky, and then he introduced the story. His ominous words were adapted from the opening of the 1898 science-fiction novel by Wells (no kin), who had come under the influence of Percival Lowell. In his novel, Wells the author had pictured a race of "intellects vast and cool and unsympathetic," who "regarded this earth with envious eyes, and slowly and surely drew their plans against us." Welles the actor intoned: "We know now that in the early years of the twentieth century this world was being watched closely by intelligences greater than man's and yet as mortal as his own."

So began the most stunning single program ever broadcast on radio. It set off a brief wave of mass hysteria. The Martians were coming! The Martians had invaded the United States. They were monstrous, and they were killing thousands of people with ray guns, spreading poisonous black smoke, and setting fire to the countryside, from New Jersey to the north and west and south.

The program's verisimilitude could not have been more effective. In adapting the novel for radio, Welles and his scriptwriters transferred the site of the invasion from England to New Jersey at this very moment, and they chose to relate events in a sequence of breathless radio news bulletins and simulated on-the-scene reports. They created an illusion of reality that drove many unsuspecting people into the streets in panic.

It began with an introduction and an ordinary weather report, and then the announcer said the program would be continued from "the Meridian Room in the Hotel Park Plaza in downtown New York, where you will be entertained by the music of Ramon Raquello and his orchestra"—innocent enough, for dance-band "remotes" were a staple of radio in those days. Then the music was interrupted for a news bulletin, as listeners had also come to expect from time to time.

"Ladies and gentlemen," the announcer said, "we interrupt our program of dance music to bring you a special bulletin from the Intercontinental Radio News. At twenty minutes before eight, Central time, Professor Farrell of the Mount Jennings Observatory, Chicago, Illinois, reports observing several explosions of incandescent gas, occurring at regular intervals on the planet Mars."

It all sounded authentic and mildly exciting: Never mind that there was no such band or hotel, no Professor Farrell or observatory in Chicago. The tempo picked up as further bulletins interrupted the orchestra. A Professor Pierson, played by Orson Welles, gave a conventional description of Mars. Then came the announcement that a flaming object had crashed on a farm near Grovers Mill, a pastoral crossroads in New Jersey. On the scene, or so it seemed, was the radio newsman Carl Phillips. This was actually another actor in the studio, but he had immersed himself in transcriptions of the legendary eyewitness account of the zeppelin *Hindenburg*'s explosion the year before. The appalled and distraught announcer that day, abandoning journalistic objectivity, had wept at the horror of the disaster.

The "Carl Phillips" reporter gave a similarly excited description:

> Ladies and gentlemen, this is the most terrifying thing I have ever witnessed—wait a minute! Someone's crawling out of the hollow top—someone or . . . something. I can see peering out of that black

hole two luminous discs. Maybe eyes, might be a face. . . . Good heavens, something's wriggling out of the shadow like a gray snake. Now it's another one. . . . They look like tentacles. . . . I can see the thing's body now—it's large as a bear. It glistens like wet leather. But that face, it's . . . it's . . . ladies and gentlemen, it's indescribable; I can hardly force myself to keep looking at it, it's so awful. The eyes are black and gleam like a serpent; the mouth is . . . kind of V-shaped, with saliva dripping from its rimless lips that seem to quiver and pulsate. The monster or whatever it is can hardly move; it seems weighted down possibly by gravity or something. . . .

Phillips continued his running account of the invasion until he was suddenly cut off the air, presumably a victim of a death ray or the poisonous gas. More bulletins followed, and then came the announcement that seemed to leave no doubt as to the imminent peril:

A Martian invader hovers, from H. G. Wells's The War of the Worlds. *(Bettmann Archive)*

Ladies and gentlemen, as incredible as it may seem, both the observations of science and the evidence of our eyes lead to the inescapable assumption that those strange beings who landed in the Jersey
farmlands tonight are the vanguard of an invading army from the
planet Mars. . . . The monster is now in control of the middle
section of New Jersey and has effectively cut the state through its
center. Communications lines are down from Pennsylvania to the
Atlantic Ocean. Railroad service from New York to Philadelphia
is discontinued, except routing some of the trains through Allentown and Phoenixville. Highways to the north, south, and west
are clogged with frantic human traffic. Police and Army reserves
are unable to control the mad flight. . . .

Alien craft were descending everywhere, it seemed, and a voice
resembling that of President Franklin D. Roosevelt came on with
emergency instructions to the public. Even though CBS made four
announcements during the show that it was "only a play," many
listeners did not hear them or were already too confused and panicked
to comprehend the cautionary disclaimer. As it happened, many of
the listeners, an estimated three to six million, had tuned in the
Mercury Theatre about twelve minutes into the show to escape an
obscure guest singer who was holding forth on NBC's competing
"Chase & Sanborn Hour" instead of the tremendously popular Edgar
Bergen and his dapper dummy Charlie McCarthy. The first words
they probably heard were those of Phillips describing the cylinders
of unknown origin crashing to Earth "with almost earthquake force."

Panic immediately swept New Jersey. In Newark, families fled
their homes, pressing wet handkerchiefs to their faces as protection
against the reported poison gases. Thousands of telephone calls
poured into the Newark police headquarters; some of the callers were
terror-stricken and wanted to know where to flee, while others were
physicians and nurses volunteering their services. A Newark hospital
reported that fifteen men and women were treated for shock and
hysteria. Scores of people ran out of their houses in Jersey City and
stood in the streets looking apprehensively toward the sky. A bar-
tender in West Orange, New Jersey, hearing that everyone was to be
evacuated, put his customers out, closed the tavern, and drove home
to rescue his wife and children. Armories were swamped with calls

from National Guardsmen wanting to know where and when to report for the general mobilization they had heard about on the radio. Several motorists arrived at the police station in Maplewood, New Jersey, to inquire how they were to get back to their homes in New York City now that the Pulaski Skyway had been blown up.

In a sociological study of the panic conducted later by Princeton University, some of the people interviewed recalled the confusion and terror of that evening. The story of a Newark housewife was typical:

> We listened, getting more and more excited. We all felt the world was coming to an end. Then we heard, "Get gas masks!" That was the part that got me. I thought I was going crazy. It's a wonder my heart didn't fail me because I'm nervous anyway. I felt if the gas was on, I wanted to be together with my husband and nephew so we could all die together. So I ran out of the house. I guess I didn't know what I was doing. I stood on the corner waiting for a bus and I thought every car that came along was a bus and I ran out to get it. I kept saying over and over again to everybody I met: "New Jersey is destroyed by the Germans—it's on the radio!"

One of the panicked listeners also recalled:

> When the Martians started coming north from Trenton we got really scared. They would soon be in our town. I drove right through Newburgh and never even knew I went through it. . . . I was going eighty miles an hour most of the way. I remember not giving a damn, as what difference did it make which way I'd get killed.

Another New Jersey housewife said:

> I knew it was something terrible and I was frightened. But I didn't know just what it was. I couldn't make myself believe it was the end of the world. I've always heard that when the world would come to an end, it would come so fast nobody would know—so why should God get in touch with this announcer?

A laborer in Massachusetts was so upset that he spent his savings trying to escape the disaster. He wrote to the Princeton investigators:

I thought the best thing to do was to go away, so I took $3.25 out of my savings and bought a ticket. After I had gone sixty miles I heard it was a play. Now I don't have any money left for the shoes I was saving up for. Would you please have someone send me a pair of black shoes, size 9B.

In New York City, the hysteria sent people running to police stations asking where to go to be evacuated. They milled in the streets and cast worried eyes toward the west for signs that New Jersey might be under Martian siege. A caller to a Bronx police station cried: "I went to the roof and I could see the smoke from the bombs, drifting over toward New York. What shall I do?" The switchboard at *The New York Times* was overwhelmed with 875 calls, including one from a man in Dayton, Ohio, who asked: "What time will it be the end of the world?"

Elsewhere, the reaction was much the same. People gathered in churches to pray. In Rhode Island, people demanded that the power companies disconnect all electricity so that the Martians might overlook their little state. In Pittsburgh, a husband rushed in just in time to prevent his panicked wife from swallowing poison. Some people in Boston swore they could see the red glow in the sky as New York burned.

Steve Allen, the entertainer, recalls that he was among those fooled by the radio show. "I was seventeen, and I was on the ninth floor of a run-down hotel on the Near North Side of Chicago with my mother and aunt," he said. "Take three otherwise normal people who believe the world is about to end, turn them loose in Chicago, and you have a situation comedy." They raced down the corridor to escape the hotel, with his aunt crying, "They're up in the air!"

Allen was reminded of that night as he prepared for a re-creation of the famous broadcast fifty years later, on October 30, 1988. Jason Robards played the Welles role, Douglas Edwards was the studio announcer, and Allen broadcast "remotes" from a rooftop near Wall Street. Some updating adjustments were made: Intercontinental Radio News became Satellite News. Crowded interstate highways replaced parkways, and lasers, Amtrak, and jet fighter planes were added. There was another difference: no panic this time.

At Grovers Mill, a few people remember the village's one night of fame and take pains to point out that no one there went berserk. The only people out and about that night were said to be some fishing buddies who had spent the day reeling in pickerel and bass. On the drive home, they turned on the radio and heard something about the invasion from space. "Gee, Ed, I didn't see anything," one of them said. "Did you?"

Esther Engelke, a lifelong resident, remembers the broadcast. "I heard them say the Martians had landed and told my parents," she said. "My father said, 'Let's go around and see.' We asked the police. They didn't know, so we drove around and then we went home and didn't think any more about it."

At least one person in Grovers Mill apparently did panic. A gunman fired at the village's cone-shaped water tower, thinking it was the Martian invasion craft. The tower is still standing, and next to the landing site is a pond that has turned green (from algae, not Martians). Soon, there will be a bronze monument commemorating the night the Martians landed. It will show a spaceship along with Welles at a microphone and a family huddled around a radio. The inscription will read: "One million people believed it."

In the original broadcast, Welles, as Professor Pierson, spent the last twenty minutes bringing it all to a reasonably happy ending. The Martians were finally killed off by terrestrial bacteria. By then, however, the CBS studio was threatened with an invasion of its own. Policemen and news reporters were outside demanding to know what was going on. Presently, the radio network and Welles issued a statement expressing regret for any misunderstanding. Welles left the studio that night astonished by what had occurred and fearful that it might have wrecked his career. "I'm extremely surprised to learn that a story which has become familiar to children through the medium of comic strips and many succeeding novels and adventure stories should have had such an immediate and profound effect upon radio listeners," Welles said.

The Martians brought him national fame and a lasting place in American drama. Without the Martians, it could be argued, there might never have been the classic movie *Citizen Kane*. The chief scriptwriter for the program, Howard Koch, would go on to be co-author of the script for the legendary movie *Casablanca*.

In the aftermath, psychologists made the point that in the fall of 1938

Orson Welles, after his realistic broadcast of The War of
the Worlds *on October 30, 1938. He explained that he never
meant to spread terror and cause panic. (Associated Press)*

the world was on the brink of a nervous breakdown. Heywood Broun,
the newspaper columnist, was apparently the first to suggest this
interpretation. Writing two days later, he said: "I doubt if anything
of the sort would have happened four or five months ago. The course
of world history has affected national psychology. Jitters have come
home to roost. We have just gone through a laboratory demonstration
of the fact that the peace of Munich hangs heavy over our heads, like
a thundercloud."

Hadley Cantril, the professor at Princeton who conducted the
sociological study of the panic, adopted the same line of explanation.

People had been hearing on the radio an unrelieved flow of frightful news about impending war in Europe. Nazi Germany had taken over Austria in March and, after the "peace in our time" conference at Munich, had sent troops and tanks across the border of Czechoslovakia on October 1. People were becoming conditioned to the idea of invasion, death and destruction, and perhaps global catastrophe. One month it might be Hitler, the next Martians.

HERBERT GEORGE WELLS was only one of many writers who perpetuated the idea of a populated Mars—a Lowellian Mars. When he wrote *The War of the Worlds* (as an 1897 magazine serial, which was published as a book the next year), stories about space flight and

H. G. Wells, right, strolls outside his Mediterranean villa with Julian Huxley. They collaborated on The Sciences of Life. *(P&A Photo)*

life on other worlds, which were then called science romances and only later would be called science fiction, were well established and growing in popularity.

A prototype was Jules Verne's *From the Earth to the Moon*, published in 1865, which was remarkably prescient in that it anticipated by a century a manned launching from Florida with a splashdown in the Pacific Ocean. Earlier, Edgar Allan Poe had written a tale of Hans Pfaal, who fled from Earth toward the Moon in a homemade balloon to escape his debts. There was even a precedent for the public being taken in by an elaborate and seemingly authentic journalistic report about extraterrestrial beings.

In August 1835, the New York *Sun* published a series of articles that came to be known as the "Moon Hoax." They purported to be the reports of John Herschel, the astronomer son of the famous William Herschel, about telescopic observations made at the Cape of Good Hope revealing the existence of intelligent lunar creatures. The amazing report went on to describe these "rational beings" that had built a magnificent temple, were glimpsed conversing and gesticulating around their fires, and seemed to be living in the "universal state of amity among all classes of lunar creatures." Professors at Yale University were said to have read the articles "with unexampled avidity and implicit faith," and Poe told of a professor of mathematics in Virginia who had "no doubt of the truth of the whole affair." Soon it was revealed that the articles were in fact written by a journalist, Richard Adams Locke, as a satire on the notion of extraterrestrial life. But people, it seemed, had been too eager to believe the articles to recognize them as satire.

Fictional attention shifted from the Moon to Mars after the "canal" discoveries. In 1880, for example, a British writer, Percy Gregg, published a two-volume novel, *Across the Zodiac*, which was about a voyage to Mars in a spaceship that "resembled the form of an antique Dutch East-Indiaman." Gregg's Mars was like an older Earth with pale green skies and orange foliage. With the next major novel about Mars, *On Two Planets* by Kurd Lasswitz, a German professor of mathematics, the idea of Martians invading Earth enters literature. After all, if the Martians possess a higher intelligence, they would be the ones making the first interplanetary voyages. The 1897 book deals with Martians who establish a base at the North Pole from which they set out to take over Earth with the help of Martian sympathizers. Americans eventually learn the secret of Martian technology, build a fleet of their "atmosphere ships," and at last bring about a truce between the two planets, with equal rights for humans and Martians alike.

Like so many other writers, Lasswitz employed science romance not only to entertain but to deliver a serious message. The conflict between Martians and Earth people served as his critique of European power politics. Likewise, Wells invented his invading Martians as a morality tale about Victorian arrogance. As his son, Anthony West, writes in *H. G. Wells: Aspects of a Life,* a "central idea" informed the story and it was this: "Suppose that living creatures were to come to earth from another planet—from Mars, say—beings so far ahead of earthlings technologically and in every other way as to make it impossible for them to think of us as fellow creatures. And suppose that they were to treat earthlings as Europeans had treated the backward peoples that they had come upon in the earth's far corners—the Tasmanians had been run off their native grounds and exterminated in fifty years; the Belgians were doing something of the same kind in the Congo; and the Zulu nation had been treated almost as vilely. Suppose these Martians had our racial arrogance and had come to clear our planet for colonization, as Tasmania had been cleared."

As Wells observed in the novel: "Are we such apostles of mercy as to complain if the Martians warred in the same spirit?"

On the fiftieth anniversary of the radio broadcast, Philip Klass, professor emeritus of English and comparative literature at Pennsylvania State University and author of eight books of science fiction under the pseudonym William Tenn, wrote of Wells's interplanetary parable. "Our kind has triumphed not only as biological competitors, but also as creatures with consciences and religious commitments, with ethical systems and awareness of guilt," he said. "I believe we are at least subliminally aware of a special, shared guilt. Even knowing that natural law recognizes extenuating circumstances, we are still waiting for justice to arrive, demanding payment of us in our turn. When H. G. Wells's novel of 1898 came through to Orson Welles's America of 1938—and people learned that creatures had arrived who were more intelligent and better-armed than we—of course there was a panic. Our time had come at last. I think H. G. Wells might have seen it as a headlong flight from justice."

Edgar Rice Burroughs and his wife on their honeymoon. (Wide World Photos)

Although in the novel Wells described a similar panic ensuing in the English countryside, one of the first actual reactions to the book took the form of a literary counterattack on the Martians. In the same year, an American writer, Garrett P. Serviss, published *Edison's Conquest of Mars.* The book described an American space fleet, armed with weapons quickly invented by Thomas Alva Edison and other clever Yankees, which went to Mars and exacted swift retribution from those who dared to invade Earth. Wells's anti-imperialist message was apparently too subtle for many Americans, who in Cuba and the Philippines were asserting their own might on the world stage for the first time.

IT WAS A HACK writer, Edgar Rice Burroughs, whose stories of Mars left an even more enduring mark on the human mind. Many scientists and engineers of the American planetary exploration program have confessed that they first experienced the lure of Mars not from reading scholarly tomes but in those long childhood hours spent soaking in Burroughs' romantic tales of the gentleman-adventurer John Carter and his exploits on Barsoom, which was the local name for Mars. They yearned to share with Carter the love of the beautiful Dejah Thoris, Princess of Helium. When they grew up, they wanted to visit Barsoom, and in a sense, they did. Ray Bradbury, the modern science-fiction writer, has called Burroughs the spiritual father of the space age.

The first of eleven Mars books by Burroughs, who also wrote the Tarzan adventures, was published in 1911, at the time of Lowell's influence on popular thinking. The book, *Princess of Mars*, had appeared originally as a story in one of the "pulp" magazines, where people in a pretelevision society looked for their escapist entertainment. Burroughs did not bother with the technological support systems invented by other writers. He simply has Carter, a dashing soldier of fortune from Virginia, stand in the Arizona desert, close his eyes, and wish himself up and all the way out to Mars. There he visits the spired cities and travels along the canals with their domed pumping stations. He encounters herds of eight-legged beasts of burden, the thoats, and a tall green fighting man named Tars Tarkas. And, of course, he woos and wins the fair Dejah.

Without Burroughs, says Bradbury, *The Martian Chronicles* would never have been written. Burroughs, he says, "took me out under the stars in Illinois and pointed up and said, with John Carter, simply: Go there."

The Martian Chronicles is arguably the best book ever written about Mars. Published in 1950, it is a collection of dreamlike folk tales about the last days of the old Martian civilization and the arrival of colonists from Earth. It is by turns humorous and poetic, pessimistic and optimistic. Bradbury is unsparing in his depiction of the dark side of man the spoiler. His colonists from Earth desecrate the crystalline cities of the Martians, shattering the towers in target practice. His Martians are described with more sympathy. They have brownish skin, yellow-coin eyes, and soft musical voices, but they are ultimately eradicated by chicken pox. As human life begins to flourish on Mars, nuclear war comes to Earth. The colonists, Bradbury writes, "stood on the porches and tried to believe in the existence of Earth, much as they

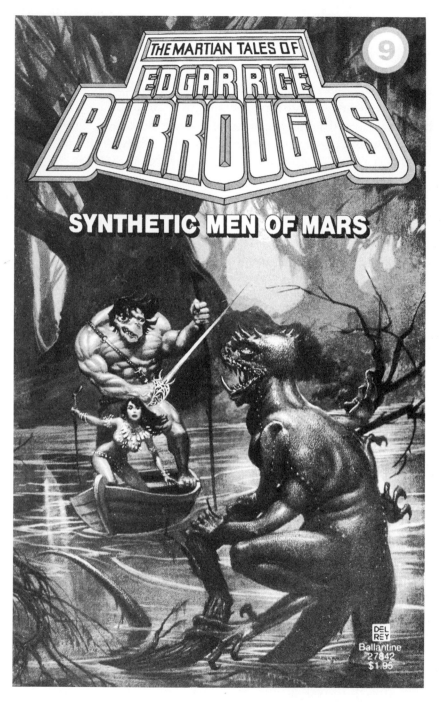

THE MARTIAN TALES OF

EDGAR RICE BURROUGHS

9

SYNTHETIC MEN OF MARS

DEL
REY
Ballantine
27842
$1.95

The Martian novels of Edgar Rice Burroughs are still in print.

had once tried to believe in the existence of Mars." They realize what they must do. They all pack up and rocket back to the home planet, and the nuclear holocaust.

Bradbury was writing after World War II, in the early gloom of the mushroom cloud of nuclear power that imperiled the species. Mars was once again a landscape for allegory. Bradbury saw Mars as a human refuge. Concluding on an optimistic note, he has two families escape the wasted Earth and make it to a Mars promising human survival and renewal. The newcomers are standing by the reflective waters of a Martian canal.

> "I've always wanted to see a Martian," said Michael. "Where are they, Dad? You promised."
>
> "There they are," said Dad, and he shifted Michael on his shoulder and pointed straight down.
>
> The Martians were there. Timothy began to shiver.
>
> The Martians were there—in the canal—reflected in the water. Timothy and Michael and Robert and Mom and Dad.
>
> The Martians stared back at them for a long, long silent time from the rippling water. . . .

The scene has become etched deep in the human consciousness. If there is no life on Mars now, someday there will be. The vision at the canal, or some variation, is implicit in much thinking about Mars that reaches beyond the first reconnaissance and first explorations.

RIGHT UP TO the eve of the first comprehensive spacecraft exploration of Mars, in November 1971, the Mars of Lowell and of science-fiction writers cast long shadows. No longer did anyone seriously believe in the canal builders or fear invasion from the forces of Wells and Welles. But it was hard to forsake old romantic attachments. Scientists who believed that some forms of microscopic life might still be found on the planet celebrated the fictional Martians for their indispensable role in keeping the dream alive. Those who were more skeptical at least paid the Martians the compliment of criticizing their role in fostering unrealistic expectations.

Bruce C. Murray, a geologist and professor of planetary science at the California Institute of Technology, complained that scientists as well as the general public had long been guilty of wishful thinking about Mars. At a symposium on the Caltech campus in Pasadena the night before the Mariner 9 spacecraft was to go into an orbit of Mars, Murray cast himself as the realist among a panel of romantics.

> Mars [Murray said] somehow has extended and endured beyond the realm of science to so grab hold of man's emotions and thoughts that it has actually distorted scientific opinion. We want Mars to be like the Earth. There is a deep-seated desire to find another place where we can make another start, that somehow could be habitable. . . . It has been very, very hard to face up to the facts, which have been emerging for some time, that indicate it really isn't that way, that it is just wishful thinking. It hasn't been just the science-fiction writers who have used that deep-seated feeling among human beings to do other things and give other messages. The people who have really fallen on this have been the scientists themselves, who have misunderstood the significance of their observations. . . . My own personal view is that we are all so captive to Edgar Rice Burroughs and Lowell that the observations are going to have to beat us over the head and tell us the answer in spite of ourselves.

Murray's position was indisputably close to the truth, though Mars was waiting with a few surprises to be glimpsed by Mariner 9's cameras. Murray was not arguing against a robust program of Mars exploration; quite the contrary. He merely wanted to emphasize that it was not necessary to be looking for life on Mars to justify the effort.

"I think what we are doing with Mars is very important," Murray said. "We are exploring. We as a people, as a nation, are spending our money on an uneconomic endeavor. We will not recover a product. We won't get military benefits. Instead, we're doing something that really has cultural value. The Mariner spacecraft up there is a cultural edifice dedicated by this country to an idea, to the idea of exploration, to learning about something we don't know. . . . The fact that we as a people have advanced far enough to explore another planet is something of which we should be very proud."

At the moment of Mariner 9's arrival at Mars, Murray was making a valid point. It was time for the Mars of romance to give way to the real Mars. We no longer needed to imagine Mars; we could now see it up close and soon would be going down and touching its surface. But it was a romantic, a writer of science fiction, who won the most enthusiastic hand from the symposium audience. They applauded Ray Bradbury when he said: "I think it's part of the nature of man to start with romance and build to a reality."

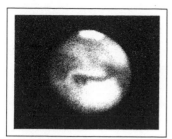

CHAPTER 4

FIRST
ENCOUNTERS

AS SOON AS flight in space became possible, beginning in 1957, it was taken for granted that missions to Mars would command a high priority. Engineers assumed their rockets would soon be capable of boosting small unmanned spacecraft as far as Venus and Mars. Scientists, with new tools of discovery at the ready, were brimming with curiosity. They had inherited much unfinished business from the days of Lowell.

It was time for a revival. There had been only one burst of post-Lowellian fervor, and that was back in the 1920s. Guglielmo Marconi, the Italian physicist who invented wireless communications, announced in 1921 that he had received mysterious signals that included the Morse code letter *V*. Martians were immediately suspected, either seriously or humorously. Did the letter stand for "Volstead," asked a *New York Times* editorial, and were the Martians warning us against prohibition? (The Volstead Act enforced the prohibition of alcoholic beverages in the United States.) Martians do inspire whimsy. Advertisements like this one ran in many newspapers in 1924: "Mars is peopled . . . And they want Kirk's American Family Soap."

In 1922 and again in 1924, when Mars was especially close, the United States government requested all radio stations to observe complete silence for a certain period while operators listened for any signals from Mars. Navy stations across the Pacific stopped transmitting on the night of August 22, 1924, and remained silent for three days, hoping to pick up a signal. (Looking back, this was remarkable not so much because people would go to such lengths to try to intercept supposed messages from Mars; it was remarkable that people once felt sure enough of peace on Earth that they would suspend key military communications for three days for a scientific exercise.) Standing by to translate any messages was William F. Friedman, chief of the code section of the Army Signal Corps. He would later score one of the code-breaking coups of World War II, deciphering the Japanese diplomatic code just before the attack on Pearl Harbor. But Friedman's skill went untested this time. The failure in 1924 to tune in on Mars discouraged even Flammarion, the French astronomer, now in his eighty-third year, who had given enthusiastic support to Lowell. He told reporters: "Perhaps the Martians tried before, in the epoch of the iguanodon and dinosaur, and got tired."

In subsequent years, planetary astronomy lapsed into a moribund state and remained so until the space age. Telescopic observations of Mars were few and yielded little that was new. And some of what was learned turned out to be incorrect.

In 1947, for example, Gerard P. Kuiper, the Dutch-American astronomer, determined for the first time that the primary constituent of the Martian atmosphere was carbon dioxide. This was accomplished by a technique known as spectroscopy, which is an analysis of the spectrum of light reflected off the planet; since different elements reflect light differently, spectroscopic analysis yields clues to the composition of the reflecting agent. But Kuiper erred when he went a step further and calculated that the atmospheric pressure on Mars was such that the polar ice caps there could not be made of frozen carbon dioxide; they most probably were frozen water. Other astronomers tended to accept the erroneous findings.

Gérard de Vaucouleurs, a French astronomer, reported in the 1950s that studies of the light-scattering properties of gas molecules, as determined by telescopic observations, indicated that the atmospheric pressure on Mars was probably one-tenth that of Earth at sea level. This was almost exactly the pressure assumed by Lowell, and it left open the possibility of water existing there in liquid form.

Other investigations also seemed to keep alive some aspects of the Lowellian Mars. In 1958, working with the 200-inch telescope at Mount Palomar in California, William M. Sinton examined reflected light in the infrared wavelength and found what he said was evidence that the seasonal waves of darkening on Mars could well be caused by vegetation.

Certainly there were no Martians in the Burroughs mold, and perhaps there had never been any canal-building civilizations. Yet scientists at the start of the space age were not ready to dismiss the possibility of some forms of life on Mars. Earl C. Slipher of the Lowell Observatory wrote in 1962:

> Our knowledge of Mars steadily progresses. Each opposition adds something to what we knew before. Since the theory of life on the planet was first enunciated some fifty years ago, every new fact discovered has been found to be accordant with it. Not a single thing has been detected which it does not explain. Every year adds to the number of those who have seen the evidence for themselves. Thus theory and observations coincide.

In his quietly eloquent book *To Utopia and Back: The Search for Life in the Solar System,* Norman H. Horowitz, emeritus professor of biology at the California Institute of Technology, cited Slipher's optimistic statement as an example of a view prevalent just before the Mariners began flying to Mars. Horowitz deplores the inordinate influence such thinking exerted on public expectations and the planning of early missions to Mars and suspects wishful thinking even now of distorting our approach to planetary exploration. But the optimism about possible life on Mars, he said, could be defended in 1962—and often was. A panel of scientists convened by the National Academy of Sciences to advise the National Aeronautics and Space Administration noted in 1961 the presumed evidence for water ice at the Martian poles and water vapor circulating globally. Although the panel did not accept Sinton's evidence for vegetation, its report concluded:

> The evidence taken as a whole is suggestive of life on Mars. In particular, the response to the availability of water vapor is just

what is to be expected on a planet which is now relatively arid, but which once probably had much more surface water. The limited evidence we have is directly relevant only to the presence of microorganisms; there are no valid data for or against the existence of larger organisms and motile animals.

According to Horowitz, the "delowellization" of Mars began with a single observation at the Mount Wilson Observatory near Los Angeles in April 1963. The spectrogram showed clear infrared evidence of carbon dioxide and, for the first time, water vapor in the Martian atmosphere. But there was only a trace of water, not enough to encourage theories of life. In their analysis of the findings, Lewis Kaplan, Guido Munch, and Hyron Spinrad, of the Jet Propulsion Laboratory and Caltech, determined that the atmospheric pressure was much lower than had been estimated and that its carbon dioxide content was considerably higher than once thought. Nitrogen might still be detected in the atmosphere, and prove to be the major component, as the pro-life forces among scientists wanted to believe. But the Mount Wilson spectrogram indicated that there might be little else in the tenuous atmosphere but carbon dioxide. Lowellian models had assumed a thicker atmosphere containing much more life-supporting water vapor as well as oxygen and nitrogen.

The prospects of finding life on Mars seemed to diminish—literally—in thin air. They would be dealt a severe blow in the summer of 1965.

IT WAS THEN that Mariner 4 became the first spacecraft to succeed in exploring Mars. The mission followed many exasperating failures.

The Soviet Union, maintaining a vigorous launching pace and showing early ambitions to explore the planets, had already made several attempts. Two craft launched in 1960 failed to reach Earth orbit. One launched in 1962 reached Earth orbit, but was stranded there. None of these flights was announced by embarrassed Soviet officials. The next attempt, designated Mars 1, appeared headed for success after its launching on November 1, 1962. But at the end of March, just ten weeks before the expected flyby of Mars, the craft's transmitter went silent, and nothing was heard of Mars 1 again. Likewise, a craft named Zond 2, launched at about the same time as Mariner 4, suffered a total loss of communications halfway to Mars. The inexplicable tendency of Soviet craft to fail halfway to Mars inspired American planetary engineers to joke about the "Great Galactic Ghoul," a mythical deity lurking out there, waiting to consume intruding spacecraft.

The Soviet experience with the Ghoul did not augur well for American chances. In 1962, American engineers scored one success in two attempts to fly by Venus; Mariner 1 failed at lift-off, but Mariner 2 passed within 21,600 miles of cloud-shrouded surface for the first spacecraft encounter with another planet. In November 1964, the Americans got off to a discouraging start in their first try for Mars. Shortly after Mariner 3 reached space, the cylindrical nose fairing designed to protect the spacecraft during the initial ascent failed to break away. The solar panels could not be deployed to convert sunlight into electricity for spacecraft systems, and so a dead Mariner 3 headed away from Earth. After some quick modifications of its protective shroud, Mariner 4 was launched three weeks later, November 28. About halfway to Mars, it, too, experienced some anomalies and for a few days the Ghoul was no laughing matter. But Mariner survived and cruised almost flawlessly the rest of the way across interplanetary space.

By today's standards, Mariner 4 was simple and small, weighing a mere 575 pounds. With its four solar panels extended, the craft looked like a flying windmill. It measured 22 feet 7½ inches across to the tips of the vanes and 9½ feet to the top of its antenna. The solar blades shone purple from the thin sapphire-glass coating that protected their thousands of tiny solar cells. The craft's silvery octagonal body, made of an alloy of magnesium and aluminum, carried 138,000 delicate electronic components ranging from a computer to a 10½-watt transmitter. On board were six scientific instruments to investigate cosmic rays, solar wind, magnetic fields, and micrometeorite populations in outer space. But the success of the mission, to scientists as well as the public, would depend on the performance of Mariner 4's single television camera.

Mariner 4 traveled a long, curving trajectory out to Mars. The way to go from one planet to another is not by a straight line; in space, where planets move in elliptical orbits, there is no natural straight-line trajectory, and to try to follow the most direct route would require a tremendous amount of rocket energy. Early in the century, a German engineer, Walter Hohmann, figured out how to plot the best possible trajectory—in terms of the shortest travel time and the least amount of rocket energy required—for a spacecraft going to another planet. Such trajectories are called Hohmann transfer orbits and are used in nearly all interplanetary travel. For a mission to Mars, for example, launching time must be set and a trajectory chosen so that the spacecraft, leaving a moving Earth, will travel a curving course outside Earth's orbit and inside Mars's orbit. It will intersect the orbit of Mars at the time of rendezvous with the planet. At that time and point, the spacecraft will find itself at Mars on the opposite side of the Sun from where Earth was at the spacecraft's launching. The spacecraft thus travels a curving orbit halfway around the Sun, and it is the gravitational pull of the Sun on the craft, not any expenditure of rocket power except for minor course adjustments, that draws it to a rendezvous with its planetary target. In this way, Mariner 4 cruised 325 million miles in 228 days to reach Mars. At its arrival on July 14, 1965, the straight-line distance from Earth to Mars was 134 million miles.

Mariner 4 approached the southern hemisphere of the planet, passing within 6,118 miles, and over a twenty-five-minute period took 22 photographs that would stun and disappoint those who had clung to visions of a Mars hospitable to life. The images of a bleak, cratered world came from the spacecraft slowly but relentlessly. As the craft sped by Mars, the pictures had been taken in rapid sequence, recorded in the digital code of computers, and then played back for transmission to Earth on subsequent days. Because of the great distance and the craft's weak radio, it took 8 hours 35 minutes to transmit the coded data that made up a single photograph. Computers at the Jet Propulsion Laboratory digested the pictures, digit by digit, and "developed" them by translating the numerical values into the correct shades of light to be projected on a photographic film. Thus the first close-up views of Mars, covering less than 1 percent of the planet's total surface, took shape over ten suspenseful days.

Frame Seven was the shocker. The first clear, unambiguous image, it showed nothing but craters, and subsequent frames revealed more of the same. The seas of Barsoom were broad craters, old and bone dry. No canals crossed the surface; not an oasis in sight. One conclusion was inescapable: Mars looked like nothing so much as our own lifeless Moon.

In its first formal statement, the Mariner photo-interpretation team, led by Robert B. Leighton of Caltech, concluded: "Man's first close-up look at Mars had revealed the scientifically startling fact that at least part of its surface is covered with large craters." The scientists further observed that "the remarkable state of preservation of such an ancient surface leads us to the inference that no atmosphere significantly denser than the present very thin one had characterized the planet since that surface was formed." Noting this absence of any serious erosion, they found it "difficult to believe that free water in quantities sufficient to form streams or to fill oceans could have existed anywhere on Mars since that time." But the scientists hedged their conclusion. They said that, as had been anticipated, the photographs "neither demonstrate nor preclude the possible existence of life on Mars."

Even so, Mariner 4's findings were disheartening to scientists who specialized in the emerging field of exobiology, the study of extraterrestrial life. Spacecraft instruments could not detect any magnetic field around Mars. As the spacecraft was disappearing behind the planet, it beamed radio signals back to Earth through the Martian atmosphere. By examining changes in the amplitude and frequency of the radio waves as they arrived at Earth, scientists obtained a more definitive measure of the atmospheric density. It was even less than earlier estimates—no more than 1 percent of the atmospheric pressure at sea level on Earth. The lack of a magnetic field combined with a very thin atmosphere leaves the surface of Mars virtually defenseless against a bombardment of cosmic rays and ultraviolet radiation in addition to the evident rain of meteorites that blasted out all those craters.

The Mars of Mariner 4 did not appear promising as a place to live or to visit. Bruce Murray, the Caltech geologist, reflected the disappointment. "We were all shocked by seeing such large lunar-like craters," he said. "It meant that Mars had not recycled its surface the way the Earth does. There must have been no rainfall, no weathering, in any way comparable to that of Earth's for billions of years, in order for Mars to resemble the Moon."

Carl Sagan cautioned his colleagues not to consider the Mariner 4 findings definitive. The spacecraft, flying by at a distance of thousands of miles, might have completely overlooked a thriving civilization. To buttress his warning, Sagan offered an assortment of pictures of Earth taken by a weather satellite. In a report entitled "Is There Life on Earth?" he pointed out that only one of those pictures, showing a snow-covered highway cutting through a forest, revealed indisputable evidence for man's presence on this planet.

T W O M O R E S O V I E T attempts to reach Mars failed in 1969, and two American spacecraft, Mariners 6 and 7, succeeded. The two Mariners were identical, slightly larger than Mariner 4, and each carried more scientific instruments than their predecessor. While the Apollo 11 astronauts were still in quarantine at Houston, following their return from the first landing on the Moon on July 20, Mariner 6 passed within 2,120 miles of Mars on July 31 and obtained 75 photographs. Mariner 7's flyby was almost as close, on August 5, and produced 126 photographs. Altogether, the photographs covered about 20 percent of the Martian surface, along the equator and in the southern hemisphere, but they showed scenes that were no more inviting. Mariners 6 and 7, like Mariner 4, afforded us only distant, fleeting, and partial views of Mars.

Again, image after image contained craters, although some differences from the Mariner 4 views began to appear. An area centered in the southern hemisphere, called Hellas on telescopic maps, turned out to be broad featureless terrain. No area of comparable size and smoothness had ever been seen on the Moon. Perhaps extensive erosional processes, probably wind, were indeed at work on Mars. Surrounding Hellas were mountain chains. Lowell and most other observers had believed Mars to be generally flat and smooth. Other regions were characterized by what geologists called chaotic terrain, which was jumbled and irregular and reminiscent of terrestrial landslides. Some of the slumped topography inspired speculation that subsurface water may exist in the form of permafrost; when it melted, the surface above would collapse and leave the jumbled terrain.

The camera photographed a hood of clouds over the south polar cap, and infrared instruments measured temperatures there as low as −193 degrees Fahrenheit. This is close to the temperature at which carbon dioxide solidifies when atmospheric pressures are as low as they are on Mars. There might be some frozen water there, but the south pole was covered mainly with frozen carbon dioxide—dry ice. Elsewhere, temperatures were also quite chilly. Another instrument detected the presence of a slight fog of water vapor. But the atmosphere appeared to consist almost entirely of carbon dioxide. Not a trace of nitrogen, so vital an ingredient of Earth's atmosphere, was detected in the thin air of Mars.

For a while, though, hopes were revived by an announcement from one of the Mariner scientists, George Pimentel of the University of California at Berkeley. The infrared spectrometer had appeared to detect temperatures at the edge of the south polar ice cap that were much too high to be from frozen carbon dioxide. It was thus assumed that at least the edge of the cap was composed of water ice. Furthermore, the atmosphere at the polar margins seemed to contain some methane and ammonia, hydrogen-rich gases that could be biological products. A buzz of excitement ran through the control room and out into the back rooms at the Jet Propulsion Laboratory where scientists pored over the data. But in a few days came the letdown. It became clear that the measurements had been misinterpreted; there was no evidence of possible biological activity. Had it been a case of wishful thinking?

If Mars still appeared to be more lunar-like than Earth-like, Caltech's Robert Leighton said, the new Mariner pictures and data showed the planet to be, well, "like Mars." The ancient craters might resemble the Moon's surface, but elsewhere the surface was more like an extremely dry and cold desert. Many of the features, Leighton said, "were unknown and unrecognized elsewhere in the solar system."

At the time, Norman Horowitz, who advised the Mariner team on biology, said: "We have certainly seen no signs of the noble race of beings that built the canals or launched the satellites of Mars. I'm pretty sure they don't exist."

Horowitz conceded that, poor as the prospects were, the search for life on Mars must be continued. "Anyone who is carrying out this work because he is sure he is going to find life, I think, is making a mistake," he said. "The search is sustained by the tremendous importance that a positive result would have, scientifically and philosophically, and until then we are obliged to continue the search."

BY CHANCE, THE first three Mariners had caught glimpses of the most unprepossessing parts of Mars. It was left to Mariner 9 in 1971–72 to reveal all the rest, but it had to wait out a dust storm that obscured the entire planet for several weeks after the spacecraft's arrival in orbit of Mars. Patience was rewarded, and Mariner 9's astonishing discoveries put an entirely new spin on thinking about Mars.

Both Soviet and American engineers sought to take advantage of the especially close opposition of 1971. Two Soviet craft, Mars 2 and 3, made it into orbits of Mars, each carrying landers. The craft were rigidly preprogrammed and so had no choice, in the face of the raging dust storm, but to deploy their landers for descents to the surface. The Mars 2 capsule crashed. The Mars 3 lander touched down, but data transmission from it ceased after only twenty seconds, long enough to send only one useless photograph. The craft had presumably been damaged on landing or overwhelmed by the dust. For all their successes in Earth orbit and in visits to Venus, the Russians were having no luck at all with Mars.

The first American attempt at this time was hardly encouraging. Mariner 8 suffered a rocket malfunction shortly after lift-off and plunged into the Atlantic off Cape Canaveral. Three weeks later, on May 30, 1971, the sister craft, Mariner 9, took off and went on to become the first man-made object to orbit another planet.

After a journey of 167 days, Mariner 9 arrived at the planet and swung into orbit on November 13. A larger and more sophisticated version of the earlier Mariners, it weighed 1,200 pounds and carried an additional 1,000 pounds of fuel for the rocket-firing maneuver that slowed it down for the entry into orbit. Of critical importance was the craft's compact on-board computer. It was designed with a flexibility to allow for many mission changes (in contrast to the Soviet vehicles), and this capability was put to an early test by Mariner 8's failure, which required that Mariner 9 assume many of the other's planned tasks, as well as by the delay in orbital operations caused by the dust storm. The craft's flexibility and durability enabled scientists to wait out the storm and still get almost a year of observations covering the entire planet. Mariner 9 took and transmitted more than

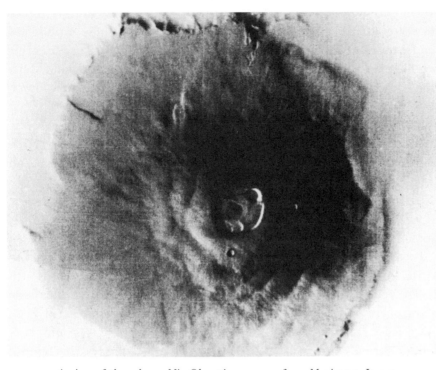

A view of the volcano Nix Olympica, as seen from Mariner 9. It was renamed Olympus Mons. (Jet Propulsion Laboratory)

7,000 pictures to provide cartographers with material for the first detailed map of the entire globe of another planet. Someone at NASA figured out that the 31 billion bits of information sent back by the spacecraft were more than had been received from all earlier planetary missions put together. This was, NASA pointed out, equivalent to 36 times the entire text of the *Encyclopaedia Britannica.*

David C. Pieri, a planetary geologist at the Jet Propulsion Laboratory, recalls the suspense and surprise. He was a graduate student at the time Mariner 9 arrived in Mars orbit, and the pictures of Mars shaped his career. He and many other scientists are still trying to interpret the messages borne by the Mariner 9 pictures, which he says represented "the quantum leap" in modern Mars studies.

"A better script could not have been written," Pieri said one day while pondering a globe produced from the Mariner 9 mapping data. "Mariner arrived at Mars, and the planet was shrouded in a big dust storm. Slowly but surely, almost grudgingly, Mars began giving up its secrets. The cloud dissipated, and there were these wonderful landscapes just laid out there, tremendously puzzling. There was this whole other half of the planet that we'd missed on the previous Mariners. We didn't expect the other hemisphere would be that much different."

Pieri pointed to the globe. "But there it is," he said, "there's one startling difference—the huge volcanoes of Tharsis. And Valles Marineris, the canyon stretching across the middle of the planet. And these great channels focusing into Chryse Planitia. The pictures of this area were very evocative, very influential in stimulating people to rethink Mars. So now we have a new version of Mars that comes out in the early 1970s."

By the end of January 1972, the winds abated and the dust began to settle. At first Mariner 9's cameras could make out only the south polar cap and four dark spots rising above the dust in the northern hemisphere and near the equator. One of the dark spots had been observed by astronomers during the dust storms of 1924 and 1956. Under normal conditions, as observed through telescopes, this feature had appeared as a bright white spot and was thus named Nix Olympica, the Snows of Olympus. As visibility improved, this and the other three spots turned out to be high mountains with craters at their summits. Clouds sometimes enveloping the summits accounted for their white appearance in early telescopic observations.

Geologists, recovering from their astonishment, concluded that these were none other than volcanoes. Recognition of these towering volcanoes on Mars, said Michael H. Carr, a Mariner scientist from the United States Geological Survey, was "one of the first and most significant results of the flight of Mariner 9."

The greatest of these is Nix Olympica, which was renamed Olympus Mons (mountain). Olympus rises some 13 miles above the surrounding plains, more than twice the elevation of Mount Everest above sea level. The crater at its summit is about 50 miles wide. The base of the mountain is more than 300 miles across, about the size of Missouri, and is surrounded by steep cliffs. Beyond is a depression caused by the enormous weight of the volcano resting on the Martian crust. The depression is largely filled with lava. With its gently sloping upper flanks and roughly circular summit crater, Olympus resembles the shield volcanoes of Hawaii, which formed by relatively quiet eruptions of fluid lava, rather than a volcano like Mount St. Helens in Washington, which was shaped by repeated explosive eruptions of ash. But there is nothing on Earth to compare in size with Olympus. Mauna Loa in Hawaii is the largest volcano on Earth, with a base 72 miles across, a summit crater only 1½ miles wide, and an elevation of 6 miles above the ocean floor. So Mariner 9 had discovered the largest known mountain and volcano in the solar system.

Olympus Mons lies at the western margin of the Tharsis uplift, a bulge in the Martian crust that extends more than 2,500 miles across. The other three spots were also revealed to be volcanoes, smaller than Olympus but by no means insignificant; they, too, dwarf their terrestrial counterparts. The volcanoes, named Arsia Mons, Pavonis Mons, and Ascraeus Mons, run at a diagonal across the equator along a ridge known as Tharsis Montes. As inferred from effects on the orbital course of the spacecraft, the entire volcanic region has the largest known positive gravitational anomaly; it is an area of great mass where gravity is stronger than in other parts of Mars.

Many smaller volcanoes were soon identified elsewhere on Mars. To geologists volcanoes mean that a planet is not—or at least has not always been—a dead world. At some time in its past Mars had been alive with internal heat. Perhaps there were some internal stirrings yet. In a chapter for the book *The Planets,* Carr wrote:

> The immense size of Olympus Mons and other Martian volcanoes is a result, in part, of the stability of the Martian crust. The Earth's crust is mobile. Differential movement of different sections of the crust creates much of Earth's surface relief, such as the ocean deeps and the linear mountain chains like the Andes and the Himalayas. Because of the constant movement terrestrial volcanoes are short-lived. Old volcanoes become extinct and new ones form on time scales measured in hundreds of thousands of years. In contrast the Mars crust is very stable and volcanoes continue to erupt for hundreds of millions of years, thereby growing to immense sizes. Olympus Mons and some of the other large Martian volcanoes may still be active. Eruptions are probably widely spaced in time, occurring only every few thousand years.

Scientists disagree on whether the volcanoes are extinct or merely dormant. Most of the slopes are gouged with craters from impacting meteorites, indicating that no fresh lava has flowed in a long, long time to smooth off the surface.

Another surprising and spectacular discovery of Mariner 9 is the great chasm beginning southeast of the Tharsis volcanoes and running some 2,500 miles along the equatorial region. Mars may not have canals, but its canyons are apparently unmatched anywhere in the solar system. The equatorial canyon system, named Valles Marineris, honoring the discovering spacecraft, is more than 100 miles wide in places and some of the chasms are as deep as Mount Everest is high. If it were on Earth, Valles Marineris would extend from Los Angeles to New York City. Some of its tributaries alone are deeper and wider than the Grand Canyon.

These canyonlands are presumably the result of a massive fracture in the planet's crust, possibly related to the turmoil associated with the formation of the Tharsis bulge and the volcanoes. The faulting perhaps released groundwater, accounting for the evidence of erosion, landslides, and jumbled terrain throughout the canyons and beyond. As Clark R. Chapman, a scientist at the Planetary Science Institute in Tucson, has written: "Such extraordinary canyonlands imply Martian geological forces like those in the Earth. The moonlike terrains were but a relic from Mars's ancient past, like the old cratered lake districts of Canada. The young canyons and volcanoes reestablished Mars, like the Earth, as a geologically fascinating world."

Arden L. Albee, a planetary scientist at the California Institute of Technology, recalls the surprise of the Mariner 9 revelations. "After the mountains began poking through and we began seeing evidence of Valles Marineris and all the rest," he said, "we looked at each other and said, hey, it isn't like the Moon—Mars is different."

Mariner 9's third major discovery also stunned scientists. East of the chasm and also north in Chryse Planitia the surface is cut with meandering valleys and channels that look like river valleys on Earth, such as the arroyos of the American Southwest or African wadis. Some of the channels included teardrop-shaped islands, the only known explanation for which is the eroding action of a flowing material.

The channels are dry now, and scientists who first examined the photographs resisted drawing the obvious conclusion. Perhaps these were smaller cracks in the crust, more evidence of faulting. Perhaps they were the channels where volcanic lava once flowed. But they certainly looked more like channels formed by flowing water. Once again, water on Mars was becoming an issue of scientific discourse.

Many of the channels differ from most terrestrial valleys in one respect, Carr observed. They emerge full-size from the chaotic terrain, have no tributaries, and maintain their size downstream. This reminded scientists of large terrestrial flood features rather than typical river valleys. At some time in Martian history, colossal floods of water swept across vast regions of the planet. The speculation fit neatly with new discoveries about one of the most devastating floods known to have occurred on Earth.

Early in this century, J. Harlen Bretz, a University of Chicago geologist, suggested that the barren, heavily scarred region of eastern Washington known as the Channeled Scablands had been created by a flood of phenomenal dimensions. The idea remained controversial until photographs from mapping satellites produced conclusive evidence of both the cause and the effect of the flood. It happened about 18,000 to 20,000 years ago during the last ice age. A lake containing half the volume of a Lake Michigan collected behind an "ice cork" that plugged drainage of western Montana into Idaho. When the ice dam collapsed, several thousand cubic miles of water rushed down the valley of the Spokane River across the site where the city of Spokane now stands, then turned south across central Washington, leaving scars clearly visible in the space photography.

The Mariner 9 pictures were coming in just as Victor Baker, then at the University of Texas, completed the analysis of the Spokane Flood. Baker recognized many similarities between eastern Washington and Mars, notably the deep channels and teardrop-shaped islands. Few geologists today doubt that flooding shaped most of the channeled landscape of Mars. But the floods of Mars were probably greater than anything known to have occurred on Earth.

Scientists are still trying to figure out where the water came from and where it went. Mariner 9 confirmed that Mars is now arid and extremely cold. Photographs revealed evidence of some frost and some clouds of water vapor but no liquid water on the surface. The caps of ice on both poles of Mars, which Mariner 9 surveyed in more detail than ever before, were found to be composed primarily of carbon dioxide. The presence of any water ice could not yet be established. Because Mars has a pattern of seasons similar to Earth's, the northern ice cap expands and the southern ice cap recedes when it is winter in the northern hemisphere—and vice versa during the northern summer. What is happening, though, is a transformation of carbon dioxide in the atmosphere to a frozen state at the poles, and then back again to a vapor. This could not be a source of flowing liquid over the surface.

The curious laminated appearance of the ice caps prompted speculation that Mars had undergone successive periods of drastic climatic change. Dust deposited on the ice cap during prolonged ice ages could have left a kind of "tree ring" record of past conditions. If the present atmospheric pressure and temperature on Mars are such that water cannot be present as a liquid on the surface, those who still harbored hopes for Martian life suggested that the poles could have melted periodically and released great amounts of carbon dioxide into the atmosphere, raising atmospheric pressure to a point where water could exist in a liquid form on the surface and also creating a much warmer climate. If it was warmer and had surface water, then it was possible to imagine that Mars was a much different world millions or billions of years ago. Could this be? What happened to change the Martian climate? The questions are important to scientists because a more watery past on Mars raises anew the possibility that life might have arisen there at one time and then vanished with the onset of the present dry and cold climate.

Perhaps there remain somewhere on Mars pockets of moisture where life in some simple, hardy forms could persist to this day. Hope springs eternal among the "pro-life" scientists studying Mars. The prospect, however remote, encouraged scientists who were planning the Viking missions to Mars in 1976.

Meanwhile, geologists puzzling over the dry channels and other signs of water erosion began to center their thinking on permafrost. Dwayne Anderson of the State University of New York at Buffalo pointed out the probability that most water on Mars is frozen in the ground, much like the permafrost under the tundra of Siberia, Alaska, and northern Canada. At present temperatures on Mars, the ground is permanently frozen to a depth of a mile at the equator and even deeper at higher latitudes. This frozen layer could act as a seal, trapping liquid water under pressure at greater depths. If the permafrost seal was somehow disrupted by faulting or a meteorite impact, Carr of the Geological Survey explained, then water could erupt to the surface in a massive flood. The rushing water would carve out the channels. And the subterranean space where the water had been trapped, empty now, would collapse to form the chaotic terrain that is seen over much of the Martian surface.

Mariner 9 left scientists with other puzzles. For example, why are the northern and southern hemispheres apparently so different? This hemispheric discontinuity is what fooled scientists on the early Mariner missions. The planet's southern half, which was viewed by Mariners 4, 6, and 7, is highly cratered and extremely ancient. Planetary surfaces are dated by the abundance of craters and how saturated by craters the surface is. The southern half of Mars is a saturated surface, perhaps as ancient as the Moon's surface—as much as 4 billion years old. The northern half is distinguished by the presence of volcanoes, canyons, flood channels, and broad plains. "One half is very active and the other is very inactive," Albee of Caltech said recently. "I don't think there's a universally accepted explanation for this difference. Nobody has attempted a global theory."

The timing of the events that shaped the Martian surface remains a mystery. How early or how recent were the floods? Or the climate changes and volcanic eruptions? "We're frustrated," said David Pieri of the Jet Propulsion Laboratory, "because we don't really know the early history of Mars, which was probably the most active period."

One school of thought holds that Mars has been an active planet until quite recent times, but the activity has been local and episodic. Geologists see evidence for this in some of the eroded channels, which they believe experienced fluid flows not too long ago. But erosion and cratering on the mountain summits indicate that volcanism had been active for perhaps two-thirds of Mars's 4.6-billion-year history, but not in a long time. Many scientists tend to believe that surface water played an active role on the planet quite early and not much has happened since.

After Mariner 9 spent 349 working days in orbit of Mars, the spacecraft ran out of attitude-control gas and tumbled out of control on October 27, 1972. But it had operated long enough to accomplish its mission. If scientists were still mystified by Mars, it was not because they knew so little, but because they had now seen so much. The real Mars had at last come into focus.

Bruce Murray conceded that "Mars turned out to be different from what any of us thought, and demonstrated that I personally have, to some extent, been a victim of my own prejudices about the planet." Before Mariner 9, he had wisely cautioned against letting Lowellian ideas color our expectations, but his own thinking had been too restrictive. "Mars," he confessed, "has proved to be an even more interesting planet to explore than I had thought a year ago."

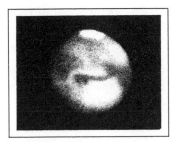

CHAPTER 5

THE MOONS
OF MARS

WHILE MARINER 9 waited for the dust of the global storm to settle, flight controllers hastily revised mission plans and reoriented the spacecraft. Its cameras were focused for a time on two chunks of rock orbiting Mars. The result was an important scientific bonus: the first close-up observations revealing the true size and face of the two Martian moons, Phobos and Deimos.

As satellites go, they are drab and seemingly insignificant objects. They are so dark and small as to go undetected for centuries, even after the introduction of telescopes. For a long time textbooks had routinely placed the notation "no moons" by the name of Mars, and astronomers had all but abandoned the search. Yet the moons of Mars had enjoyed an illustrious history even before their discovery. Their existence was imagined before they were first seen in 1877.

As early as 1610, Kepler had predicted that Mars must have two satellites. He was correct, we know, but his reasoning was fallacious, a case of Kepler the believer in orbital harmonies (and caster of horoscopes) ascendant over Kepler the genius who recognized the laws of planetary motions. His prediction was a reaction to Galileo's discovery of four large moons orbiting Jupiter. If, as all observations seemed to show, Venus had no moons and Earth had one, Kepler deduced that

Mars, being intermediate between Earth and Jupiter, would have two moons. This fit neatly with his passion for geometric progressions and the harmonic order of orbiting bodies, what came to be known as the music of the spheres. But geometric progressions do not always obtain in nature. Besides, subsequent telescopic and spacecraft observations have revealed that Jupiter has many more than four moons.

Given Kepler's stature, the supposition of two Martian moons persisted, notably in literature. In a story published in 1727, entitled "The Voyage to Laputa," Jonathan Swift has his hero, Dr. Lemuel Gulliver, visit the people of Laputa, an island in the sky. Gulliver described the Laputans as skilled astronomers who have "discovered two lesser stars, or satellites, which revolve about Mars, whereof the innermost is distant from the centre of the primary planet exactly three of its diameters, and the outermost five." They had also timed the orbits. The inner moon, Gulliver reported, completed an orbit every 10 hours and the outer moon, every 21.5 hours. It was a good guess; Phobos circles Mars every 7.7 hours and Deimos does it in 30.3 hours. How did Swift know this? Although some writers have sought to attribute the knowledge to visits from ancient astronauts or the powerful telescopes of some ancient civilizations, the most likely source was nothing more than Kepler's speculations.

Voltaire also perpetuated the idea of Martian moons. In a novel, *Micromégas,* published in 1752, he told of a visit to the solar system by a being from Sirius, the dog star. "Our travellers crossed a space of about a hundred million leagues and reached the planet Mars," Voltaire wrote. "They saw two moons which wait on this planet, and which have escaped the gaze of astronomers. . . . How difficult it would be for Mars, which is so far from the sun, to get on with less than two moons!"

After William Herschel looked in 1783 and failed to find any Martian satellites, few astronomers made the effort again until 1877, the time of the favorable viewing opportunity when Schiaparelli saw the "canals." Asaph Hall, an astronomer at the Naval Observatory in Washington, decided this was the year to renew the search. He had available the observatory's new 26-inch telescope, one of the best in the world then and especially equipped to establish positions of the fainter satellites in the solar system.

Methodical observations of satellites were important because they

*Asalph Hall, the discoverer of Martian moons.
(U.S. Naval Observatory)*

provided astronomers with data for determining more accurately the mass of the parent planet. From the orbital perturbations of the satellite caused by the planet they could calculate the gravitational influence of the planet and thus its mass. If satellites could be found orbiting Mars, the planet's mass could be established with greater certainty. As it was, astronomers had to make a rough estimate of Martian mass based on its own perturbations due to the gravitational pull of Earth and Jupiter.

Hall's search began in early August. At first, he examined faint objects at some distance from the planet. No luck; they all turned out to be fixed stars. On August 10 Hall set his sights closer to Mars, struggling to overcome the planet's glare. "This was done," he explained, "by keeping the planet just outside the field of view, and turning the eye-piece so as to pass completely around the planet." But he saw nothing the first night. He tried again the night of August 11 and at last glimpsed a "faint object" on the east side and a little north of the planet. Hall had no time for a detailed examination, for just then fog rising off the Potomac obscured his vision. After a frustrating string of cloudy nights, Hall caught sight of the object again on August 16. It was definitely moving around the planet. He had discovered a moon of Mars.

"Until this time I had said nothing to anyone at the Observatory of my search for a satellite of Mars," Hall wrote in a manuscript that was recently uncovered in the Naval Observatory's archives. "But on leaving the Observatory after these observations of the 16th, at about three o'clock in the morning, I told my assistant, George Anderson, to whom I had shown the object, that I thought I had discovered a satellite of Mars. I told him also to keep quiet as I did not wish anything said until the matter was beyond doubt."

Hall could not contain his excitement, however, and at lunch that day he told Simon Newcomb, the scientific head of the observatory. Back at the telescope that night, Hall and Anderson saw another moon even closer to the planet. Other astronomers, including Newcomb, joined Hall the night of August 18 and confirmed "beyond doubt the character of these objects." The next morning, the observatory announced the discovery of two Martian satellites.

According to Steven J. Dick, historian of the Naval Observatory, who has studied the Hall manuscript, some questions about the inner object persisted for several days after the discovery. The inner object would appear on different sides of the planet on the same night, leading Hall to believe that there might be two or three inner satellites. A few nights later, Hall discovered what Swift had imagined long before. Hall wrote that he "saw that there was in fact but one inner moon which made its revolution around the primary in less than one third the time of the primary's rotation—a case unique in our solar system."

As discoverer, Hall had the honor of naming the new moons. At the suggestion of Henry Madan, a scholar at Eton in England, he chose the names Phobos for the inner moon and Deimos for the outer one. In the fifteenth book of Homer's *Iliad*, Phobos (Fear) and Deimos (Flight) are the attendants of the war god Ares, as Mars was called by the Greeks. As Homer wrote: "He spake, and summoned Fear and Flight to yoke his steed, and put his glorious armor on." Phobos and Deimos are now generally translated as Fear and Panic.

When the photographs from Mariner 9 were examined, two substantial craters scarred the surface of Phobos. Scientists named the smaller one Hall and the larger one Stickney, after Hall's wife, the former Angeline Stickney, whom Hall credited with encouraging him to keep looking for the moons of Mars. The two most prominent craters of Deimos were named Swift and Voltaire.

LITTLE ELSE WAS learned about Phobos and Deimos for many decades. They were simply too faint and too close to Mars for observations revealing much more than their orbital timetables. These were established after years of study by astronomers at the Naval Observatory, which had a proprietary interest, and the Pulkovo Observatory near St. Petersburg, now Leningrad.

Deimos orbits in the plane of Mars's equator, about 12,470 miles above the surface. Phobos moves in an almost perfectly circular orbit no more than 3,720 miles above the planet's equator. To astronomers this meant that Phobos appeared to exist on the inner limit of possibility. If it came much closer to Mars, the planet's gravitational forces would tear Phobos asunder. The orbit of Phobos thus lies precariously close to what is known as the Roche limit for Mars. This is a theoretical boundary, the critical distance inside which tidal disruption would keep any swarm of interplanetary debris from collecting to form a single body or would disintegrate any existing object. The orbit of Deimos also is unusual. Deimos is near the outer limit for an object to be orbiting Mars; beyond that limit, the planet's gravity would be too weak to hold on to the moon. Also, Deimos lies just outside what is known as the stationary orbit position, which is the point where a satellite's period of revolution exactly equals the planet's period of rotation, so that from the surface of the planet the satellite appears to hang motionless in the sky.

The first astronauts to land on Mars will see Deimos, like the Sun, rise in the east and set in the west. Because the moon has a revolution period of 30 hours 18 minutes, its progress almost keeps pace with the rotation of Mars. But Deimos is not quite motionless in the sky. Moving ever so slowly, it takes about 60 hours to move from one horizon to the other. The little moon will be only as bright as Venus is in the Earth's sky. But Phobos, by contrast, will rise in the west.

Alone among the known moons of the solar system, Phobos is so close to its planet that it circles it in less time than the planet takes to revolve on its own axis, which accounts for its rising in the west. It will then cross the sky in only 4 hours 15 minutes and set in the east. The intervals between risings would be 11 hours 6 minutes. Phobos will be 40 times brighter than Deimos, appearing to anyone on Mars as a pale oval that would seem to be two-thirds the diameter of Earth's Moon.

From Earth it has been impossible to make out anything about the shape or surface detail of Phobos and Deimos. They are merely points of light. By analyzing the reflection of sunlight off their surfaces, however, astronomers estimated that Phobos was probably no larger than 10 miles in diameter and Deimos about half that size. This was based on the assumption that both were much like Mars in composition and were, therefore, dark and not efficient reflectors of sunlight.

But what if the composition of the moons is nothing like that of Mars? What if Phobos and Deimos are not natural satellites? The questions were raised because of some puzzling observations that led to one of the most startling propositions in modern astronomy.

Something peculiar about the orbit of Phobos was reported in 1945 by B. P. Sharpless of the Naval Observatory. His analysis of past observations of the positions of the moons indicated that Phobos seemed to be accelerating ever so slightly, pulling ahead of its predicted position. It appeared that Phobos was gradually falling closer to Mars and thus moving faster in its orbit; a lower orbit is a faster one. Phobos was behaving in a way that, in theory, artificial satellites of Earth would as they fall victim to drag from the upper atmosphere and begin to drop out of orbit.

Scientists proposed and rejected several possible explanations. The satellite's orbit might be degraded by a thin Martian atmosphere extending farther out than previously assumed. Perhaps the cause was interplanetary dust, solar pressure, electromagnetic forces, or tidal interactions between Phobos and the equatorial bulge of Mars. Someone even suggested that a meteorite could have knocked Phobos off course, though this was unlikely because the acceleration was not sudden, but cumulative.

In 1960, the Soviet astrophysicist Iosif S. Shklovskii reviewed the evidence and came up with an explanation that, if nothing else, proved that Martians lived on in the human consciousness. First, he revived the assumption that air drag could have been responsible. In all previous discussions, drag was ruled out because it was supposed that the density of Phobos was like Mars and Earth, about three to four times as heavy as water. Such a heavy object would not be affected by friction from the extremely thin Martian atmosphere. But if Phobos was much less dense, perhaps it would be light enough for atmospheric drag to pull it in closer to the planet. Shklovskii calculated that Phobos would have to be 1,000 times less dense than water for it to be so affected. What could be that light? Since no known object is that light, Shklovskii reasoned that Phobos must be hollow, and if so, it could not possibly be a natural satellite. It must, therefore, be an artificial satellite, a space station several miles across, lofted into an orbit of Mars by some earlier Martian civilization. Deimos was presumably also an artificial satellite. The Martians may have disappeared, but not their two orbiting space stations.

Shklovskii's proposal caused a brief sensation among those who believed in extraterrestrial life. Shklovskii, too, was a champion of unorthodox ideas and of the view that life has originated not only on Earth but also elsewhere in the universe. His book on the subject, *Intelligent Life in the Universe,* was amplified and introduced to American readers in 1966 by Carl Sagan, who entertained similar views. But few astronomers came to the support of arguments that the moons of Mars were actually artificial satellites. Shklovskii later insisted that he had not meant for the suggestion to be taken seriously.

The entire idea was laid to rest in August 1969, when the Mariner 7 spacecraft photographed Phobos from a range of 82,000 miles on its flight past Mars. The silhouette of Phobos outlined against the disc of the planet showed the moon to have a highly irregular shape, hardly the spherical or cylindrical shape one would imagine for an artificial satellite. Nor did it have a shiny, metallic appearance. The surface of Phobos was so dark that it was only half as reflective of light as the Earth's Moon.

Mariner 9 transmitted 27 photographs of Phobos and 9 of Deimos, all of which were much clearer and more revealing than any previous images of the moons. One of the pictures of Phobos was taken at a range of 4,000 miles, the closest approach. American scientists said Phobos looked like "a diseased potato." Deimos was also seen to be a

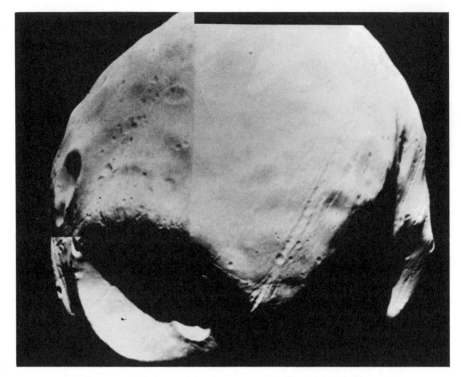

A close-up of Phobos, a Martian moon. (Jet Propulsion Laboratory)

lumpy object. If these were artificial satellites, Mariner scientists re-marked, they were cleverly disguised.

From the photographs scientists determined that the two moons were slightly larger than had been estimated. The principal diameters of Phobos are 17, 14, and 13 miles. For Deimos the measurements are 10, 7, and 6 miles.

The Mariner photographs, and subsequent ones from the two Viking missions in 1976, provided the first views of the surfaces of the two moons: Beaten and battered the two moons are, their surfaces pocked with a profusion of craters large and small, young and old.

Joseph Veverka, an astronomer at Cornell University, reported that the craters come in a variety of shapes. One elongated crater looks like a keyhole. Others are perfectly circular. The largest, Stickney, is 6 miles wide, almost one-third the size of the moon itself; it is a wonder Phobos survived such a massive blow. Presumably some powerful

A close-up of Deimos. (Jet Propulsion Laboratory)

impacts did actually knock off chunks of the moon, contributing to its irregular shape. Some craters have sharp rims, suggesting a fresh impact. Others are worn down and shallow from the erosion of the ages. With no wind or moisture on the moons, the most probable source of the erosion is steady bombardment of micrometeorites and charged gases of the solar wind on the unprotected surface. Some of the newer craters have undoubtedly overlaid and obliterated earlier craters, frustrating scientists in their attempt to use crater counts as a measure of the moons' age. The best they have been able to do is produce gross estimates of age ranging from 2 billion years to 4.6 billion years, which is the age of Mars itself and the other planets.

Two other surface features—grooves radiating out from the larger craters of Phobos and the presence on both moons of a blanket of dirt or dust—have been particularly puzzling to scientists.

Some of the grooves on Phobos are hundreds of feet wide and

roughly parallel, running out from craters like Stickney. At first, geologists guessed they must be cracks in the surface caused by the shock of the huge meteorite impact that created the crater. It was considered unlikely that these lines were gouged out by the rocky rubble blasted out from the crater, although that kind of action has occurred on Earth's Moon. With the negligible gravity of the little Martian satellites, scientists assumed, the ejecta would have escaped into space. But the subsequent discovery of a covering of dust (geologists call this a regolith) on the moons has complicated the issue.

Mariner 9's examination of heat and reflected light from Phobos and Deimos resulted in the surprising discovery of rubble and dust all over the surfaces. How could the low-gravity bodies hold on to this impact debris? No one has an answer, only theories. Perhaps the crater-making impacts are somehow weak, low-energy phenomena. Thus, not all fragments blasted free would be traveling at a velocity (13 miles per hour) sufficient to escape the satellites' gravity. Or perhaps the fragments do escape the satellites' gravity but are not traveling fast enough to escape the stronger gravity of Mars. Much of the debris would then go into an orbit of Mars in the vicinity of the satellites. There the material may be captured again by one satellite or the other, where it would collect as a kind of soil on their surfaces. In a variation of that idea, the impact debris may experience multiple collisions as it is flying away from the moons. The collisions produce showers of small particles that fall back on the moons. Scientists have arrived at calculations showing that this collision process could account for some of the smaller impact craters, perhaps also some of the grooves on Phobos.

An analysis of Mariner 9's observations did settle one matter of controversy and speculation. Phobos is indeed accelerating. Scientists at the Jet Propulsion Laboratory determined that, assuming the acceleration continues at its present rate, Phobos should come crashing down on Mars in about 100 million years. After a further examination of telescopic observations, Soviet astronomers confirmed the estimate. The most likely explanation is tidal drag. The lumpy interior and bulging equator of Mars cause a slight unevenness in its gravitational pull. Consequently, the gravity differentials on the front and back of Phobos cause it to lose some energy and descend gradually toward Mars. By contrast, Deimos in its higher altitude appears to be pulling away gradually from Mars and someday may escape the planet's gravitational embrace.

There is plenty of time, therefore, for spacecraft to probe the moons and find out what they are made of. Only then are scientists likely to answer the question of where two such small and odd moons came from. If they are not artificial satellites of the ancient Martians, what are they?

THE SIMILARITY of their equatorial orbits and, more important, the similarity of their light reflectivity, suggesting the same dark surface, have led scientists to assume that Phobos and Deimos have a common origin. The argument is over how they originated. Two leading hypotheses—capture and accretion—emerged from the Mariner 9 and subsequent Viking investigations.

When they saw the density data and the low light reflectivity, or albedo, scientists began to suspect that Phobos and Deimos were not ordinary moons formed in conjunction with the parent planet. The two moons are among the darkest objects in the solar system, reflecting only 6 percent of the incoming sunlight. Such an albedo indicates that the moons are much darker—more like coal—than the reddish Mars. Could the moons and Mars possibly be formed out of the same primordial material? The orbiting Viking craft, sensing the gravitational pull of the moons, obtained the first accurate measure of their densities. Each has a density about twice that of water, which makes them half as dense as Mars. This raised even more eyebrows.

All these clues suggested that Phobos and Deimos quite possibly were asteroids that had wandered by and been pulled in by the gravity of Mars. Variations on this hypothesis are that a single asteroid might have been captured and then broken into two pieces, or perhaps a large asteroid passing close to Mars was fragmented by gravitational stresses, with at least two of the larger chunks being drawn into the planet's orbit.

The asteroid-capture hypothesis has a special appeal. For, if true, it promises to give us easy access to examples of some of the most intriguing objects in the solar system. To take a trip to a moon of Mars would thus be to visit a place that might have been the home of the Little Prince, the enchanting creation of Antoine de Saint-Exupéry.

Phobos and Deimos are larger, of course, than B-612, the name grown-up scientists gave to the Little Prince's world, but not by a lot on the cosmic scale. They are without the flower the Little Prince nurtured under a glass globe, the baobab seedlings he pulled up to ward off catastrophe, or the two small volcanoes where he heated his breakfast. But in the moons of Mars, if they are asteroids, grown-ups will learn, if not the wisdom the fox imparted to the Little Prince, at least something about the many little worlds in the vast spaces between the planets.

Asteroids are the primitive rocky remnants of planet formation. More than 4,000 of these objects, each usually only a few miles in diameter, have been observed long enough to plot their orbits, and their total number may be as high as 100,000. They are most abundant in a belt between Mars and Jupiter. But some, known as Apollo-type asteroids, swing in on long orbits that cross the orbit of Earth, posing a threat of collision. A few craters on Earth bespeak massive collisions in the past, and geologists have gathered substantial evidence that a 6-mile-wide object, either an asteroid or a comet, slammed into Earth 65 million years ago, possibly causing a global darkness and contributing to the mass extinctions of dinosaurs and other life. New discoveries suggest that a similar impact may have caused other mass extinctions, including the most recent one 11 to 13 million years ago.

The darkness and density of the moons remind scientists of a certain type of carbon-rich meteorite known as carbonaceous chondrites. They are of prime scientific interest because they have been found to contain amino acids that are considered basic building blocks for life on Earth. But carbonaceous chondrites rarely reach Earth intact; they either burn up in the atmosphere or, if they reach the ground, are diminished as scientific specimens by rain and other contamination. But they are believed to be common in space, especially between Mars and Jupiter. Finding such objects in Mars's orbit would facilitate the exploration of asteroids and help resolve a long-simmering controversy in science. Conventional wisdom has it that asteroids are mainly unchanged remnants of the cosmic debris out of which the planets formed. In recent years, however, revisionist astronomers have argued that many asteroids are anything but pristine relics of primordial material; many of them may have undergone just as much alteration by extreme heat as have the planets and so may not preserve evidence of conditions at the beginning of the solar system.

The asteroid hypothesis has its weaknesses, however. It is hard to conceive of how captured asteroids could have wound up in circular orbits of the planet's equator. They would more than likely be in orbits sharply tilted with respect to the equator. When spacecraft are sent to the Moon, for example, it requires carefully programmed rocket firings to inject them into a circular orbit. Otherwise, they either fly past the target or crash into it.

The other leading hypothesis supposes that the two moons were formed by accretion of material left over after the birth of Mars. The material could have coalesced into two separate bodies or a single larger satellite that eventually broke apart. Perhaps the breakup occurred when a passing asteroid collided with the satellite and then proceeded on its way, leaving some satellite fragments escaping into space and at least two remaining in an orbit of Mars. It could be that Phobos and Deimos are the sole survivors of many small moons, perhaps fragments of a larger satellite, that once surrounded Mars. Some geologists contend that the shapes of some impact craters along the Martian equator suggest they could have been created by earlier moons that came crashing in. But the accretion hypothesis, in whatever form, suffers because of the apparent dissimilarities in color and density between the moons and Mars.

Finding out how the Martian moons came into being could help explain the origin of Earth's Moon. Even after all the Apollo landings, the dispute over the Moon's genesis goes on. Is it a "sister" or a "daughter" of Earth? Or a "captive"? A fundamental similarity between Earth and the Moon in the chemical composition of their rocks strongly suggests the two were formed together. Yet the Moon is different from Earth in its bulk composition, notably the absence of a large metallic core and thus its low density. If anything, the lunar composition reminds scientists of that of Earth's upper layers, prompting speculation that the Moon was formed from material gouged out of Earth by a massive impact—the daughter theory. A related proposal is that when Earth was young it was rotating very rapidly; this created a misshapen bulge that was eventually spun off in one big mass, the Moon. The sister theory suggests that Earth and the Moon formed in close proximity from a spinning cloud of dust, in much the same way that scientists believe the large satellite systems of the outer planets originated. But why would Earth and the Moon have such compositional differences? Our Moon, moreover, is an oddity in the solar system because it is much larger, relative to its parent body, than any of the other satellites. Astronomers have thus proposed that the Moon originated elsewhere and was captured. A more recent version of this theory involves what might have been a grazing collision of a Moon-sized body with Earth. In the heat and force of the collision, material from Earth's mantle was thrown out into a ring around Earth, mixing there with fragments of the colliding body to form the Moon that we know today.

Little has changed, that is, since Harold C. Urey, the Nobel Prize–winning chemist, observed: "All explanations for the origin of the Moon are improbable."

With even more yet to be learned about the moons of Mars, exploration of them was accorded a high priority by Soviet scientists. Two Soviet spacecraft were launched in July 1988 on missions to orbit Mars and rendezvous with tiny Phobos. Unfortunately, the first craft went out of control in early September, and the surviving companion made it to Mars orbit, only to drop out of communication as it maneuvered into a position to land scientific instruments on Phobos. Scientists will thus have to wait to learn the composition of the moons and get strong evidence of their origins.

There is a practical, as well as scientific, objective. Those who look to the future of human exploration and colonization of Mars see Phobos and Deimos as potentially indispensable staging bases. They would make stable observation platforms. Landing on one of the moons would be as easy as the docking of two spacecraft. In the weak gravity on either moon, the descent velocity of a craft would be little more than that of a parachutist hitting the ground on Earth. And lifting off again would require a minimum of propulsive energy. An astronaut on Phobos could even throw objects with sufficient velocity for them to escape the moon's gravity.

If the moons are indeed carbonaceous chondrites, or even some other type of asteroid, scientists estimate they may contain about 20 percent of their weight in water, as well as some carbon. With these resources in mind, engineers have already drawn up preliminary plans for manufacturing facilities that could be deployed on one of the moons to produce oxygen, water, and propellants for use on Mars and by spaceships making stops between Earth and Mars. Voyagers to Mars would thus carry only enough oxygen and propellants to get to Phobos and count on being resupplied there for the rest of the journey to Mars and back to Earth. Never again would the moons of Mars be dismissed as odd and insignificant.

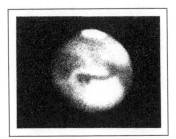

CHAPTER 6

VIKING AND
THE SEARCH
FOR LIFE

ONE YEAR SHY of a century after Schiaparelli had sighted those "canals," the two Viking spacecraft arrived for the climactic event of man's search for life on Mars. No one expected the mission to encounter intelligent life on the planet, not after the Mariner observations. Nor did anyone seriously expect to find large organisms. But there was still a chance that somewhere in the arid sands, on an ancient floodplain or perhaps in the ooze of some thawing permafrost, microbes were making the best of a hostile environment. Some hardy lichen, sustained by water vapor in Martian air, might be growing on a sheltered rock here and there. Or, more likely, there would be nothing living there at all. The prospects of finding life were admittedly dim. But not to pursue the search with an empirical test, now that this was possible through space flight, was absolutely unthinkable. Americans had invested $1 billion in the pursuit, and in the summer of 1976, the two Viking spacecraft reached Mars for the first systematic *in situ* experiments investigating the possibility of extraterrestrial life.

The spacecraft were launched from Cape Canaveral in August and September of 1975 amid the usual trepidations. Once again, the Soviet experience had been discouraging. A year earlier, the Mars 4 craft had

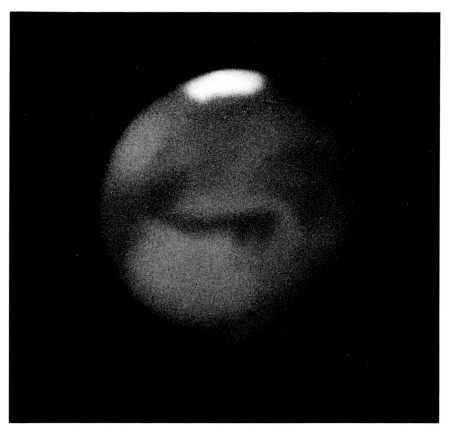

Given the distances covered and technological limitations, the quality of some images in this section may suffer, but not the impression they convey of a world being revealed to human eyes. Above, Mars as photographed by a ground-based telescope before the Viking explorations. Polar ice cap is seen at top. (Robert Leighton, California Institute of Technology)

Mars as captured by a Viking camera while the spacecraft raced toward the planet. Craters and canyons are visible. (Jet Propulsion Laboratory)

The first color photograph taken by Viking 1 from Chryse Planitia. (Jet Propulsion Laboratory)

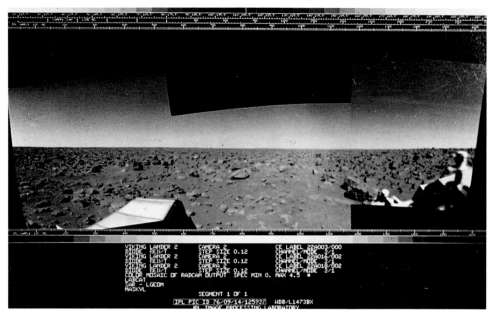

VIKING LANDER 2   CAMERA 2   CE LABEL 22A003/000
DIDIE BEW/1   STEP SIZE 0.12   CHANNEL/MODE   2/1
VIKING LANDER 2   CAMERA 6   CE LABEL 22A01?/002
DIDIE BEW/T   STEP SIZE 0.12   CHANNEL/MODE   1
VIKING LANDER 2   CAMERA 2   CE LABEL 22A018/002
DIDIE BEW/1   STEP SIZE 0.12   CHANNEL/MODE   2/1
COLOR MOSAIC OF RADCAM OUTPUT SPEC MIN 0. MAX 4.5 ■
LABCAT
SAR → LGEOM
MASKVL
                    SEGMENT 1 OF 1
         IPL PIC ID 76/09/14/125933   WDB/L1473BX
               IPL IMAGE PROCESSING LABORATORY

Horizon at Chryse Planitia, photographed by Viking 1. The computer-processed image, as seen at the flight control center, is accompanied by identifying data. (Jet Propulsion Laboratory)

Viking 1 with its robotic arm extended to dig a trench in the red Martian soil. (Jet Propulsion Laboratory)

Viking 1 orbiter's image of Valles Marineris, the huge canyon system on Mars. (Jet Propulsion Laboratory)

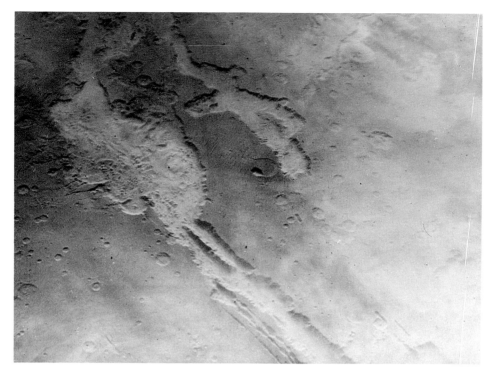

A canyon in Valles Marineris. The area suggests earlier fluid movement on Mars. (Jet Propulsion Laboratory)

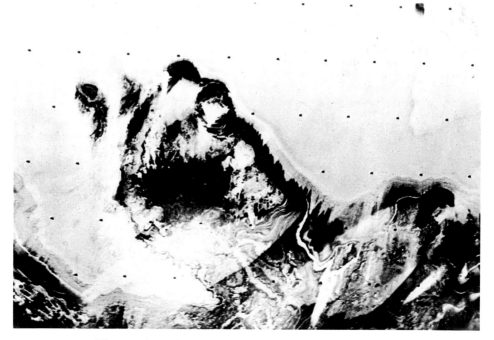

The great ice cliffs near the Martian North Pole, as seen from orbit by a Viking spacecraft. (Jet Propulsion Laboratory)

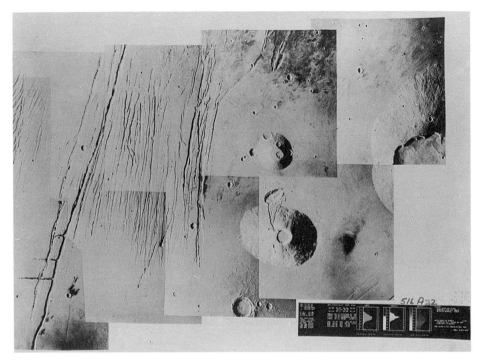

A mosaic of Viking orbital pictures showing volcanic peaks in the Tharsis region of Mars. (Jet Propulsion Laboratory)

A self-portrait of Viking 2 as it rests on Utopia Planitia. (Jet Propulsion Laboratory)

Martian terrain, as Viking 2 saw it. (Jet Propulsion Laboratory)

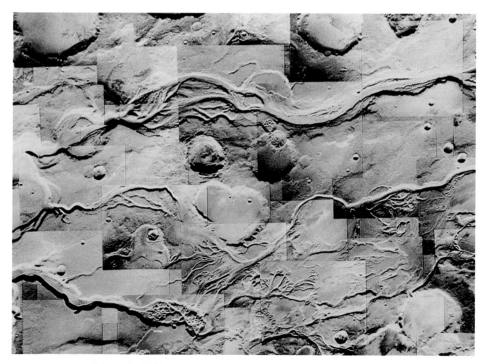

Mangala Valley, a region of Mars with sinuous channels. (Jet Propulsion Laboratory)

Olympus Mons, the great volcano, seen from a Viking orbiter's camera. (Jet Propulsion Laboratory)

failed to make it to an orbit of the planet, and its companion, Mars 5, operated in orbit for no more than 10 days. Mars 6 and 7 were supposed to deliver landing craft. The first crashed into the surface, and the second missed the planet altogether. The continuing lack of Soviet success gave Americans an opportunity and a challenge. They now had the chance to land the first operating craft on another planet and to be the first to seek the answer to the big question: Is there life on Mars? But they would have to do better than the Russians. They would need a little luck.

Each Viking was really a double spacecraft. The main vehicle was an orbiting craft based on Mariner 9 technology, including a full complement of television cameras and remote-sensing instruments for surveying the entire planet. Attached to this vehicle was a biologically sterilized landing craft built by the Martin Marietta Corporation in Denver in a project managed by NASA's Langley Research Center at Hampton, Virginia. Over the previous eight years, some 10,000 people had worked on Viking, under the stern gaze of James S. Martin, Jr., the project manager, designing, building, testing, and operating these craft of exploration.

The first Viking spacecraft, Viking 1, went into an orbit of Mars on June 19, 1976, in time, it was hoped, to attempt a landing on July 4 as a cosmic flourish to the American Bicentennial celebration. Geologists consulting Mariner 9 maps and photographs had already identified a landing site on Chryse Planitia, the Plain of Gold, chosen because it appeared once to have been inundated by a great flood and was thus a promising place for life to have arisen. It also seemed to be a smooth and safe place for a landing. But when the Viking 1 orbiter's more powerful cameras examined the area, scientists were both elated and shocked. The pictures were sharper and more detailed than anyone had dared expect, but they bore bad news. "We could see the site was full of craters," Harold Masursky of the U.S. Geological Survey said. "So we decided very soon that there was no way that we could land on our original choice."

The Viking orbiter was instructed to go looking for more suitable sites, while photo-interpretation teams at the Jet Propulsion Laboratory, where the flight was being controlled, worked day and night examining the new photographs. Some 800 pictures covering territory about the size of Texas were reviewed. As good as the pictures were, the resolution was not good enough to reveal boulders and small ravines that could destroy a landing craft. Something as big as the Rose Bowl would have gone undetected, and the scientists at JPL had only to look down the hill to see how big a hidden obstacle that could be to the Viking lander. "What if we land on a big boulder?" said a worried Gentry Lee, director of science analysis and mission planning. "What if we land on the side of a crater? The lander can't stand up on a slope of more than thirty degrees. What if it just sinks in the dust?"

To supplement the photography, radar beams from Earth were bounced off different sites to measure their comparative roughness. "That was quite a circus," David Pieri, a member of the mapping team, recalled. "We'd get the new data at ten o'clock each evening, and we'd stay up all night preparing a new site map to present to the mission management." Three potential sites were rejected before one was finally chosen, 560 miles away on the edge of Chryse Planitia. By this time, however, Viking had missed its July 4 landing opportunity.

The date finally set, July 20, also had historical overtones. On that day, seven years before, Neil A. Armstrong and Edwin E. Aldrin, Jr., had landed on the Moon, stepped from their craft, and put man's footprints on another world for the first time.

Early in the morning of July 20, 1976, flight controllers at JPL radioed the command—a single coded word, KVUGNG—to initiate a sequence of preprogrammed instructions in Viking 1's computer. It took 19 minutes for the command to travel the 200 million miles to Viking, which responded obediently. Pyrotechnic devices were fired to release the lander from the orbiter. Three sets of springs gently pushed the lander, a 1,300-pound vehicle about the size of a jeep, a safe distance away. The firing of small rockets on the edge of the lander's aeroshell, its dome-shaped protective covering, oriented the vehicle and braked it so that Martian gravity could pull it downward out of orbit and toward the surface. The descent to landing took 3 hours 13 minutes.

After a long coasting period and just before reaching the upper fringes of Martian atmosphere, the lander was reoriented so that its heat shield faced the angle of attack. The shield's corklike coating was designed to protect against entry heat of up to 2,700 degrees F. Atmospheric drag and lift further slowed down the craft's descent and kept it from plunging in too fast or too steeply. At an altitude of 19,400 feet, a large parachute deployed, braking the descent to about 100 miles an hour. At 4,600 feet, three rocket engines fired to ease the gangling three-legged craft to a soft landing.

It was late afternoon on a midsummer day at the landing site. It was 4:53 a.m. at the control room in Pasadena. But it would be another 19 minutes, the transit time for Mars-to-Earth radio signals, before anyone would know the fate of the Viking 1 lander.

"Touchdown! We have touchdown!" The voice of Richard A. Bender, one of the flight controllers, broke the tension. The craft had landed in excellent working condition. It had come down near the center of its target area. Mark the spot on all future maps of Mars. The first successful landing of a man-made craft on Mars occurred on the western slopes of Chryse Planitia, at 22.3 degrees north latitude and 47.5 degrees west longitude.

Viking dutifully began photographing its surroundings. The first

An artist's rendering of the Viking lander perched on the Martian surface. (Jet Propulsion Laboratory)

razor-sharp image showed one of the lander's three footpads, confirming its solid footing and calibrating the camera's performance. Details as fine as pea-sized rivets on the footpad and individual grains of soil showed up clearly in the picture. A few hours later, the second camera took and transmitted a 300-degree panorama. Slowly, line by vertical scan line, the picture filled the screens at the control room. It took 36 minutes to complete the picture, but it was worth the wait.

Off in the distance there were sand dunes, a depression that could be an eroded crater, bright patches of fine soil, and some low ridges. The horizon two miles away was a ridge that looked like the rim of a large impact crater. At one point, his excitement rising, Thomas Mutch, head of the photo-interpretation team, said with a sigh: "You just wish you could be standing there, walking across that terrain." To many viewers, the scene was reminiscent of the deserts of the southwestern United States. They could even imagine they were seeing sagebrush in the distance; closer examination revealed that the clumps of sage were rocks. Everywhere there were rocks of all shapes, shades, and sizes. At the sight of one field of boulders, Mutch grinned and said: "As we sophisticated geologists say, those are dark rocks."

All those rocks were a sobering sight. "The most striking impression is one of a lot of rocks," Mutch said, "and this automatically brings to mind the fact that we had a good deal of luck, because some of these rocks are about two or three meters across and had the spacecraft landed on those rocks, it would probably have been permanently disabled." Indeed, not thirty feet away sat a ten-foot boulder, which geologists nicknamed Big Joe. A landing on Big Joe would have been disastrous.

Looking at the desertlike panorama, the effervescent Mutch commented: "You can almost imagine the camels coming up over the dune into our view. Unfortunately, we do not see any camels or any other animals for that matter."

THE SEARCH ON Mars for life had begun. The Viking 1 lander, resting on a gentle slope of a boulder-strewn plain, was the most sophisticated robotic craft ever built, a machine designed to duplicate human senses and carry out experiments that human logic deemed most likely to detect the presence of microbial life.

The lander had two eyes, identical television cameras capable of seeing stereoscopically almost 360 degrees around the craft. The cameras stood about five feet above the ground, providing a view much like what a person standing there would see. The cameras could take and transmit pictures in black and white, color, and also infrared.

Those first color pictures revealed that the sky is not blue, but salmon pink. The Martian sky is pink for the same reason that on Earth the sky will turn yellow in a raging sandstorm. Because the atmosphere is so thin, its light-scattering properties, which determine color, are dominated by the relatively large dust particles that hang suspended in the sky for months, the result of periodic dust storms. The sky proved to be a washed-out duplicate of the soil coloration that gives the planet its ruddy complexion, as seen from Earth. While the rocks ranged from gray to reddish, the soil all around Viking was uniformly red. It reminded geologists of rust, and for good reason. Examination with the X-ray fluorescence spectrometer showed that silicon and iron accounted for about two-thirds of the soil's content. Magnets on Viking's mechanical arm picked up the soil in a way confirming its iron-rich nature. Oxidizing processes in the porous rocks had presumably caused mineralogical reactions producing the rust that gives Mars its distinctive hue.

Bristling from the lander were antennas for communicating with flight controllers on Earth (either directly or relayed through the orbiter overhead) and transmitting the pictures and scientific data; a mechanical arm that could reach out 10 feet with a scoop to pick up soil for analysis; and a meteorology boom with instruments for measuring temperature, humidity, and wind speed. Soon after the lander touched down, the meteorology boom sprang into an upright position, ready to deliver the first weather report from Mars.

The report for Viking's first day on Mars: "Light winds from the east in the late afternoon, changing to light winds from the southwest after midnight. Maximum wind was 15 miles per hour. Temperature range from −122 degrees F. just after dawn to −22 degrees F., but we believe that was not the maximum. Pressure steady at 7.70 millibars."

The part about the winds seemed routine enough, but the rest was definitely unusual. The observed temperature range was comparable to that in the high interior of Antarctica, where lichens and mites manage to survive. At the landing site, however, it was summer, and presumably these temperatures were about as warm as it ever gets at these latitudes. Although the cameras occasionally showed wisps of clouds in the sky and an early-morning covering of frost on the ground, with those low temperatures the chance of precipitation on Mars the next day—or any other day—was zero.

On the eighth day, the lander's mechanical arm, controlled by radioed commands from Earth to the spacecraft computer, began digging into the Martian soil. As the soil was trenched and probed and shaken to collect samples, the cameras recorded the marks, trenches, and clods of soil. By studying these pictures, scientists were able to determine that Martian soil was about as firm as good farming soil on Earth. The soil of Mars sticks together in about the same way, too. Smaller particles clump together into larger clods, and the walls of shallow trenches remain straight and show little tendency to collapse. In some places, wind had scoured away the fine reddish soil, exposing gray bedrock. Closer examination of some rocks by the cameras revealed that they were pitted with vesicles, holes once filled by bubbles of gas in cooling rocks. The pitted rocks looked as if they had come from lava produced by erupting gas-rich volcanoes. The bedrock, scientists concluded, was probably created by ancient Martian lava flows.

But everyone, layman and scientist alike, was more interested in what the soil revealed about the prospects of life on Mars. Biologists were mildly encouraged by findings of the mass spectrometer, one of the lander's instruments. On the descent, the instrument sampled the atmosphere and detected evidence that it contained as much as 3 percent nitrogen, which is considered an essential ingredient for life. (Carbon dioxide, as expected, made up 95 percent of the thin atmosphere.) Mariner 9's far-off measurements had detected less than 1 percent nitrogen, probably too little to nurture life. Even though Earth's atmosphere has almost 80 percent, as little as the 3 percent nitrogen they now detected might be sufficient for life, scientists decided, as they looked forward even more eagerly to the lander's biological investigations.

"Many of the Viking instruments could have detected life," wrote Gerald A. Soffen, a biologist and the mission's chief scientist, in *The New Solar System,* a book that came out in 1981. "The orbiter camera could have seen cities or the lights of civilization. The infrared map-per could have found an unusual heat source. The water-vapor sensor could have detected watering holes or moisture from some great metabolic source. The entry mass spectrometer could have identified gases that were wildly outside the limits of chemical equilibrium (as oxygen is on Earth). Seismometers could have detected a nearby elephant. But Viking's search utilized three main tools on each lander: a pair of cameras, the pyrolytic gas chromatograph and mass spectrometer, and the biology experiments."

The first soil sample grabbed by the mechanical arm was dropped through a funnel on top of the craft. The soil was then sieved automatically, divided, and delivered to several "laboratories" for different kinds of analysis, chemical and biological. The material was examined by the gas chromatograph–mass spectrometer for signs of organic molecules. Another sample was analyzed by the X-ray fluorescence spectrometer to determine the element-by-element chemistry. The rest of the soil sample was measured out in three separate portions for each of the experiment chambers in the $50 million biology laboratory in the core of the craft. Additional samples were collected and tested in the following weeks. They were submitted to experiments designed after careful consideration by hundreds of biologists who asked themselves the tough question: How do you look for life if you are not sure what the life looks like?

OVER THE YEARS scientists addressing the question had suggested four fundamental ways to detect life on another planet. First, we can look from Earth for major changes on a planet like Mars that we might ascribe to another civilization—the Lowellian strategy. Second, we can listen at various radio wavelengths for signals produced by another civilization—the method tried systematically in the hope of receiving something from Mars in the 1920s. In describing these two methods in their book *The Search for Life in the Universe,* Donald Goldsmith and Tobias Owen noted, however, that they would have failed until quite recently to signal the presence of life on Earth to a Martian with the same technology that we possess. "The distorting effects of the Earth's atmosphere," they wrote, "would obscure our planet's surface so much that humanmade changes in the landscape could not be seen, and the nighttime glow of our cities would not have reached the level of easy detection. Similarly, no radio transmission would have been detectable, since humans began to generate large amounts of radio power only in the 1920s."

The third test, Goldsmith and Owen said, would have yielded positive results, even if no civilizations had arisen on Earth. This test involves analyzing the composition of the planet's atmosphere, using advanced spectroscopic techniques, to spot subtle changes caused by the presence of life. Martians, for example, could have thus detected the presence of oxygen molecules in the Earth's atmosphere, as well as a small amount of methane. Both are telltale signs of living processes. But neither observers on Earth nor the early spacecraft had found such evidence on Mars of the conditions that mark Earth as a biologically active world.

All that was left was to try the fourth approach: Go to Mars to perform experiments that test for the presence of microbial life.

Only a few scientists had not given up entirely on the idea that larger organisms, macrobes, were possible. Joshua Lederberg, a Nobel Prize–winning biologist then at Stanford University, and the ever-optimistic Carl Sagan had suggested that the environment of Mars might be too hostile for small organisms but somehow tolerable to much larger creatures. Polar bears, after all, do very well in the Arctic. Lederberg and Sagan were exercising their imaginations more than their scientific judgments. They were also trying to keep open minds about what might exist on Mars. Sagan, however, may have been more serious about macrobes. In *The Search for Life on Mars*, Henry S. F. Cooper, Jr., quoted Sagan as saying before the Viking mission: "I keep having this recurring fantasy that we'll wake up some morning and see on the photographs footprints all around Viking that were made during the night, but we'll never get to see the creature that made them because it is nocturnal. I wanted a flashlight on Viking, but I didn't get it." Mutch said that he had tried to get a lighting system for Sagan. It might have been useful, Mutch said, in observing the predawn formation of frost. But the request was rejected. Mutch added: "Carl, by the way, also talked about putting out bait."

Nearly all scientists believed that if there was any life at all on Mars, it would be microscopic, rare, and extremely hard to find. "Microbes are the last survivors in a harsh environment," Norman Horowitz noted. The history of life on Earth also pointed to the hardihood of microbes. These tiny organisms—bacteria, yeasts, and molds—were the first life to emerge on Earth and for several billions of years were the only life. They still outnumber larger organisms by an incalculable margin.

"The dirt in your backyard contains more organisms than the number of stars in our galaxy," Goldsmith and Owen wrote. "We have no reason to expect another planet with life to differ from Earth in the overall development of living systems, so we greatly increase our chances of finding life when we include a search for microorganisms. This realization underlay the design of experiments to find life on Mars."

In planning Viking, scientists had the freedom to conceive of more advanced life-seeking experiments than anything they had entertained before. One of the proposals for Mariner 4, for example, had been typically clever but crude. The idea, dubbed Gulliver, was to parachute a one-and-a-half-pound package to the surface as Mariner flew by. On contact two sticky, 23-foot-long coiled strings, like a No-Pest Strip, were to shoot out of their containers and reel back in, picking up microbes along the way. Anything sticking to the strings was supposed to multiply in a solution of sterile beef broth, vitamins, malt extract, and distilled water—producing radioactive carbon dioxide in the process. A Geiger counter would detect the gas, and a small radio would transmit the findings to Earth. Although Gulliver was abandoned, the concept contained a germ—so to speak—of the idea that informed scientific thinking for Viking's life search.

Scientists felt it was reasonable to assume that the fundamental chemistry of Martian life would be like that of Earth life, which is based on the element carbon and thrives by transforming carbon compounds. Carbon is abundant in the cosmos, having been found in meteorites and detected in spectroscopic analysis of interstellar dust and gas. Such studies, as well as laboratory experiments, show that organic (carbon-based) compounds like those found in living matter seem to be prevalent in the universe. Carbon, more than other elements, has the ability to make strong chemical bonds, which renders it especially suitable for the construction of large molecules. "Carbon is almost infinitely flexible," Soffen explained. "Not only can carbon atoms make long chains, but they have hooks that can attach many other atoms and make an endless number of configurations. Only carbon can provide the incredible variety of molecules needed by any living organisms we can conceive of." On Earth, for example, compounds of carbon with hydrogen, nitrogen, and oxygen form the substances of the genetic system. If life exists elsewhere, biologists concluded, it is probably based on carbon chemistry.

Since organic molecules, which are built around a carbon base, are fundamental to all known living things, one instrument on the lander, the gas chromatograph–mass spectrometer (GCMS), was designed to detect and identify any organic matter in the surface soil. The instrument was developed by Klaus Biemann, an organic chemist at the Massachusetts Institute of Technology. A soil sample placed in a tiny oven is baked at extremely high temperatures. The heat drives off gases into the chromatograph tube, where the molecules are separated into their component parts. These are then identified as they pass through the mass spectrometer. The mass of each gaseous fragment is measured by accelerating it through electrostatic and electromagnetic fields. After careful analysis, scientists can name the component parts and also determine the original molecules from which they came.

Finding organic material by means of these experiments would not provide a definitive answer to the life question. Nearly all organic matter found on Earth is biological in origin—including our hydrocarbon fuels, which are the remains from life several hundred million years ago. But this is not the case elsewhere. The organic compounds in meteorites are nonbiological, and since Mars is close to the asteroid belt, it was assumed that over the ages collisions with these objects could have left a residue of organic material on the Martian surface. If so, the GCMS should find the traces; the instrument could detect a few parts per billion of substances containing more than two carbon atoms. The results of the experiment, it turned out, would be unambiguous and prove critical in evaluating the findings of the three experiments on the lander designed specifically to search for signs of life.

THE LANDER's biology instrument compartment, measuring scarcely more than one foot high, wide, or long, housed three automated laboratories built by the TRW Corporation of Redondo Beach, California, to the specifications of three separate teams of scientists. Each laboratory was designed for experiments based on a different set of premises.

One characteristic of terrestrial organisms, large or small, is that they give off gases produced by their metabolic activity. Plants give off oxygen, animals give off carbon dioxide, and both exhale water. The gas exchange test, known facetiously as the "chicken soup" experiment, was designed by Vance Oyama, a biologist at NASA's Ames Research Center, with this principle in mind. Some nutrients—vitamins, amino acids, purines, and organic acids—were mixed with water. This broth was then dripped on a soil sample inside a sealed chamber. The chemical composition of the gas above the soil was continuously analyzed by the gas chromatograph for changes that might indicate biological activity. On Earth the experiment would reveal the presence of life through distinct changes in the amount of oxygen, carbon dioxide, or hydrogen in the air, which would be the result of the microbes digesting and processing the nutrients added to the soil. Would there be any Martian microbes to hungrily consume Oyama's chicken soup and expel telltale gases?

The second experiment was based on the fact that terrestrial animals consume organic compounds and give off carbon dioxide. Designed by Gilbert V. Levin of Biospherics Incorporated, a private laboratory in Rockville, Maryland, the labeled release experiment, as it was called, involved adding a variety of nutrients in which radioactive carbon atoms were substituted for some of the ordinary carbon atoms. The radioactive atoms served as labels for tracing the course of the compounds should any of the nutrients be consumed by organisms. During an incubation period any microbes that function by metabolism should consume the nutrients and release gases that contain some of the labeled wastes. As the soil was moistened with the nutrient solution, gases above the sample would be tested to see if any carbon dioxide or methane bearing the radioactive traces had been released by organisms.

But Mars is exceedingly dry, and these two experiments involved watery solutions. What if Martian organisms were "drowned" in the aqueous nutrients applied to the soil? What if some of the solutions were poison to Martian life?

The third experiment, developed by Norman Horowitz of Caltech and called the pyrolytic release test, sought to test the soil in the dry, carbon-dioxide-rich conditions that exist on Mars. Radioactive-labeled carbon dioxide was added to the atmosphere in the laboratory chamber. A soil sample was then exposed to this atmosphere, and the illumination from a xenon lamp roughly simulated sunlight on Mars. Any biological process that converts carbon dioxide to organic matter is called carbon assimilation; photosynthesis is one such process. Plants use sunlight to turn carbon dioxide and water into organic matter, emitting oxygen as a waste product. After giving any organisms in the soil a chance to live for a while, the sample would be exposed to intense heat. Any organisms should be roasted, and any organic material would be vaporized. A living organism in the chamber would have assimilated some of the radioactive carbon from the atmosphere. The heat-released vapors, once analyzed, should bear the radioactive traces of such biological activity.

Care was taken to avoid contaminating the soil at the landing site. The rocket engines used in the Viking landers were redesigned to minimize surface heating. Tests on Earth demonstrated that rocket exhaust did not kill soil bacteria. And to be sure of getting an undisturbed sample, the mechanical arm picked up soil 10 feet away from the lander, well beyond the range of rocket exhaust.

The scientists, therefore, felt sure they were working with pristine Martian soil. They checked and double-checked their instruments and were certain they were functioning properly. But when the first results of the experiments trickled in, the scientists were at a loss to explain what they were seeing. All three experiments yielded seemingly positive results. The data indicated some kind of activity in the Martian soil. But were these signs of life?

On the tenth day after the landing, the gas exchange experiment gave the scientists their first surprise. Analysis of gas in the sealed chamber showed that exposure of the chicken soup to the soil had released large amounts of oxygen. Although it was clearly a positive result, the scientists were not jumping to conclusions. The oxygen seemed too abundant to be a product of microbial metabolism.

The next day the labeled release experiment also reported positive measurements. When the radioactive nutrient solution was applied to the soil, there was a surge in the radioactivity of gases in the chamber, and then it tapered off.

Reports from the third experiment were eagerly awaited. After an incubation period of five days, data from the laboratory showed a small but definite rise in radioactive carbon—another positive finding. Just possibly some organisms were processing carbon dioxide and releasing radioactive-tagged carbon into the chamber's atmosphere. But the scientists remained cautious, even skeptical.

Their skepticism was rooted in the knowledge that the GCMS had failed to turn up the slightest hint of any organic material in the soil. The positive results from the three biology experiments had to be weighed in the light of these negative data. How could there be life on Mars that did not leave some organic traces? Horowitz said that this negative discovery, made by instruments that were not actually charged with life-seeking responsibilities, was confirmed in repeated tests and became "the most important single biological finding of the Viking mission."

The lack of organic evidence forced the scientists to consider seriously nonbiological explanations for their observations. Harold P. Klein of the Ames Research Center, who headed the Viking biology team, summed up the prevailing attitude. "Life is the most complex peak of evolution that we have seen," he said in those post-landing days. "Therefore, we must try every other possibility to explain the responses by physical means, by chemical means, before absolutely being driven, you might say, to the conclusion that we can only explain it by a living reaction."

The scientists soon hit upon nonbiological explanations. The oxygen recorded by the gas exchange experiment was probably the result of chemical reactions between water in the chicken soup and something in the soil. The rise in radioactive gases in the labeled release experiment was likewise attributed to chemical processes. In both cases, most of the scientists concluded, the reactive agents in the soil were almost certainly peroxides and superoxides unlike anything occurring naturally on Earth. Their existence on Mars had been predicted because of unusual chemical processes that could be operating where the atmosphere is cold and thin and the Sun's ultraviolet radiation beats down unfiltered on a soil rich in iron oxides. Add water to superoxides and they start behaving like microbes.

As for the third experiment, the production of some radioactive carbon in the chamber continued even after the soil was exposed to intense heat that would have killed off any terrestrial organisms.

Repeated tests seemed to rule out a biological interpretation. But if these were chemical reactions, they must be different from those observed in the other two experiments. Even Horowitz, the most skeptical of biologists on the issue of Martian life, had to concede that "until the mystery of the results . . . is solved, a biological explanation will continue to be a remote possibility."

Viking 2 was unable to clarify matters. This companion craft rocketed into an orbit of Mars on August 7 and dropped its lander to the surface on September 3. The lander, equipped with an identical complement of life-seeking experiments, came to rest on Utopia Planitia, a dusty red plain much like the Chryse site and bearing not the slightest resemblance to the ideal land envisioned in the sixteenth century by Sir Thomas More. Viking 2's place on the map of Mars was 47.5 degrees north latitude and 226 degrees west longitude, putting it on the opposite side of the planet from the Viking 1 lander and in a more northerly region. The lower elevation, as well as higher latitude, promised greater amounts of water in some form. Even so, the second Viking's tests yielded similarly puzzling results, suggesting that the apparently lifeless but chemically reactive soil is widespread. Windstorms have presumably mixed soils from place to place and distributed them over most of the planet. Only in the iced-over polar regions is it likely that conditions are markedly different.

SO THE TWO Viking missions, though dazzling engineering and scientific successes, failed to give a conclusive answer to the big question. If the old fantasies of Martian life were no longer tenable, it was entirely possible for scientists to marshal Viking data and choose different sides on the question, their positions in the argument usually depending on their respective inclinations toward optimism or pessimism.

The official reports wisely avoided dogmatic assertions. The Viking results, the biology team declared, "do not permit any final conclusion about the presence of life on Mars." A panel of the National Academy of Sciences issued an equally indisputable assessment, noting that the results lowered the possibility of life on Mars.

Some Viking scientists had to ovecome personal feelings of disappointment before arriving at similar conclusions. Soffen, the project's chief scientist, had devoted most of his career as a biologist to the question. "I began with a very optimistic view of the chances for life on Mars," he said. "I now believe that it is very unlikely." Having said that, however, he raced down one possible avenue of escape. Life should not be ruled out at least until the polar regions of Mars have been visited. Viking 2's orbiter had discovered that the permanent ice cap over the north pole was mostly frozen water. "I have always believed," Soffen said, "that in the search for life you must go where the water is."

Finding water on Mars, and there resuming the search for life, present or past, may well motivate future explorations of the planet. Nearly every discussion of Mars by scientists includes, as we shall see, some kind of "water proviso."

In *To Utopia and Back*, Horowitz summarized the most pessimistic post-Viking view on the life question:

> Viking found no life on Mars, and, just as important, it found why there can be no life. Mars lacks that extraordinary feature that dominates the environment of our own planet, oceans of liquid water in full view of the sun; indeed, it is devoid of any liquid water whatsoever. It is also suffused with short-wavelength ultraviolet radiation. Each of these circumstances alone would probably suffice to ensure its sterility, but in combination they have led to the development of a highly oxidizing surface environment that is incompatible with the existence of organic molecules on the planet. Mars is not only devoid of life, but of organic matter as well.

Even though the evidence did seem to argue against the presence of any life on Mars, the irrepressible Carl Sagan said that Viking, while putting to rest any notions of macrobial life, had not changed his mind about the possibility of microbial life on Mars. "For the entire history of the question," Sagan said, "it has been demonstrably true that the scientific consensus has been wrong" in times of optimism as well as pessimism. He was warning, once again, against a rush to judgment.

One of the principal Viking scientists, Gilbert Levin, has continued to dispute the chemical explanation for the observed reactions and to insist that the soil tests did not close the case on Mars biology. "The accretion of evidence has been more compatible with biology than with chemistry," Levin said in 1977. "Each new test result has made it more difficult to come up with a chemical explanation, but each new result has continued to allow for biology." And he, too, has not changed his mind. Chemical laboratory tests on Earth since the mission, he said, have failed to replicate the strange reactions in the soil that were observed by Viking. How, then, can biology be ruled out?

A year after the first Viking landing, Harold Klein, the biology team leader, who had often found himself mediating arguments among his colleagues, seemed to believe that the search for life on Mars had come up with an unsatisfying but perhaps not unsurprising answer: We can't be sure. "These are the facts we have," Klein said. "They do not rigorously prove the existence of life on Mars. They do not rigorously exclude the presence of life on Mars. My feeling is, we'll not be able to prove any more until we go back to Mars."

THE FOUR VIKING spacecraft—the two orbiters and the two landers—proved to be durable explorers. If their operations had ended in November 1976, only a few months after reaching Mars, their missions would have been officially declared a full success. The craft were designed and built to last at least that long, and the scientists had carefully planned their experiments and measurements to meet their primary test objectives in that time. Anything beyond November would be a bonus, and it was quite a bonus the Vikings awarded their controllers on Earth.

Viking 2's orbiter was the first to expire, but not until a leak caused it to run out of steering fuel on July 25, 1978. Its lander continued operating another two years, until its batteries malfunctioned. Viking 1's orbiter survived 1,509 days. The two orbiters had combined to transmit more than 51,000 pictures of Mars, mapping 97 percent of the surface in even greater detail than had Mariner 9. And Viking 1's lander exceeded all expectations by lasting until November 1982—after working 2,299 Earth days (2,238 sols, or Mars days).

The lander's last transmitted image, taken on November 5, showed a gloomy scene. Shadows, dark and foreboding, stretched across the Chryse landscape. Another of those fierce dust storms was sweeping the Martian plains. Flight controllers radioed commands for the lander to report in again on November 19 with more on the storm. The appointed day came, but no message from Chryse Planitia. The mission that had started with the familiar bang at Cape Canaveral in August 1975 had ended with an electronic whimper, unheard. The lander was never heard from again. "It's like losing an old friend," George Gianopulos, a project manager, said. "How do you express it?"

The first phase of Mars exploration had come to a close. So disappointing was the apparently negative result of the life-seeking experiments that, after the Vikings radioed their final weather reports and took their last pictures of those magnificent pink skies, Mars was abandoned for years as a destination.

But Tim Mutch, for one, had already been moved by the grandeur and lingering mystery of Mars to dream of returning. He was an alpinist, as well as a geologist, and more than most Viking scientists, he saw planetary exploration of the late twentieth century as an adventure of the human spirit and equated it with geographical exploration of an earlier time. His wish, on the morning of the first Viking landing, was that he could be walking over those rocks and out to the horizon at Chryse Plain. In 1981, Mutch was killed in a climbing accident in the Himalayas, and as a memorial the Viking 1 lander was named the Thomas A. Mutch Station. He had had other plans for the lander. In a book on the mission, *The Martian Landscape,* Mutch concluded with this vision of the future:

> A tractor drive vehicle, slightly larger than Viking, could roam up to several hundred kilometers, sampling geological and biological environments inaccessible to Viking . . . followed by an unmanned sample return mission. Even if the immediate future is uncertain, I have no doubts about the distant years. Someday man will roam the surface of Mars. Those wonderful Viking machines will be crated up, returned to Earth and placed in a museum. Children in generations to come will stand before them and struggle to imagine the way it was on that first journey to Mars.

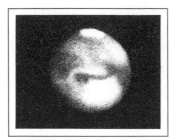

CHAPTER 7

AN INVENTORY
OF KNOWLEDGE –
AND QUESTIONS

IF THE EARLY voyages to Mars dispelled some of the myths, they revealed a world no less fascinating to scientists. It was a world of unsuspected splendor and variety. Conway W. Snyder, a Viking scientist at the Jet Propulsion Laboratory, once compiled a list of descriptive words geologists have applied to the varied surface features: bedded, bulbous, chaotic, cratered, etched, fractured, fretted, furrowed, grooved, hackly, hilly, hollowed, hummocky, knobby, layered, mantled, mottled, patterned, pitted, ridged, rolling, smooth, streaked, striped, textured, and troughed. Rising above the landscape is a volcano, Olympus Mons, higher than any known mountain in the solar system. There is also a chasm wider and deeper than the Grand Canyon and as long as the continental United States is wide. There are deep channels that resemble dry riverbeds, stretches of sand dunes greater than the Sahara, global permafrost, and vast, ice-coated polar landscapes. It is a cold, arid world, though perhaps not as dry as once thought. It has been subjected to massive volcanic eruptions and spreading lava flows, periodic climate changes, and, in all likelihood, enormous floods.

Even if there are no canals of ancient civilizations or any apparent signs of life, the sum of recent discoveries is an enduring mystery that begs for further exploration. The mystery has to do with water. As the Viking scientists found, the braided channels and other evidence of floods, the chaotic terrain and other signs of permafrost, and the polar ice all bear witness to the influence of water in the planet's past and its continuing, if diminished, presence on Mars today. Emerging from the Viking findings is a more coherent picture than had been possible of how water once must have been abundant on Mars, how it became locked in the permafrost and ice caps, and how this has changed thinking about life on Mars. In a wetter past, life might have evolved, and then vanished in the dry wind. Life might just possibly be hanging on in some watery enclaves. The prospect of finding life, Fred L. Whipple, the Harvard astronomer, said in a review of Viking results, "is not very encouraging except for the clear evidence that water has been widespread on Mars, at least periodically. Will we finally discover life forms in the 'oases' or in the bottoms of the great canyons such as Valles Marineris?"

Increasing attention is being given to the water question, as it could affect the prospects for life on Mars in the future. Mars, though bleak and forbidding by any terrestrial standard, still reminds us enough of Earth to inspire visions of human outposts rising on its dusty red plains. The supply of water will be the key to any realization of such a vision. But is there any reality to the vision? Or is this the myth of a new generation contemplating Mars? Will the vision of humans becoming Martians turn out to be as much a chimera as Lowell's canal builders?

Now, at least, we have a solid foundation of knowledge for planning future explorations and contemplating ideas of Mars as an abode of human life. After the Viking missions, scientists summarized their findings and produced the following inventory of the Mars we know now.

Size, Shape, and Structure. The diameter of Mars is about half that of Earth—4,200 miles, compared with 7,926 miles. Less mass results in a correspondingly weaker gravitational force. In the weak Martian gravity, persons will feel only 38 percent of their normal weight.

Like Earth, Mars is slightly pear-shaped. Without liquid water, surface irregularities cannot be measured in relation to sea level. But a sort of hypothetical "sea level" has been defined—called the Mars datum surface. Most of the southern hemisphere, except close to the

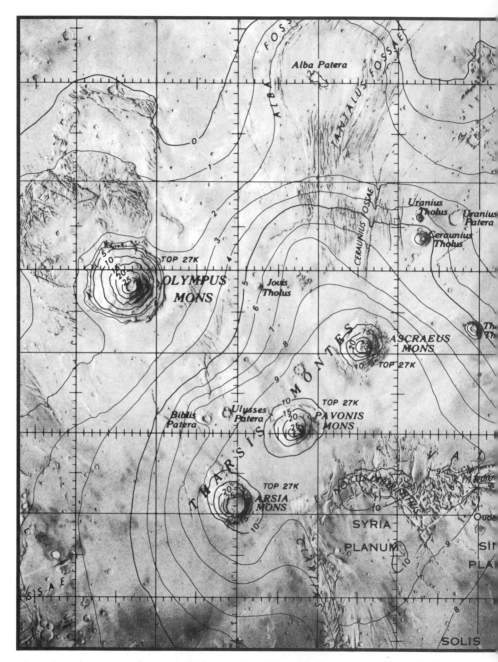

A portion of a topographic map of Mars produced from Mariner 9 photography. It shows Olympus Mons, the largest known volcano in the solar system, and the huge canyon Valles Marineris, in the equatorial region. (U.S. Geological Survey)

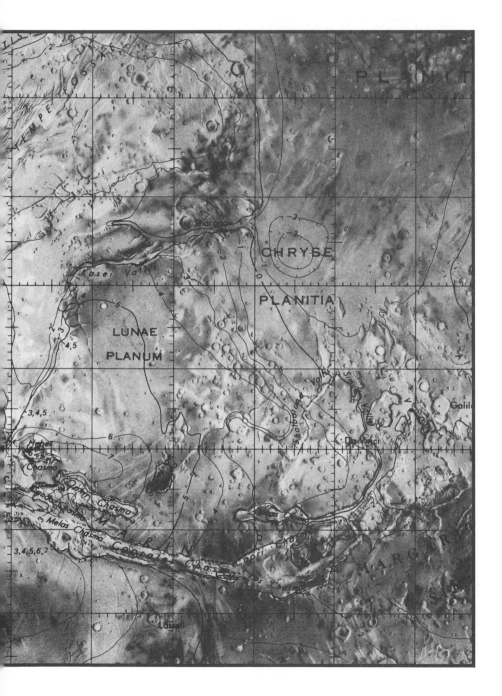

pole, is elevated in relation to the datum surface; by as much as 1.5 to 4 miles above the datum surface between 20 degrees and 75 degrees south latitude. By contrast, most of the northern hemisphere is depressed, sometimes by as much as 1.5 miles. No one understands the reasons for this "hemispheric discontinuity."

The planet's interior is poorly understood, though some clues can be derived from exterior evidence. The crust is believed to be thick and rigid; no evidence of the shifting crustal plates, the tectonic plates, that characterize the Earth's protean surface. There is only a weak magnetic field, which suggests that if Mars has a hot liquid metallic core at all, it is extremely small. Earth's much stronger magnetic field is believed to be generated by the convective forces of a large molten core acting as a dynamo. The size of Mars also militates against a hot interior. With less mass, it has presumably cooled off more thoroughly since its formation, losing much of its heat of accretion 4.6 billion years ago and its original radioactive heat. The Martian interior thus could be cool and solid all the way down.

Volcanoes. The Martian interior must have been hotter and more active long ago, for volcanic mountains are among the most conspicuous features of the planet's landscape. Most of the biggest volcanoes lie in a region called Tharsis, centered on the equator. But another line of volcanoes is found on the opposite side of the planet, and much of the cratered terrain in the southern hemisphere shows signs of volcanic activity in the distant past. Towering above all the others is Olympus Mons, 90,000 feet high and more than 300 miles across at its base. The crater at the pinnacle appears to be about 50 miles wide and 10,000 feet deep with wall slopes of about 32 degrees. The mountain is so massive that its weight has caused a sagging of the crust, leaving a broad "moat" that completely surrounds the central volcanic structure. The few impact craters on the outer slopes and in the lava plains below indicate that Olympus Mons and the other major volcanoes may be relatively young features, although it is unclear whether some volcanism continues to the present day.

The Tharsis region, the site of Olympus Mons and several other large volcanoes, is the center of an inexplicable bulge in the Martian surface. The Tharsis bulge extends over an area 2,500 miles wide and its uplift has produced general elevations of as much as 5 miles above the Mars datum surface. Tharsis is thus a striking exception to the generally depressed terrain of the northern hemisphere.

The great size of the volcanoes is important evidence of the dynamics of Mars. On Earth, volcanoes form on top of the huge tectonic plates, which are slowly shifting as part of the drift of continents. It is believed that the magma, or molten lava, that produces the volcanic eruption remains in a stationary location under the plate. As a plate moves, the volcano gradually moves away from the source of the magma. The result is that volcanoes on Earth die out before they can build to tremendous heights and breadths. But the crust of Mars is fixed. A volcano there will continue to build up in one place as long as the underlying magma is available. The Hawaiian volcanoes, for example, grew over a period of perhaps one million years. But on Mars, geologists estimate, volcanoes probably remained active for hundreds of millions of years, thereby growing to immense size with the accumulation of cooled lava. A second reason for the large size of Martian volcanoes is the planet's thick crust, which means that the magma feeding the volcanoes must come from greater depths and thus at greater pressures. The greater the pressure forcing the magma to the surface, the higher the volcano can grow.

The Great Canyon. Although geologists do not understand what caused the Tharsis bulge, they can see one of the consequences stretching about 2,800 miles along the middle of Mars, just south of the equator. This is Valles Marineris, a canyon that is as much as 3 miles deep and 150 miles wide. Its proximity to the west end of the Tharsis bulge suggests that the stresses of the uplifting and volcanic forces fractured the equatorial crust. The canyon floors are sparsely cratered, implying either a young age or, more likely, a recent or continual renewing of the floor surfaces by erosion or deposition. In some areas, the floors are covered by landslides resulting from the slumping of canyon walls. The slumping could have been triggered by quakes or caused by melting groundwater. (The seismometer on the Viking 1 lander failed; the seismometer on the other lander worked but did not detect any Mars tremors.) Indeed, movements along the fault could have released floods of groundwater into the canyon and beyond. Layered sediments seen in the canyon appear to have been deposited by water.

Channels and Valleys. The most compelling evidence for running surface water sometime in the Martian past is seen in the prevalence of meandering valleys, with tributary channels and teardrop-shaped islands, that resemble nothing so much as river systems on Earth.

Some of the larger channels are several hundreds of miles long and 60 miles or more wide. They are usually widest and deepest at the source and have few tributaries, and thus are more like terrestrial flood features than typical river valleys. For this reason, geologists have termed them outflow channels. They generally emerge from the areas known as chaotic terrain, shallow depressions cracked and covered with jumbled boulders. A rapid release of subsurface water from these areas could have caused enormous floods that carved out these channels.

The second and more numerous class of channels exhibit features that are smaller and tend to be sinuous and have a braided appearance, similar to that produced by intermittent flooding of desert streambeds on Earth. Even more abundant are the small dendritic channel networks, the third type of channels. These most nearly resemble river systems on Earth. They start small, increase in depth and width downstream, have branching tributaries, and eventually fan out like the Nile and Mississippi deltas. Their great age (perhaps as much as 3.8 billion years old) and the absence of any obvious source suggests to some geologists that these small channels could have been fed by rainfall or snow. Certainly these channels in the ancient cratered lands seem to have been created when the Martian atmosphere may have been more conducive to surface water flow. Most geologists, however, tend to believe that melting groundwater, not rainfall, is the more likely source.

Impact Craters. Meteorites have left their marks all over the Martian surface, particularly in the southern hemisphere, where the ancient cratered terrain looks so much like the Moon. The largest circular basin on Mars is Hellas Planitia, which is 1,000 miles wide and some 4 miles deep, making it the most distinctive feature in the southern highlands. Its heavily eroded walls indicate that Hellas is extremely ancient, perhaps 4 billion years old. A multitude of craters of more moderate size generally have flat floors and appear to be of all ages. Some of the strangest craters, unlike anything on the Moon, are seen in the northern hemisphere. They are called pedestal craters. Wind apparently has eroded the terrain all around the crater, leaving it standing there like some lithic toadstool.

Plains. Some 40 percent of the Martian surface is described as plains. Some plains are the smooth floors of ancient craters, such as

Hellas. Much of the Tharsis bulge, beyond the volcanic mountains, is a relatively featureless plain. Most of the plains appear to be covered with lava flows. But they are not entirely smooth, as the Viking landers discovered. Boulders, ridges, and eroded craters give them texture. And their predominant color is, of course, red.

Winds and Dust Storms. At least once every Martian year, the entire planet is shrouded by a dust storm, raised by hurricane-speed winds that seem to begin developing in the southern hemisphere when Mars comes closest to the Sun. Winds are apparently generated by the extreme difference in temperature between day and night (normally as much as 150 degrees F.). The air may be thin, but the winds can be powerful, reaching estimated speeds of as much as 200 to 300 miles an hour and transporting surface dust everywhere.

The influence of wind and dust is pervasive. Every pebble, boulder, and hummock has its fillet of dust left behind by the last storm. Every rock face is worn by blizzards of dust grains, though geologists express surprise that wind erosion has not worn down the surface even more. Sand dunes are common, the most extensive of them bordering the northern polar cap.

Wind erosion and some trick of light and shadow probably account for the Sphinx-like face that, in some Viking pictures, stares outward from the Cydonia region of northern Mars. The "face" stands out in sharp relief over an area more than a mile wide. When they first examined the pictures, Viking scientists concluded that the feature was an interesting natural phenomenon at most and should not be given anthropomorphic interpretations. A few Mars buffs have done just that, however, and in 1988 they called a news conference in Washington to announce the results of a computerized enhancement of the pictures that, they said, strongly suggested the "face" was a monumental relic of a civilization that has since disappeared. Carl Sagan, asked by a newspaper reporter for a comment, said that scientists have seen several other features resembling faces. "There's a wonderful happy face in the middle of a crater," he said, "from which I do not deduce that there are people who live on Mars who make happy-face buttons."

Wind erosion, it turns out, has played other tricks on observers. For decades the seasonal changes visible on Mars were interpreted as signs of seasonal growth and decline of vegetation, one important piece of the evidence encouraging speculation about Martian life. Bright streaks on the surface are now believed to result from the deposition of light-colored dust on a darker terrain by relatively low-velocity winds. The dark streaks result from the removal of dust by high winds to expose the underlying rock. Some of the dark splotches seen in crater floors turn out to be sand dunes.

Atmosphere. Martian air is exceedingly thin, no more than 1 percent as dense as Earth's atmosphere at sea level. The atmospheric pressure is so low—the equivalent of Earth's atmosphere at an altitude of 100,000 feet—that water cannot exist in liquid form. Humans would have to wear pressure suits to keep their blood from boiling, as well as to supply oxygen for breathing. On Earth the air is composed mainly of nitrogen and oxygen. The Martian atmosphere is entirely different: 95 percent carbon dioxide, 2 percent nitrogen, 1.5 percent argon, 0.1 percent oxygen, and traces of water vapor, carbon monoxide, neon, krypton, and xenon. The total mass of the atmosphere undergoes major seasonal variations as great amounts of carbon dioxide "snow out" and accumulate at the winter pole and then are released from the receding summer polar cap. By analyzing the composition of the isotopes of nitrogen in the Martian atmosphere today, scientists have deduced that in the past Mars must have had a much denser atmosphere in which rainfall and flowing water on the surface could have been possible.

Weather. Besides the periodic windstorms, Martian weather is notable for its freezing temperatures. At the poles, temperatures can plunge as low as −280 degrees F. Mean surface temperatures range from −225 degrees F. to a rare 63 F. Even at the equator conditions are usually frigid. Each night, equatorial temperatures plummet from afternoon's comparatively balmy 0 F. to a bitter −150, far colder than it ever gets on Earth. Water vapor, though not plentiful (a few molecules per 10,000), produces some Earth-like effects. Clouds often form in the summer mornings over Tharsis, sometimes covering large areas and leaving only the tops of the volcanoes visible. Spiral cloud formations sometimes develop at the high northern latitudes. In the valleys and canyon floors, atmospheric water freezes out during the night and then vaporizes again when the Sun rises, forming local patches of white fog. Frost often covered the rocks in the morning at the Viking landing sites.

Soil. Direct observations show that the soil is composed of silicon

(21 percent), iron (13), aluminum (3), magnesium (5), calcium (4), sulfur (3), chlorine (0.7), titanium (0.5), and potassium (less than 0.25). Indirect analysis suggests that the balance of the soil composition is oxygen (42 percent) and traces of other elements, such as sodium and hydrogen. This composition corresponds to that of a terrestrial or lunar basalt lava, but with some striking differences. The Martian soil contains less aluminum than a terrestrial basalt and less titanium than a lunar basalt. The high iron content accounts for the soil's rusty reddish hue.

To the astonishment—and initial puzzlement—of the Viking scientists, Martian soil is rich in superoxidized material. Ultraviolet radiation from the Sun beats down on the planet with virtually no atmospheric intervention. Upon striking the surface, the radiation interacts with mineral grains to produce caustic vapors, or superoxidized matter. Earth has two defenses against such a phenomenon. The thick atmosphere, particularly the layer of ozone in the stratosphere, screens out most ultraviolet rays, and water inhibits the development of unusually oxidized materials. Mars has no such protection. With the accumulation of superoxidized materials in the topsoil, Mars's surface must be self-sterilizing. As Sagan has said, the surface of Mars is "antiseptic with a vengeance."

This would seem to explain two of the most surprising findings of the two Vikings: the absence of any organic, or carbon-based, molecules in the soil and the strong chemical reactions touched off when soil samples were mixed with the watery nutrients in the experiment chambers. The superoxidized minerals were reacting with the Viking molecules, breaking up the complex compounds and liberating some oxygen gas and even more carbon dioxide gas. Much the same reaction occurs when hydrogen peroxide is poured on a cut. The soil must have behaved like any organic material that ever reached the surface of Mars, as undoubtedly has happened often with the arrival of carbon-rich meteorites. The carbon is swiftly converted to carbon dioxide gas that blends into the Martian atmosphere. No organic material survives in the soil.

With the soil so inhospitable to carbon molecules, scientists were hard put to conceive of how at present there could be any life on Mars. Of course, some life might exist beneath the superoxidized topsoil. Just how deep this oxidizing zone reaches is a question to be addressed in future explorations.

Polar Caps. The ice at the poles, formed from both water and carbon dioxide, has been called "frozen club soda."

Because of the eccentricity of Mars's orbit around the Sun, winter and summer durations and temperatures are not the same at the two polar regions. Summer temperatures at the north pole are about −95 degrees F.; at the south pole, −165 F. Consequently, their ice caps are not symmetrical. The south polar cap, for example, is larger in the winter (extending halfway to the equator) than the northern cap ever gets. It also disappears more rapidly in the spring, and is smaller in the summer than is the northern cap. The ice is mostly frozen carbon dioxide—dry ice—which freezes out of the atmosphere in the winter.

Viking orbiter observations found that at the north pole the residual cap, the ice sheet that remains in the summer, is water ice. When the dry ice sublimes in the summer sunshine, all that is left is the still-frozen water. At the south pole, conditions are different and not well understood, but indirect evidence suggests that the residual cap there is primarily frozen carbon dioxide. The residual caps at each pole occupy most of the area inside the 80 degree latitude. The exposed edges of the ice caps reveal terraces of alternating layers of dust and ice, a feature that has no terrestrial analogue. These terraces, or laminated terrain, could be an archive of the planet's climate history. The thickness of the residual ice has not been determined, but it has been estimated at anything from 30 feet to half a mile.

Permafrost. Even greater amounts of water are presumably frozen in the Martian ground, just below the surface, like the layers of permafrost underlying the Arctic landscapes of Earth. Estimates of subsurface temperatures on Mars indicate that at the poles the permafrost may be as much as 5 miles thick and come within an inch or two of the surface. Even at the equator, permafrost may be 2 miles thick and lie within 10 feet of the surface.

The evidence for Martian permafrost is indirect but, in the minds of most scientists, compelling. The apparent riverbeds bear witness to running surface water at various times in the past. Where did the water come from, in such a dry, cold world, and where did it go? Analysis of Viking photographs has produced some clues. To geologists the so-called chaotic terrain has all the marks of a place where permafrost melted and flowed away, causing the overlying terrain to collapse into the subterranean void left where the permafrost had been. The widespread networks of small, branching channels are believed to be the result of water seepage and sapping; that is, from groundwater that was in some fashion liberated and progressively undermined rock, a phenomenon that produced the canyons of the Colorado Plateau. There are also signs of mudslides. And many craters on Mars are surrounded by rim material that looks as if it had been wet when it was flung out by the impact. Some of the ejected material reminds geologists of cow pats. These features go by the descriptive name of splosh craters. Since they have also been observed on Ganymede, the icy Jovian satellite, this suggests to some scientists that meteorites hitting Mars have often penetrated an upper crust saturated with water ice.

THE BIG QUESTION about Mars still concerns life. But it is now being asked from the post-Viking perspective in which scientists recognize that the Mars we see today is not necessarily the planet as it always was. The landscape everywhere evokes learned speculation about the planet's early history. The channels and canyons, the evidence for permafrost, and the volcanoes testify to a time when Mars was a much different planet, more active geologically, wrapped in a thicker atmosphere, warmer, and presumably well watered. The question of life on Mars—past, present, or future—thus cannot be addressed until there are some answers to the subsidiary questions related to water. Did Mars ever have standing water, and for how long? What happened to the water?

"We see evidence of large channels; we see evidence of valley networks; we see evidence of polar caps with layered terrain; we see evidence of buried water," David Pieri said, enumerating the aqueous clues. "What does that tell us of the initial inventory of water on Mars? My gosh, that tells us we had not ten meters, or a hundred meters, but thousands of meters of water distributed over the planet. This surface geology is trying to tell us a story, a surprising story, and we may not be ready to accept it."

Although some geologists suggest that episodes of flowing surface water could have recurred in local areas until recent times, most scientists believe that the water epoch on Mars was largely confined to its first billion years, between 4.6 billion and 3.6 billion years ago.

According to estimates based on the amount of water believed to be frozen in the poles and below the surface, the total amount of water on Mars at that time may have been equivalent to a planet-wide layer of water as much as half a mile deep. Erupting volcanoes vented enormous volumes of carbon dioxide, producing a denser atmosphere that could absorb and retain solar heat and hence create and sustain a warmer environment. Such conditions would have been conducive to liquid water on the surface. Much of the water must have come from the volcanoes (water and carbon dioxide are the most abundant gases emitted by terrestrial eruptions) or could also have arrived on Mars through the steady bombardment of comets that is thought to have occurred in the solar system's youth. But Mars is a small planet and far from the Sun. Being small, it soon lost most of its interior heat, and the resulting diminution of volcanic activity sharply reduced the planet's source of atmospheric gases to replenish those becoming locked in the carbonate rocks or escaping into space. With its weaker gravity, also a consequence of the planet's smallness, Mars was less able than Earth to hold on to its atmosphere. With a progressively thinner atmosphere, and being farther out from the Sun, Mars was gradually plunged into the deep chill that exists there today. Much of the surface water presumably vaporized and vanished into space. But some of the water froze at the poles and, as it appears, settled into the ground as icy permafrost.

In many respects, Mars in its first billion years or so may not have been all that different from Earth at the same time. Indeed, one argument for further exploration is to examine Mars's possible early similarities with Earth. Mars may be a world frozen in time, virtually unchanged in the last several billion years. Two-thirds of its surface, the heavily cratered regions, seems to be 3.8 billion years old or older. Earth, on the other hand, has undergone continual change that has obliterated much of its early history. To study Mars may be to learn something of what Earth was like when life first emerged.

In a reversal of its traditional philosophy of uniformitarianism, geology in recent years has come to recognize that the present is not necessarily the key to the past. The physics of what is going on now, geologically, is identical to the physics of what went on before; the laws of gravity and thermodynamics are immutable. But without violating any laws of nature, dramatic changes are possible over time.

The Earth is a case in point. In its first billion years, scientists now realize, Earth shared with Mars such similarities as surface water, a carbon dioxide atmosphere, moderate temperatures, and more extensive volcanism. Earth was a brutal place, too, but it was in this time and under these conditions that life emerged on Earth.

Perhaps life developed on Mars then, under similar conditions. There was an atmosphere of essential gases, liquid water as the medium for prebiotic chemical reactions, and the energy from the Sun's ultraviolet radiation and lightning to drive the formation of organic molecules. But as Mars gradually lost most of its atmosphere and grew colder, conditions were no longer so hospitable to life, while on Earth things got better. Earth's internal heat kept the crust shifting and the volcanoes spewing more gases into the atmosphere. And the early life forms, consuming carbon dioxide and expelling oxygen, transformed Earth forever. The atmosphere became oxygen-rich and developed a protective layer of ozone that screens out most solar ultraviolet radiation. "Our microbial ancestors," Pieri said, "really did a job for us, creating a fairly pleasant place for us."

Christopher P. McKay, a research scientist and exobiologist at the Ames Research Center, offers three possible scenarios for the history of biology on Mars. One, life began on Mars much as it did on Earth and remained for a billion years or more. Two, prebiotic evolution occurred and possibly primitive organisms developed, but conditions deteriorated and life became extinct before it had a chance to flourish. Three, prebiotic evolution never occurred on Mars.

McKay, citing the lack of liquid water, doubts that any active life exists on Mars today. But there could have been ice-covered lakes on ancient Mars, and there life might have evolved for a time. McKay and Robert Wharton, a biologist at Ames, made a study of seven lakes in Antarctica and compared them with photographs of dry beds of what may have been large lakes long ago on the floor of Valles Marineris. The Antarctic lakes, situated in an arid, frigid environment, are perhaps the closest terrestrial analogue to the ancient Martian lakes. The thick ice covering traps heat and concentrates dissolved gases to maintain water temperatures as high as 77 degrees F. and support microorganisms such as algae, bacteria, and fungi. The same life-sustaining process could have been operating on ancient Mars, McKay and Wharton concluded, but if so, the life probably would have been destroyed billions of years ago when the planet cooled and lost much of its atmosphere.

McKay and other scientists, therefore, propose looking for evidence of past Martian life in the form of fossils. "Our whole approach to looking for life on Mars has changed in recent years," McKay said. "We are no longer looking for extant life. Rather, we are looking for evidence of extinct life."

Sedimentary rocks in the dry riverbeds might be a promising place to begin the hunt. These fossils might be stromatolites, the layered rocks made from colonies of blue-green bacteria that are sometimes found on Earth. Fossil hunting on Mars will not be easy, but the absence of disruptive forces like tectonic activity and severe water erosion there should improve the chances of success, if there have been any fossils to be preserved.

Some scientists, however, insist that the search for present Martian life should not be abandoned. If you dig deeper, they say, you may find life forms that have access to water and are protected from the fierce solar radiation. Pieri was only half joking when he advised: "One of the first things people had better do, when they start drilling and getting water, is they better boil it before drinking. You never know."

Soviet scientists, in particular, believe that the Viking results should not be regarded as the last word on Martian life. "Various types of brines and solutions found inside Mars might be a suitable environment in which to look for life," said Mikhail Ivanov, director of the Soviet Institute for Microbiology, "so the question of the existence of possible oases on Mars should not be ruled out." Yuri Surkov, a Soviet expert on space chemistry, said: "Obviously one has to get to the permafrost in order to respond to the question of whether there are any forms of life on Mars."

Investigating the history of water on Mars could point to discoveries of broad philosophical and scientific import. If it leads to the discovery of some kind of life, active or fossil, we will have expanded our knowledge of the conditions under which life can evolve and survive in the universe. Extraterrestrial life will move from the realm of theory and speculation to reality, and we will be able to contemplate with rising anticipation the possibility of life, perhaps even intelligent life, on other worlds in other planetary systems. No longer will exobiology be disparaged as a science without a subject. If, even after probing the permafrost and other possible oases, no life is found, this, too, will increase our understanding of the limits to life and narrow the thermal band around a star where we can expect to find life. Earth will seem that much more special.

The search for water on the planet will also have a crucial bearing on the prospects for establishing life on Mars in the future. Explorers, especially those pioneers with colonization on their minds, will want to pitch their camps near reservoirs of frozen water. Living on Mars will depend on accessible supplies of water, preferably water near the equator (where it is warmer and otherwise better suited for a colony) and in permafrost that reaches close to the surface. On Mars water will be especially vital to explorers and colonists. It will be their source not only of drinking water but also, through extraction processes, of oxygen for life-support systems and hydrogen and oxygen for rocket propellants.

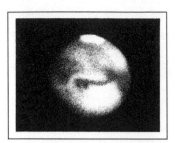

CHAPTER 8

THE RUSSIANS
ARE GOING

IN THE CLOSING years of the 1980s, it seemed possible to dream again and, flexing the human mind and the technologies of its creation, to anticipate a heady revival of Mars exploration. For the first time since the Viking launchings in 1975, two spacecraft embarked for Mars, while scientists and engineers shaped plans for other expeditions to follow in the years remaining to this century. Not all of their plans will come to fruition as soon as they might wish. Lapses of human judgment and shortcomings of flight machinery will disrupt some of the best-laid plans, as happened at the outset of this new and more ambitious phase of the human experience with Mars.

Occasional setbacks must be expected. But they should not obscure a notable change in the dynamics of mankind's response to the beckoning Mars.

A prominent scientist, speaking at a symposium in 1987, personified this surprising and promising change. The many questions about the biological, geological, and climatic history of Mars, he said, had given rise to "the present enormous interest" in the planet and to the emergence of a challenging agenda for exploration. He said that the study of Mars "should be done first by robots." He spoke of the need to examine the Martian atmosphere from orbiting spacecraft and balloons, to deploy automated rovers on the surface for collecting soil and rock samples, and to bring samples back to Earth for analysis. "Perhaps not all of the questions can be answered even by delivering samples from Mars, or by their study with rovers," the scientist added. "The human mind so far is still irreplaceable. Probably, therefore, a time will come when, in order to increase our knowledge, man on Mars will be necessary." That time, he said, would come "somewhere beyond the year 2000."

This vision of the future was not so much remarkable because of its content or confident tone. The scientific questions about Mars had been raised before. The need to proceed first with more robotic missions was indisputable. A belief in the inevitability of human expeditions in the twenty-first century was becoming an accepted article of faith. What was remarkable, then, was the speaker himself: Valery L. Barsukov, director of the Vernadsky Institute of Geochemistry and Analytical Chemistry in Moscow. Here was one of the foremost scientists in the Soviet space program addressing an international forum, freely describing his nation's aspirations and plans, inviting others to join in the continued exploration of Mars, but leaving no doubt that the Soviet Union was bidding for leadership in mankind's reach for the Red Planet.

In the middle years of the 1980s, Soviet space officials and scientists like Barsukov began showing up at international conferences, where they talked openly of their plans for a series of expeditions to Mars. We are going to Mars, they said many times in many ways at these meetings in Moscow, Europe, and the United States. These are our plans, they said with unprecedented candor. You could take part, they added in a new and sincere gesture toward international cooperation.

Both developments—the openness of Soviet officials in discussing their plans and their confident reach for international leadership in planetary exploration—marked an astonishing departure from the usual politics of the space age. Ever since the first Sputnik in 1957, the Soviet space program had operated behind a tightly drawn veil of secrecy. Plans and schedules were never disclosed. Setbacks and disasters were covered up. Successes, especially in the early years, were trumpeted as the inevitable achievements of a superior society. They were a source of pride to a long-suffering people and, with the strong military overtones, a warning to adversaries not to underestimate the Soviet Union.

But secrecy could not conceal woeful shortcomings. With a minimal industrial base for high technology, a lack of production incentives, and a sclerotic bureaucracy, the Soviet Union could not come close to matching the accomplishments of the American Apollo project to land men on the Moon and, except for some notable unmanned missions to the Moon and Venus, could never mount a widely successful drive to explore the solar system. By some counts (secrecy makes such reckonings difficult), fifteen Soviet Mars missions were launched between 1960 and 1973, and not one could be rated a success. Even so, Soviet space officials and scientists persevered and in the 1980s were emboldened by technological successes and fresh political leadership to strike out in new directions.

The change in aims and capabilities of the Soviet civilian space program began to emerge in 1980 with the early planning for the two

Roald Z. Sagdeyev of the Soviet Space Research Institute with a model of the ill-fated Phobos 1. (The New York Times/Felicity Barringer)

Vega missions to explore Venus and then rendezvous with Halley's comet. At first the sole objective had been a visit to Venus, the object of most Soviet interplanetary triumphs. But at a cocktail party, a French scientist on the project, Jacques Blamont, mentioned to the Russians that the Venus craft could easily be redirected after the Venus encounter to make a close pass by the illustrious comet. "Suddenly all hell broke loose," Blamont recalled, and in a few months the Soviet Union had its sights set on Halley's comet.

It was a rare display of flexibility and innovation for the Soviet program, and the man largely responsible for this and for organizing and directing the Vega missions was Roald Z. Sagdeyev, director of the Space Research Institute in Moscow. The institute, an arm of the Soviet Academy of Sciences, oversees many of the Soviet unmanned scientific operations in space. Sagdeyev is a physicist with powerful political connections, the charm and patience of a diplomat, the verve and courage of a reformer, and the skill to bring about surprising changes working within the Soviet establishment. Not only did Sagdeyev recognize the scientific merit of the French suggestion, but he saw the potential political benefits and marshaled all his talents to see the project through. In so doing, he laid a foundation for the revival of Mars exploration. Vega became the political and scientific model in planning a variety of Soviet missions to Mars.

The prospect of political benefits no doubt helped Sagdeyev win the support of his government for the mission. Halley's comet comes flashing by Earth only once in a lifetime, every 76 years, and this time several nations were planning to send out a welcoming party of spacecraft. The thirteen-nation European Space Agency was developing its Giotto spacecraft, Japan was preparing two small craft, but the United States had defaulted. American plans for a Halley mission were scuttled, a victim of tight NASA budgets. So this was an opportunity for the Soviet Union to play a leading role in a highly visible scientific endeavor, while the United States, the usual star, had to settle for a walk-on part. This was a chance to gain greater respect as an equal among the advanced nations in scientific and technological prowess. In the Soviet Union, where cosmonauts are exalted heroes and soaring monuments commemorate their exploits, the symbolism of achievement in space as a measure of national greatness retains much of its old power.

But the Vega missions would not be exclusively Soviet undertakings. Sagdeyev and his colleagues, realizing the complexity of the mission, sought the help of others through international cooperation. Soviet officials had already been moving cautiously in this direction. On recent flights to Venus, they had included instruments and equipment from Eastern European countries and France. It was a mutually beneficial pooling of talents and resources: The Russians had the rockets, spacecraft, and flight-control facilities, and the Europeans could supply some advanced remote-sensing instruments and electronics in return for the participation of their scientists in a major planetary expedition.

For the Vega missions the Soviet Union widened international involvement to eleven nations, including more Western Europeans this time. Although the United States, having let the Soviet-American space cooperation agreement lapse, did not take part officially and directly, an arrangement with the European Space Agency opened the way for American deep-space antennas to be used in tracking the Soviet craft in the vicinity of Halley's comet. Also, a scientist at the University of Chicago, accepting a personal invitation from Sagdeyev, provided critical comet-dust detectors for the two Vegas. But the scientist, John A. Simpson, had to resort to the subterfuge of having the instruments assembled in West Germany, and represented in mission publicity as a German contribution, to avoid possible political fireworks either in Washington or in Moscow. (American-Soviet relations, it should be remembered, were especially fragile at the time, with President Ronald Reagan calling Moscow the "evil empire" and with the Kremlin in the shaky hands of caretakers since the death of Leonid Brezhnev in 1982.) Ever the shrewd politician, Sagdeyev had taken the precaution of not divulging the modest American presence on the Vega spacecraft until after their launchings in December 1984.

In most respects, however, Sagdeyev saw to it that the Vega missions were conducted in a refreshingly open atmosphere. He established this as a policy even before the dynamic and daring Mikhail S. Gorbachev came to power in 1984 espousing *glasnost*, or openness, and *perestroika*, economic restructuring, for the entire Soviet society. With so many Western participants in Vega, the usual policy of secrecy probably could not have been enforced. But Sagdeyev had other reasons. He wanted the world to know of and share in this Soviet success. He wanted to encourage Westerners to join in future missions. Moreover, according to Western observers, Sagdeyev wanted to impress upon his own government the Soviet capabilities in planetary exploration and the advantages of increased international cooperation in such endeavors; in other words, he sought to secure his political position at home and build for the future. Like any leader of an expensive scientific enterprise in any country, Sagdeyev had to fight other powerful forces within the space establishment and the government at large for money, manpower, and other resources. He was carrying the fight to the world through some Western-style public relations.

Toward these ends Sagdeyev arranged for live television coverage of the Vega launchings. (Previously, most launchings were not announced in advance, and telecasts were ordinarily shown later, after the success of lift-off had been assured.) Then, in March 1986, Western scientists, including a number of Americans, were invited to the Space Research Institute to be on hand for the flybys of Halley's comet. Western reporters were allowed to mix and mingle with the scientists in an atmosphere that was reminiscent (deliberately so) of American planetary encounters at the Jet Propulsion Laboratory. For Sagdeyev it was a calculated risk. Successful or not, the Vegas and, for the first time, the Soviet planetary program were operating in full view of the world.

Fortunately for Sagdeyev and his allies, both spacecraft were scientific—and political—successes. Looking back, Sagdeyev speaks of the Vega missions as a striking experiment in international cooperation and "an island of scientific brotherhood and *glasnost.*"

Writing in 1988, Sagdeyev revealed some of his motives in reinvigorating and opening the Soviet planetary program. "One goal of *perestroika* is to break out of our recent scientific isolationism," he said. "I can remember when many years ago my young colleagues and I were admonished by an experienced administrator before going to a big international conference: 'It will be difficult to avoid contacts. Therefore, your task is to give them a kopeck's worth of information in exchange for a ruble's worth.' Such shortsighted thinking has hurt Soviet science far more than it has helped."

Cynics may argue that Sagdeyev is making a virtue of necessity. He is pursuing and advertising international partnerships, they might say, because this is the only way the Soviet Union can mount a wide-ranging, sophisticated program of planetary exploration. There is some truth in this; Soviet space technology, Western experts say, has many shortcomings. But a variation of the argument also applies to a degree to Western Europe and, judging by recent experience, to the United States as well. Although European or American technology is capable of making prodigious interplanetary strides alone, the increasing complexity and cost of such missions impose frustrating limits. Economics may become the necessity driving others to see virtue in wider cooperation.

Also, cynics may argue that Sagdeyev's ulterior purpose is to use the experience and resources of others to help build up Soviet science and technology. He is undoubtedly a loyal Russian and seeks to improve Soviet science, which was implicit in his assertion that scientific isolation had hurt Soviet science more than it had helped. In that light, it seems, his pursuit of cooperation marks him as a shrewd opportunist, an attribute much admired in leaders anywhere. By all indications, Gorbachev's entire program of reforms is a calculated and brave attempt to reverse the nation's deteriorating economy and revive its stagnating society by all available means, which include the ending of the military adventure in Afghanistan, some unilateral disarmament to show goodwill and reduce missile spending, and a vigorous campaign to encourage trade with the West.

Recent developments also emboldened Soviet space officials to be more innovative and expansionary in science and technology. A new super-rocket, the successes of the Mir space station, and the introduction of a reusable space shuttle bolstered Soviet capabilities and confidence, and impressed competitors and would-be partners. The American program was sorely troubled, and Western Europeans were restive, looking more and more beyond their customary American allies for the realization of their space objectives.

By then, as well, Gorbachev had seemed to secure his hold on the Kremlin, and programs modeled after Vega appeared to fit right in with his *glasnost* policy. Sagdeyev had become a close adviser to Gorbachev and so was in a position to press more vigorously his ideas for revamping Soviet science and space programs. "Sagdeyev and Gorbachev are aiming for intellectual power," Jacques Blamont said. "They believe in the power of science. This is a political battle of the highest importance."

In these changing circumstances, Soviet space officials and scientists let everyone know that they had big plans for the exploration of Mars.

THE FIRST OBJECTIVE was the Martian moon Phobos. Several factors contributed to the selection of this target. A flight to Mars, if successful, would build confidence that the many malfunctions that plagued earlier efforts had finally been overcome. And the scientific results, moreover, would not duplicate those of the previous American flights. Entirely new ground in the solar system would be claimed for scientific investigation.

As Aleksandr V. Zakharov of the Space Research Institute said before the mission, the study of small bodies is an "urgent" goal of solar system exploration. "All the planets and most of their moons," he explained, "have evolved due to external factors (like cratering) and, more important, internal processes (like volcanism). Such forces have drastically changed planetary materials and practically erased all traces of primordial matter. The situation with the solar system's small bodies—comets and asteroids—is radically different. Because of their size, the smaller accumulation of radioactive elements largely precluded internal heating and any subsequent tectonic activity. They exist today with much of their original primordial material, taken from the protoplanetary cloud out of which the planets formed."

Thus, by investigating a small object like Phobos, the Soviet spacecraft would be gathering information about the early stages in the formation of the solar system and about the origin and evolution of the planets, including Earth. If Phobos is a captured asteroid, as many scientists believe, then the Soviet spacecraft, Zakharov added, "will do more than study the moons of Mars—they will make the first close-up study of a new class of astronomical object: asteroids."

These were the great expectations in July 1988, when two Proton rockets were launched less than a week apart (on the seventh and the twelfth) to boost the Phobos 1 and Phobos 2 spacecraft on their way toward Mars. For the launchings Sagdeyev went even further with his open-door policy.

Scores of Western European and American officials were invited to the Baikonur Cosmodrome, 1,600 miles southeast of Moscow in Kazakhstan, to witness the Phobos 1 launching. Some American journalists were also able to see a major Soviet launching for the first time. They were given tours of the Proton processing facilities and the buildings where the manned Soyuz spacecraft were being prepared for flights to the Mir space station. The Proton rocket being readied for the next Phobos launching was also on view, bearing some incongruous marks of capitalism. Painted on the Proton's second stage were the corporate logos of two Western steel companies, Danieli in Italy and Voest-Alpine in Austria, which had paid the Soviet Union a fee to advertise themselves as "sponsors" of a space-bound rocket. Never had the land of Madison Avenue gone so far as to have rocket billboards. But the spectacle of the launching was the best advertisement of the Soviet Union's new emphasis on Mars exploration.

The Phobos mission—the first Soviet flights to Mars since 1973—was the most complex and challenging Soviet interplanetary undertaking to date. The two almost identical spacecraft, each weighing 13,700 pounds, including instruments and fuel, represented the first new model of planetary vehicles to be introduced by the Russians in eighteen years. They were designed to go into an orbit of Mars and then send small landers to the surface of Phobos. The little moon would then become the fourth extraterrestrial body (after the Moon, Venus, and Mars) on which spacecraft have touched down.

Following the Vega precedent, Soviet officials publicized details of the mission years before the launchings and included cameras, instruments, and assorted equipment from fourteen other countries. The participation of non-Communist nations was even more extensive this time, with Austria, France, Sweden, Switzerland, and West Germany, as well as the European Space Agency, helping in the development of instruments and providing scientists for the data-analysis teams.

The United States joined the project in a limited way. Its deep-space antennas were aimed for tracking the spacecraft through key maneuvers, and some American scientists—unofficially at first, then with the approval of their government—served as advisers, sharing their expertise gained in the Mariner and Viking programs. By this time, the summit meetings between Gorbachev and Reagan had thawed Soviet-American relations. In April 1987, the two nations reached an agreement resuming coordination and cooperation in certain civilian space activities. At the May 1988 summit conference, the leaders agreed to expand this cooperation, noting scientific missions to Mars as an area of possible bilateral and international partnerships.

Before this, however, American and Soviet scientists on their own had been quietly learning to work together. In an informal, nongovernment arrangement between Brown University and the Vernadsky Institute, for example, scientists of the two countries had been sharing problems, data, and plans since the early 1980s, meeting in alternate years in Providence, Rhode Island, and in Moscow. Similar arrangements were effected between planetary scientists at Caltech and their Soviet counterparts. James W. Head III, a planetary geologist at Brown, said: "It's another whole community that shares a common interest in something that is truly mysterious and beautiful."

Through these continuing contacts American scientists developed respect for their Soviet planetary colleagues and their plans for exploring Phobos. Head called the mission "incredibly imaginative." The plan was for the spacecraft to descend as low as 100 to 200 feet above Phobos and fly in a matching orbit with the small moon. Soviet researchers were pinning special hopes on a laser instrument, built with the cooperation of scientists in West Germany and Bulgaria. The laser was designed to fire its highly focused beam of light and vaporize first one spot and then another on the moon's dark surface. In the nearly perfect vacuum of space, the resulting vapors would speed away in all directions, with some of them expected to reach an instrument on board Phobos 1 that included a "reflectron" device. Its analysis of the vapors would presumably reveal their chemical makeup and thus enable scientists to reconstruct the chemical composition of the Phobos soil. Simultaneously, another instrument was to seek the same information through a different technique, developed with the help of scientists in Austria, Finland, and France. This instrument was designed to emit a concentrated beam of krypton particles directed to the moon's surface, while a mass spectrometer on board sensed and sought to identify the particles given off by the surface material in response to the bombardment.

Also, the two spacecraft were each supposed to release two small landers to the moon's surface. The larger of the two was an automated laboratory equipped with a camera and instruments for investigating the chemistry and structure of Phobos. Because the moon's gravity is so slight (a person who weighed 150 pounds on Earth would weigh about one ounce on Phobos), a harpoonlike device was to be driven into the surface to keep the lander from drifting back into orbit. The "penetrator" would be able to make soil temperature readings. The other lander—the "hopper"—was a 110-pound metal sphere, about the size of a basketball, with spring-loaded legs so that it could bound from place to place, making chemical, magnetic, and gravity observations over a wide area.

Alas, this was not to be.

A computer programming error at the flight control center caused the Phobos 1 spacecraft to lose its celestial bearings in early September, while still en route to Mars. The trouble, American experts said, betrayed an inadequately designed control system on the craft. One chance error, of the kind that threw Phobos 1 out of control and out of communication, should not have been allowed to have such consequences. On the highly successful Voyager spacecraft to the outer planets, for example, the on-board control computer is programmed to spot an unusual command and call back to ground controllers for verification. These and other defenses are built in to prevent irrevocable damage and also to permit a complete change of on-board computer instructions in response to some unforeseen problem.

Phobos 2 made it to Mars, easing into orbit in late January 1989. For almost two months, the craft traveled around the planet in various orbits, photographing the landscape and studying its atmosphere, geochemistry, and possible magnetic properties. But on March 27, when ground controllers were trying to reorient the spacecraft to take pictures of Phobos prior to the planned landing, they began receiving sporadic radio signals and then nothing at all. Phobos 2 was irrevocably lost.

It was an inauspicious start for the Soviet program of Mars exploration. Officials continued with their plans for a mission in 1994 and were studying the possibility of using spare equipment to develop another spacecraft for a new attempt to explore Phobos, possibly in 1996.

Bruce Murray, the Caltech scientist, who was a member of the international team of advisers on the mission, said the fate of the spacecraft was not too surprising. The Russians had invariably had problems on the inaugural flights of entirely new interplanetary spacecraft, which had a lot to do with their test philosophy. As in the early days of aviation, they tended to build new vehicles and, in contrast to the American and European programs, fly them with a minimum of ground testing. If they worked, fine; if not, figure out the problem, fix it, and try again. The new spacecraft that were unsuccessful in Mars flights in 1971 and 1973 were later perfected and flown without mishap many times to Venus and twice to Halley's comet. Murray said: "Their solution to failure is to do it again. They'll fly again and eventually get it right and make their landings on Mars."

If the Phobos craft is to be the prototype for future Mars vehicles, however, serious defects in its design must be corrected. Both Soviet and American experts proposed a major redesign to give the craft an adequate on-board computer intelligence to recover from the kinds of problems in communications and commands that disabled the Phobos-bound vehicles. Sagdeyev charged that delays in getting approval for the project necessitated taking some shortcuts in design and testing and that the agencies responsible for building the craft failed to consult scientists on the requirements for the mission. In the opinion of Sagdeyev and foreign observers, this exposed one of the basic weaknesses of the Soviet program. Engineering groups and industry in the Soviet Union are independently financed and are managed separately from the agencies directing a space project. No single agency, such as NASA in the United States, is responsible for the entire enterprise. Consequently, Murray pointed out, one agency will conceive and define the nature of the spacecraft, and only later will leaders of that agency negotiate with the scientific groups regarding its use. "Our style" in planning and managing space programs must change, Sagdeyev said after the Phobos failures, adding that "it seems that *perestroika* has not reached that sphere."

The failures also came at a time when the Soviet space program was coming under sharp attack at home. In another manifestation of *glasnost*, criticism of space spending was aired in the 1989 election campaign, reflecting increasing popular demand that the space program be reduced and the resources reallocated to meeting consumer needs. Newspaper articles, acknowledging that space once was a "sacred cow," carried stinging attacks and urged that the program be oriented "toward the needs of the national economy." The new public dialogue also exposed deep rifts in the Soviet space establishment. Scientists, taking their cue from Sagdeyev, openly complained of their treatment at the hands of the bureaucracy that controlled the design and production of rockets and spacecraft.

The Phobos setback could make Soviet officials more conservative in their planning and cause would-be international partners to question the advisability of putting too much faith in Soviet planetary spacecraft technology. Going to Mars, officials and scientists said, is still the Soviet goal. But getting there may take longer than the Russians had believed it would before the Phobos disappointments.

SCIENTISTS WHO visited Moscow in 1988 were handed copies of a document outlining the proposed stages of Mars studies beyond the Phobos mission. The first stage in the Soviet program, to be undertaken between 1994 and 1996, would see the investigation of the Martian surface and atmosphere with heavy unmanned vehicles carrying an orbiter, Martian rovers, a drilling device, and atmospheric probes. The second stage, between the years 2000 and 2005, would concentrate on the development and testing of future manned mission systems. This would call for unmanned expeditions using propulsion systems (including nuclear-power rockets), landing craft and return vehicles, and other equipment essential for later flights of humans. One objective would be to have the roving vehicles pick up soil samples for return to Earth. Finally, in the third stage, an expedition would carry humans to Mars.

Most of the emphasis was on planning for the 1994 mission. Its scope has yet to be determined, but scientists could see by the Soviet document that the range of possibilities for the 1994 flight was wide and challenging. Under serious consideration were plans to place two spacecraft into orbits of Mars passing over the poles. Each orbiter could carry a balloon, a small rover, and possibly other deployable equipment. Among the devices being studied were a smaller satellite to be released in Martian orbit to provide gravity data; a set of small weather transmitters to be dropped at widely scattered places on the surface to return data on temperature, pressure, and wind velocity; two penetrators that would be driven as deep as 16 feet into the planet's surface to provide information on chemical composition, soil temperature, and water content. Soviet planners have also considered equipping the orbiters with high-resolution imaging systems and Earth-return capsules to bring the film back; the latter would serve the dual purpose of returning higher-quality pictures and providing a demonstration of the propulsion, guidance, and retrieval technologies needed to return Martian surface samples on future missions. The document went beyond listing and describing the various mission components. On one page, under the heading "Cooperation," each proposed component was accompanied by the name of the country or countries that were being invited to act as designers and suppliers. Orbiter—U.S.S.R. Penetrators—U.S.A. Balloon—France, U.S.A., U.S.S.R. Martian rover—France, U.S.A., U.S.S.R., European Space Agency. And so on.

The Soviet officials may have been guilty of wishful thinking, for by early 1989—even before the loss of the second Phobos spacecraft—they were scaling down their plans. The 1994 mission might be reduced to an orbiter that would simply release a balloon in the atmosphere, deploy the small meteorological stations, and drop the subsurface penetrators. The orbiter's photography would be the basis for selecting a landing site for a roving vehicle to be deployed by a follow-up flight. In other words, details and time lines of Soviet plans for Mars had not been firmly established, and in view of the Phobos failures, the next missions are likely to have limited goals.

Balloons floating in the Martian atmosphere, however, appeared to be a certainty in Soviet plans. French designers, who were responsible for the balloons deployed at Venus by the Vega spacecraft, had already proposed a dual-balloon configuration for use in the less dense and less hostile Martian environment. A lander released by the orbiter would separate on reaching the surface, and out of one section would emerge the balloon, made of very thin polyester. The upper bag would be inflated immediately with helium. Suspended below it would be a larger parachutelike bag of aluminized polyester, a type of balloon known as a montgolfier, after a pioneering eighteenth-century French balloonist. In the cool of the night on Mars, the helium balloon would not be quite buoyant enough by itself to lift the gondola with its scientific instruments off the surface. But it would float high enough to keep itself and the montgolfier safely above the surface. In the morning, the sun would warm the atmospheric gases trapped in the montgolfier until it gained the necessary buoyancy to lift itself and the gondola to altitudes of 1 or 2 miles and then drift with the winds as much as 120 miles each day, perhaps farther. Its cargo of cameras would take close-up pictures in visible and infrared wavelengths over a wide variety of Martian landscape. It might even be possible to take pictures inside the canyons and on the slopes of the huge volcanoes. At night, when the gondola is resting on the ground, one of its instruments, a gamma ray spectrometer, would measure natural gamma rays emitted by the surface rock. From these measurements scientists believe they can determine the radioactive elements that emitted the rays and thus learn something about primordial Martian material. Other instruments should be able to study the chemical composition of the soil and the magnetism of Martian rock.

"One of the system's advantages is its mobility," Blamont of the French Space Agency said. "The presence of boulders, rocks, dust, and other obstacles on the Mars surface creates major difficulties for a rover vehicle. However, by using the atmosphere as a means of transporting a payload by balloon, we will have the mobility aspect and be able to land at several sites on the planet."

Each balloon system would be capable of operating several weeks before too much helium leaks from the upper bag and it can no longer provide its share of the lift. Geochemical data and photography would be transmitted from the gondola to the Soviet spacecraft in orbit. In addition, arrangements were being made to equip an American spacecraft, Mars Observer, so that it could also relay the French-Soviet balloon data. The Mars Observer was scheduled for a 1992 launching—and, ironically, for all the talk of the Soviet plans, it will probably turn out to be the true inaugural mission in the new drive to explore Mars.

Sooner or later, Soviet spacecraft will probably deliver remotely controlled roving vehicles to the surface of Mars. They would be a much more sophisticated elaboration of the technology Soviet engineers pioneered with the Lunokhods, rovers that collected soil samples on the Moon in the early 1970s.

According to preliminary plans, the first of these Soviet rovers to operate on Mars would weigh about 500 pounds, have a lifetime of 1 to 3 years, and range over a distance of as much as 300 miles. It would run on nuclear-electric power, have at least six large steel wheels, and be maneuvered by computers and with the help of a television system by which controllers back on Earth could plan its movements. The Mars rover would carry an assortment of instruments, besides the television camera, for making scientific investigations. The instruments would examine soil chemistry, make seismic soundings, collect weather data, and look for signs of biological activity. On later missions, a larger version, weighing more than 1,500 pounds, would carry drills capable of digging as deep as 100 feet and investigating the chemical and physical properties of the samples. The rover would also gather soil and rock from widely scattered sites and haul it back to a return vehicle, waiting to blast off and fly back to Earth with the precious cargo. Once the return vehicle reaches the vicinity of Earth, it would decelerate into orbit and rendezvous with a Soviet space station, where the samples would be examined first to make sure they contain no potentially harmful organisms. Then they would be sent on to Earth for detailed analysis. The sample-return mission could occur as early as 1998 or 2000.

SOVIET PLANS for Mars exploration raise questions about how real are their prospects. How deep and permanent are the changes in the operation and goals of the Soviet program? Are the promises of international cooperation genuine and lasting? Can the technology be marshaled for accomplishing such bold missions? What are we to expect in the future?

The openness of the Soviet program may not be complete, but Soviet officials and scientists seem to relish it as much as their Western counterparts welcome it. There is nothing like the sharing of problems and dreams to draw people together. The Soviet program, as a result, seems less monolithic and forbidding than before. In public meetings and news accounts, Soviet scientists acknowledge past mission failures and planning mistakes and argue openly over policy differences. Their shifting views on the scope and objectives of the 1994 mission have been voiced at international conferences. Bureaucratic rivalries are exposed, as when representatives of Glavcosmos, the Soviet civilian space agency, argued in favor of using the Energia super-rockets for the 1994 mission and were opposed by leaders of the

Babakin Engineering Research Center, a spacecraft production facility, who insisted on sticking with the smaller but proven Proton rockets.

Similarly, their conflicts over spending priorities sometimes come to a boil in public, as when Sagdeyev attacked the wisdom of the Soviet space shuttle. His criticism, as he acknowledged, echoed the perennial debate in the American scientific community on the same issue. In 1988, he wrote:

> We have put too much emphasis on manned flight at the expense of unmanned efforts that produce more scientific information at lower cost. Open discussion might have contributed to a more balanced program. But the United States has demonstrated that open discussion alone does not guarantee scientific wisdom. After years of debate over the advantages of manned and unmanned space missions, the United States has also put too much emphasis on the manned space shuttle program. U.S. space scientists must wait for the expensive and much-delayed shuttle to lift their payloads into space. The U.S. aerospace industry, like the Soviet industry bureaucracies, used its influence to subvert the logic of science. Open discussion helps scientists reach consensus, but scientists also must have more influence in making science-related decisions.

Carl Sagan or Bruce Murray or any number of American space scientists would agree wholeheartedly and empathize with their Soviet colleague in the battles he must be fighting. The fact that Sagdeyev could openly dispute policies of powerful government forces not only reflected the growing influence of *glasnost* in space affairs but encouraged others to feel that they can safely support Sagdeyev's plans for an expansive Mars program based on international cooperation.

There is concern among Westerners, however, about the Soviet organizational capabilities to implement bold programs. As already noted, no single agency has the authority to control all components of space missions, to the same degree that NASA does in the United States. Different agencies are in charge of building the spacecraft, the rockets, and the scientific instruments. The result, as Soviet scientists are beginning to acknowledge in public, is often inefficiency and confusion and this could thwart their plans for greater international participation in Soviet space operations. The involvement of other nations in missions like Phobos and those being planned, Head of Brown University said, "allows the Soviets to do more, to defer much of the cost, and expand the mission's scientific and technical capabilities. I think that for the Soviets space is much more a part of foreign policy than it is in our country."

The policy's continuity, of course, hinges on the fortunes of Gorbachev and Sagdeyev, who resigned in late 1988 as director of the Space Research Institute but has remained an outspoken and influential force in science and space affairs. "What we're seeing is the Sagdeyev approach," said Arden Albee of Caltech, who has worked closely with the new Soviet space leaders. "If his influence were to wane, then I suspect there might be quite a different kind of approach."

Assuming no fundamental shift in policy, the Soviet Union could well be in position technologically to accomplish its ambitious Mars goals. Nicholas L. Johnson, a specialist in Soviet space technology at Teledyne Brown Engineering, Inc., in Colorado Springs, which publishes an authoritative annual booklet on Soviet space activities and capabilities, describes current preparations as being typical of the conservative, evolutionary Soviet approach in all its space undertakings. "Little by little," he said, "they're embarking on big things. Without doubt, Mars will be the focal point of Soviet planetary exploration for the next ten to twenty years. Soviet scientists have now devised an evolutionary, multifaceted program for investigating the entire Martian system which is defensible on purely scientific grounds while simultaneously laying a foundation essential for the contemplation of a manned mission to Mars."

Although no firm commitment to undertake manned expeditions to Mars had been made, Johnson said that it is only a matter of time. The Soviet goal, he said, is nothing less than "the evolution of man into space," adding: "They really see that as inevitable, and they aim to be a large part of it, if not the leading part."

Recent developments—the Energia rocket, the Buran space shuttle, and expanding operations of the Mir space station—are steadily enhancing Soviet capabilities to mount a major program of Mars exploration.

The Energia can launch payloads of about 220,000 pounds into low Earth orbit, compared with the American shuttle's 55,000 pounds, and may be upgraded to provide an even greater capacity. (The American Saturn 5, which boosted astronauts to the Moon, could put 300,000 pounds into low Earth orbit, but was decommissioned in 1973.) The Energia's design allows for significant flexibility: The rocket can transport into orbit either the Soviet shuttle or a large cargo canister. Although it is derived from previous proven technologies, Energia represents one significant departure in that it is the first Soviet application of cryogenic fuels, such as the super-cold liquid hydrogen, which had long been employed by the United States and the European Space Agency and had also been adopted by China. Cryogenic fuels and engines, more efficient in providing heavy-lifting thrust, are probably essential for rockets sending astronauts to Mars.

In November 1988, Soviet engineers finally introduced their long-awaited space shuttle, Buran, the Russian word for snowstorm. Buran bears a strong resemblance to the American shuttle in concept, shape, and capacity. Boosted by an Energia, Buran orbited Earth twice and came to a smooth runway landing—all without any pilots on board, which American experts saw as clear evidence that the shuttles represent a major advance for Soviet flight technology in electronic controls and computerized guidance and navigation systems. Cosmonauts will take the controls on future flights of an operational version. Although Buran appears to be an approximate copy of the American shuttle, Soviet officials made it clear that they will not repeat the American policy mistake of relying almost exclusively on these reusable vehicles. The shuttle will provide a means to return large payloads to Earth, a capability the Russians had lacked. But the shuttle will not replace existing systems, such as the Soyuz manned craft and the Progress cargo carriers. It may not even be the only reusable manned vehicle in the Soviet fleet. Western analysts suspect (the Soviets still do not tell all, any more than Americans do) that Soviet engineers are developing a small, reusable space plane that would be launched by rocket but would be able to land on a standard runway. The space plane would carry two or three people into low orbit and perhaps a small payload. Its primary utility would be in transporting people to orbiting stations, in the inspection of satellites, or in service as a rapid-response rescue vehicle.

After fifteen years of plodding progress with a series of Salyut stations, Soviet engineers made a significant advance with their new-generation Mir station in February 1986. Despite its structural similarity to the Salyuts, Mir was qualitatively different, with more modern computers, increased electric-power capacity, more automatic controls, and improved communications systems. And Mir was designed to grow in space. The most important innovation was the addition of a five-port docking adapter at one end of Mir. Along with the single port at the other end, the adapter made it possible for six spacecraft or modules to be attached to the station at one time. A few months later, the Kvant science module, almost as large as the 56-foot-long Mir core itself, was docked with Mir. Kvant was another example of international cooperation, with many of its telescopes and other instruments provided by Britain, Switzerland, West Germany, and the European Space Agency. These and similar modules to be added provide the station with more working and living room, and give engineers and flight controllers experience in assembling large components in orbit, which will be critical in Mars flights.

Mir has been occupied almost continuously since its launching. In tests of the physiological and psychological effects of weightlessness, Salyut crews had systematically extended the "stay times" to 96, 140, 175, 185, 211, and finally 237 days. At the end of 1988, two cosmonauts, Vladimir G. Titov and Musa K. Manarov, returned after spending a year on board Mir, slightly more time than it might take to travel one way to Mars. The mission increased Soviet confidence that a long-duration flight to Mars was physiologically feasible for cosmonauts. As one Soviet space program manager told *Aviation Week & Space Technology* magazine: "We're one step closer to Mars."

In reviewing the expanding Soviet program, Peter M. Banks, an engineering professor at Stanford University and a NASA adviser, and Sally K. Ride, the former astronaut, asked whether these recent steps, in fact, presaged a major program to send cosmonauts to Mars. "Perhaps, but it will certainly not happen in the near future," they concluded in a 1989 article in *Scientific American*. "It is true that the development of Energia and an understanding of human response to weightlessness are necessary in order to reach out to Mars; it is also true that Soviet space representatives have been talking about Mars more frequently. But an expedition to Mars is a huge undertaking, much more demanding than the Apollo program. It would take from

15 to 20 Energia launches to put the Mars vehicle and its fuel into low earth orbit for assembly, and a new-generation space station would be needed to house assembly workers and to store, integrate and test the vehicle and its component systems. Such an extraordinary task would require a generation of dedicated effort."

If there is one trait characteristic of the Soviet space program, it is patience in the unrelenting pursuit of large objectives. The Soviet program is often seen as the tortoise to the American hare. Its strengths lie in rocketry and long-duration manned space flight. Its main weaknesses are in the nation's lagging base in high technology, especially instrumentation and the computer chips that bring delicate space probes to life. The Phobos mission was probably a victim of these inadequacies. Despite such limitations, and with help from other countries, the Soviet space program, manned and unmanned, is forging ahead at a steady pace—and its much-heralded destination is Mars.

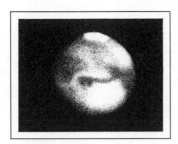

CHAPTER 9

AMERICAN
INDECISION

THE RESURGENCE of Soviet interest in Mars came at a distressingly low point in the American space enterprise. Those robotic craft exploring the planets, the long lenses of human curiosity and once the pride of American technology, were becoming an endangered species. A Pioneer spacecraft had taken off in 1978 to map Venus—nothing since. The durable Voyager 2 cruised on into the outer solar system, beyond its initial targets of Jupiter and Saturn, and had just transmitted our first close-up glimpses of Uranus before heading out to Neptune. But Voyager had left Earth in 1977 and was the product of commitments made even earlier. The mission of Galileo, a spacecraft to orbit Jupiter and its largest satellites, had barely survived the pruning knives of budget officials and was destined to remain on the ground many more years. None of the challenging proposals to return to Mars after the Viking landings had come to pass, or was likely to in the foreseeable future. And then came the most stunning blow of all—the worst disaster in space history.

On the cold and windy morning of January 28, 1986, the space shuttle Challenger lifted off from Cape Canaveral and, 73 seconds into flight, exploded in full view of spectators on the ground and, through television, the entire world. All seven on board—five astronauts, an

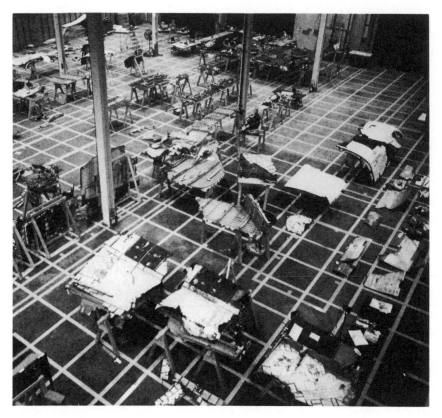

Debris from the space shuttle Challenger is laid out on a grid at Kennedy Space Center. (AP/Wide World Photos)

aerospace industry engineer, and a schoolteacher from New Hampshire—were killed.

More than the Challenger exploded in the blue sky over the Atlantic Ocean. The space shuttle was the most visible symbol of American leadership in space technology, which had been undisputed since the Apollo days. Its successes seemed to affirm our faith in NASA to transport us safely and efficiently to the new frontier of human aspirations. Then, suddenly, after fourteen years and the investment of $30 billion, in the reverberating shock of failure, we were left full of doubts not only about the shuttles and NASA's fabled competence but also about the very fundamentals of our national space policy.

As long as the launching pads bustled to the tempo of countdowns and shuttles regularly took off—twenty-four missions had been flown since 1981—it was easy to set aside the doubts. If the technology had its flaws, it certainly seemed to work well enough. If the space shuttles' widely promised potential for hauling cargoes at reduced costs had yet to be realized, just wait until they were flying twenty or thirty times a year. If shuttle costs and delays were paralyzing other space endeavors, notably science and planetary programs and new rocket systems, enabling foreign competitors to steal a march on us, this was unavoidable and only temporary. There were risks to space flight, of course, but the shuttles were making it routine enough to send a senator, a congressman, and a schoolteacher to float weightless above Earth.

With the Challenger disaster, however, there was no denying the weaknesses of both the shuttles and the policy that relied almost totally on a single launching system. The remaining shuttles—Columbia, Discovery, and Atlantis—were to sit in their hangars with nowhere to go for another three years. The nation's misfortune was compounded by a plague of setbacks to its Titan 3, Atlas-Centaur, and Delta expendable launchers. For a time the United States found itself an impotent spacefarer. This bleak state of affairs became all the more painful, even a little embarrassing, in the light of developments in the Soviet Union, Western Europe, and Japan.

In February 1986, the Soviet Union took another big step in its drive to establish a permanent human presence in space, placing its Mir space station in Earth orbit. It was the eighth Soviet station in orbit since the mid-1970s. The American Skylab, an experimental space station, was used for three missions in 1973–74 and then abandoned in orbit. Plans for a larger, more sophisticated station, though strongly endorsed by President Reagan, were meeting opposition in Congress and among scientists and the public. No American space station was likely to make it to orbit for another decade, if then.

Later in the spring, the world's scientists gathered not in Pasadena or Houston but in Moscow and Darmstadt, West Germany, to receive the first close-up images of Halley's comet. The two Soviet Vega spacecraft made the first encounters with the comet, followed by the European Space Agency's Giotto craft and two smaller Japanese probes. Americans, their resources largely consumed in building the shuttles, were on the sidelines for one of the decade's biggest events in solar system exploration.

At the same time, Western Europe, China, and the Soviet Union pushed ahead with the launchings of their conventional expendable rockets. With the shuttles out of service, they sought to seize the moment to gain an advantage in the world's emerging commercial space-launching market.

The shuttle tragedy underscored what many in the aerospace community had known for several years: The United States was involved in a new space race. Unlike the contest with the Soviet Union in the 1960s to land men on the Moon, this new race has more than two participants and more than one goal. And there is no clear winner in sight. Perhaps, in the altered circumstances, thinking in terms of winning such a race is simplistic and outmoded. But people who would continue to be spacefarers must be fully engaged and alert to opportunities. The American space program, in this moment of crisis, came up short on both counts.

Thus, the revival of interest in Mars exploration could not have come at a worse time for American space officials. They had their hands full defending past policies and the management of the shuttle program and trying desperately to get the shuttles flying again. They were not sure they could even win approval for a space station, much less for any sweeping programs of planetary exploration. Nor could they be certain that they would be keeping their jobs in the general housecleaning of NASA that followed the investigation into the Challenger accident.

But, in one sense, the timing was not necessarily inopportune. In the Challenger aftermath, nearly everyone associated with the American space program, as well as political and science leaders, was forced to recognize the need to conduct a long-overdue review of the nation's capabilities and aims in space. They were encouraged by the public reaction to the disaster. Opinion polls showed that most Americans favored continuing shuttle flights, after necessary modifications to the vehicles and launching procedures, and supported a strong space program with a bold and expansive vision. Despite some early fears, there had been no Luddite reaction against modern technology or space exploration. Instead, there seemed to be an awareness that we had been drifting too long without a clear, comprehensive policy regarding why we were spacefarers and where we could be and should be going.

IN HIS 1985 book *The Heavens and the Earth*, a critically acclaimed political history of the space age, Walter A. McDougall, a history professor at the University of California and now at the University of Pennsylvania, wrote: "Apollo was a matter of going to the moon and building whatever technology could get us there; the space shuttle was a matter of building a technology and going wherever it could take us."

It was this thinking—as close as the United States came to a national space policy in the 1970s—that led to an almost exclusive dependence on the space shuttle as the national launching system. Coming off the successful Apollo moon landings, NASA officials had sought a mandate to deploy a manned orbiting space station, to build a fleet of reusable shuttles to ferry to and from the station, and eventually to fly people to Mars in the 1980s. But hubris had clouded NASA's vision of reality. The public and the administration of Richard M. Nixon, beset by the war in Vietnam, urban decay, and economic woes, were in no mood for a new space extravaganza. The best NASA could get was approval, in 1972, to build four shuttles. This represented a revolutionary space transportation system in search of a well-defined mission. The space station was deferred indefinitely, and nothing was heard again in official circles of sending people to Mars.

At the time of the Challenger accident, some groundwork was already being laid for a national debate on space policy and goals. The National Commission on Space, established by Congress and the President and headed by a former NASA administrator, Thomas O. Paine, had been developing recommendations to guide decision makers in planning for the next fifty years of space exploration, travel, and industry. In its report, issued in the middle of 1986, the Commission invoked the spirit of explorers past and sought to wrap the space enterprise in the cloak of a new Manifest Destiny. "The Solar System is our extended home," the Commission proclaimed in its opening statement. "Five centuries after Columbus opened access to 'The New World' we can initiate the settlement of worlds beyond our planet of birth. The promise of virgin lands and the opportunity to live in freedom brought our ancestors to the shores of North America. Now space technology has freed humankind to move outward from Earth as a species destined to expand to other worlds."

More specifically, the Commission identified three national goals for the civilian space program: science, including space astronomy, planetary exploration, and a detailed global study of planet Earth; human settlement of the solar system; and the development of space commerce. To achieve these goals, the Commission recommended a "phased approach" that would start with a permanently manned space station in Earth orbit and a new series of launching vehicles capable of lifting passengers and cargo into orbit at less than one-tenth the cost of the space shuttle. This could lead in time to the construction of interplanetary factories using raw materials mined from the Moon and asteroids and ultimately to permanent outposts on the Moon and Mars.

The Commission figured that the cost of such an undertaking would nearly triple the annual civilian space budget to something like $20 billion a year (in 1986 dollars)—the NASA budget was then $7.3 billion. (NASA's budget has been increased significantly since the Challenger accident, to about $12 billion in 1989.) Though not a trivial expenditure, the Commission's proposed budget, in terms of its percentage of the gross national product, would be less than half what NASA received during the peak Apollo years.

The Paine Commission's report got a frosty reception, however. Its far-reaching proposals seemed to bear too much of a resemblance to science fiction to be embraced by political leaders. And the more modest short-term recommendations tended to get lost in the "Bridge Between Worlds" imagery of Buck Rogers spaceships. Americans in the 1980s, as much as they might say they wanted a more visionary space policy, seemed in no mood for long-term plans and investments, and their politicians, in addition, were hobbled with legislated restraints on budget increases. So the Commission's colorfully illustrated report, *Pioneering the Space Frontier,* was ignored by the White House and Congress. Another presidential commission was heard from at the same time and its findings had more immediate impact. This was the Presidential Commission on the Space Shuttle Challenger Accident, chaired by William P. Rogers, a former Secretary of State. It brought a harsh indictment against NASA and the "flawed" management of the shuttle program.

In the following months, nonetheless, momentum began gathering to make Mars the next major goal of the American program. American scientists had become aware in 1985 that the Russians were contemplating new unmanned missions to Mars of increasing complexity and were viewing these as forerunners of a manned expedition sometime in the early twenty-first century. Planetary scientists, chafing at the official neglect of their programs, saw in the post-Challenger atmosphere an opportunity to renew their advocacy of a new round of Mars exploration. In speeches, articles, and discussions with politicians, prominent scientists urged the President to declare Mars the long-term goal as a means of reasserting the nation's eroding leadership in spacefaring.

Gerald J. Wasserburg, professor of geology and geophysics at Caltech, who has served on many space science advisory boards, suggested a measured strategy that many could agree upon. He proposed a commitment to a concerted program of robotic exploration of Mars over the next fifteen years. Then it could be decided if we wanted to fix our sights specifically on manned expeditions. A revived campaign of Mars exploration with more advanced unmanned craft, he said, "would excite the world in general and would lead to major scientific discoveries of that planet and development of substantial skills and technologies in robotics and artificial intelligence." All the while, he said, it should be clearly emphasized that the ultimate goal is putting humans on Mars—at a time and in a way to be determined later. "If he's worried about his place in history, Mr. Reagan could dignify his presidency with this one act," Wasserburg remarked in 1987, urging a presidential call to explore Mars. "Whenever people finally reach Mars, he would be remembered as the President who started it all."

Aerospace officials and some public figures joined in supporting Mars as a goal. A panel of independent advisers to NASA, headed by Daniel J. Fink, a former executive of the General Electric Company, and including Michael Collins, the former Apollo 11 astronaut, said that American leadership in space "absolutely requires the expansion of human life beyond Earth" and urged that exploring Mars be made the agency's "primary goal." The advisory panel said that such a "goal, clearly stated, will result not only in increased public awareness of NASA, but will serve the internal purpose of providing a stimulus to focus and clarify programs."

Over the next few years the Mars goal was endorsed by a dozen major publications, ranging from *The New York Times* to *The New Republic*. The Planetary Society, a 125,000-member public group headed by Carl Sagan, issued a "Mars Declaration," which advocated an American space program that would lead to human exploration of Mars. Among the signers were a glittering array of such prominent Americans as Walter Cronkite, Jimmy Carter, the Nobel Prize–winning physicist Hans Bethe, and the Rev. Theodore Hesburgh, former president of the University of Notre Dame. Senator Spark Matsunaga, Democrat of Hawaii, wrote a book, *The Mars Project*, that strongly advocated the space journey. But he told a reporter: "I hope the outcome won't be an East-West race."

Support was by no means unanimous among scientists or space officials. Some feared that an all-out effort in the fashion of Apollo would seriously distort priorities and jeopardize other worthwhile projects. They emphasized the importance of expanding space operations for studying Earth's resources and the threat of the "greenhouse effect" on global climate. Christopher C. Kraft, Jr., the retired director of the Johnson Space Center, for instance, had been second to none as an advocate of vigorous manned space flight and was a leader of the Apollo project. But, reacting to some of the more ambitious Mars proposals, he said: "I believe our goals should be more modest and more aimed at solving the problems we have on Earth. The rate of progress in robotics and automation will make unmanned expeditions to the planets more productive, will provide strong technological stimulation, and will be considerably less expensive than sending humans along to do the job."

Some scientists, many of whom raised the same argument years ago against Kraft and his Apollo associates, could hardly have agreed more. They had bitter memories of other expensive manned programs, notably the space shuttle, that drained money away from science and skewed NASA's entire operations. The cost of sending people to Mars would be even more staggering, these critics contended, and would be of only marginal scientific value. One of these critics was Norman Horowitz, the biologist who had been a leader in the Viking search for life. Asked what he thought of proposals for a major effort to send humans to Mars, he responded without hesitation. "It's just as wrong as can be," he said. "It's wrong because it guarantees there won't be any space science. We know how NASA treats science as a second-class citizen when it competes with man-in-space programs."

Other influential NASA scientists and advisers weighed the policy choices and decided that it would be wiser to go back to the Moon first and use it as a test bed for the technologies of human expansion through the rest of the solar system. In an article entitled "Resist the Pull of Mars," John M. Logsdon, a political scientist at George Washington University, who is a frequent adivser to NASA, wrote:

> Establishing a permanent base on the moon is an essential stage of expansion beyond Earth. Human beings should go to Mars, but it does not make sense to bypass the moon, a celestial island just offshore that offers significant knowledge for colonizing space. Getting to the moon is a three-day hop, compared with a months- or years-long journey to and from the Red Planet, which is approximately 200 times farther away. . . . The experience gained in establishing an outpost on the moon would be unarguably beneficial to a Mars trip, particularly if the eventual intent is to establish a permanent settlement on the Martian surface. Our current level of knowledge will support only limited human operations on Mars. . . . The moon's proximity makes it a wiser choice for such experiments because a mistake made there would be easier to correct than one on Mars. Crews could come home at any time; there would be no weeks- or months-long wait for the next launch window.

Proponents of a commitment to manned Mars missions conceded the point of Horowitz's criticism and of the Moon partisans—to some degree. Eventually, they contended, the lure of Mars will be so irresistible that people will want to go there themselves. And there may be no substitute for the human brain in conducting elaborate scientific studies, prospecting for the planet's resources, or surveying the place for possible human colonization. Thus, these proponents argued, it makes sense to plan future robotic exploration with the larger goal always in mind and clearly enunciated.

Bruce Murray, the Caltech planetary scientist, was one of the earliest advocates of making Mars the nation's long-term space goal with an emphasis on the ultimate objective of manned landings. Ironically, several of the scientists who took this position and argued it most fervently came from backgrounds in the unmanned planetary program and had once looked upon manned space flight as the bully on the block that robbed them of their small change. They were now seeking an alliance with former foes that might be to their mutual benefit. A man-on-Mars goal, Murray said, would bring coherence and a new sense of mission to the nation's rudderless civilian space program. It would give a "focus and rationale," he added, for the manned space station, whose purpose NASA was having trouble justifying to Congress and the public. An orbiting station would provide experience in long-duration flight and the assembly of the large components, and would serve as a staging area for a Mars mission. Moreover, Murray argued, the goal would go a long way toward uniting scientists (who usually favor science-centered robotic flights) and engineers (who prefer the more demanding manned projects) in a joint endeavor involving unmanned precursor science missions as well as the culminating expeditions of large spaceships carrying astronauts.

In its own study of possible long-term goals, NASA neither endorsed nor rejected Mars. A NASA task force, headed by Sally Ride, the first American woman to fly in space, concluded in 1987 with the sound advice that "it would not be good strategy, good science or good policy for the U.S. to select a single initiative, then pursue it single-mindedly." The pursuit of such a goal to the exclusion of all others, the task force decided, "results in leadership in only a limited range of space endeavor."

Instead, the Ride panel cited four "initiatives" that would be worthwhile, but did not choose any one in preference over others. One strategy, described as the "Mission to Planet Earth," would use the orbital perspective to study and characterize our home planet on a global scale. A second strategy would emphasize the exploration of the solar system, retaining American leadership in robotic travel to the outer planets. The third, called "Outpost on the Moon," would focus on returning Americans to the Moon to establish a permanent scientific outpost and begin prospecting for the Moon's resources. Finally, the most ambitious undertaking would be a program aimed at sending astronauts to Mars, leading to the eventual establishment of a permanent base.

In its conclusions, the task force recommended increased Earth studies and continued solar system exploration. Rising concerns over Earth's deteriorating ecosystem give a strong impetus to programs for surveying global conditions from orbit; a major commitment to the "Mission to Planet Earth" is expected to be made by NASA in the early 1990s. The task force also suggested that the nation should move toward building the lunar outpost as a valuable endeavor in itself— "Although explorers have reached the moon, the moon has not been fully explored"—but also as a way station toward the ultimate objective of "exploring, prospecting and settling Mars." As the report said: "Settling Mars should be our eventual goal, but it should not be our next goal. Sending people to and from Mars is not the only issue involved. Understanding the requirements and implications of building and sustaining a permanent base on another world is equally important. We should adopt a strategy of natural progression which leads step by step, in an orderly, unhurried way, inexorably toward Mars."

These conclusions apparently reflected the thinking of most NASA officials and many engineers. "I think the right way to go to Mars is by way of the Moon," said James C. Fletcher, the NASA administrator. A preliminary plan developed by the Johnson Space Center envisaged American astronauts returning to the Moon by the year 2000, and a permanently occupied base could be established there by 2005 or 2010. It would cost at least $80 billion spread over two decades—roughly the same cost as the Apollo project converted to the value of current dollars.

Mars advocates emphatically disagreed. "A lunar base wouldn't be a detour on the road to Mars, but a trap," Sagan said. "We would use up [financial] resources and indefinitely delay going to Mars. Mars is so much more exciting."

PEOPLE LIKE Sagan were disappointed but not too surprised. NASA was being cautious and, some would say, sensible. Anything as bold as a let's-go-to-Mars declaration would have to come from the President, as it had when President John F. Kennedy set in motion the drive to the Moon in 1961. The motivating spirit would have to be not so much scientific and engineering as emotional and political. In the late 1980s, for all the debate over space goals and the renewed attraction of Mars and the growing possibility of a major Soviet challenge, the time was not yet right in the United States for making a commitment to go to Mars. The expansive economic and political climate of 1961 had completely changed. In the more constricted atmosphere, no President was willing to challenge the nation to invest in the future, including most especially any nonmilitary enterprise like Mars exploration. Reagan's Apollo was the speculative (and, many experts believe, ill-conceived) anti-missile program known as the Strategic Defense Initiative.

The only approved Mars project on the national agenda was the relatively modest Mars Observer, but government officials kept squeezing its budget and pushing its launching farther into the future. As planned now, the small spacecraft is scheduled to be launched in September 1992 and go into an orbit of Mars eleven months later to begin a study of the planet's surface, atmosphere, and climate over a full Martian year.

Instruments on the Mars Observer have been selected to give scientists insights into the planet's past and the role of water there, past and present. A gamma ray spectrometer will measure the abundance of elements (uranium, thorium, potassium, iron, and silicon, for example) on the surface. An infrared spectrometer will gather data for a mineralogical map of Mars and also chart the concentrations of water and carbon dioxide in the atmosphere and on the surface as frost and snow. A television camera will supply daily images for studying climate change and the dust storms. A radar system will provide more detailed maps of the planet's topographic relief. Other instruments will measure temperatures and the water content of the atmosphere and determine the nature of the magnetic field.

Although the selection of future landing sites is not one of the mission's primary goals, Arden Albee, the chief project scientist, said: "After Mars Observer, I think you can go straight to a landing for the sample-return missions." So far, however, the United States has not established any specific program to explore Mars, with either robots or humans, beyond the Observer mission.

The accession of George Bush to the presidency in January 1989, therefore, found the nation still facing a crisis in its space program and not yet committed to finding a way out of the crisis. Steps had been taken, but no long, purposeful strides. The manufacture of more

The shuttle Discovery blasts off on March 13, 1989, further evidence of a recovering shuttle program. (NASA)

powerful expendable rockets was well underway to provide a "mixed" fleet of launchers and end the total dependence on the shuttles. But efforts to develop heavy-lift expendable launch vehicles had made little progress. NASA was studying designs for adapting the shuttle as an unmanned cargo carrier, and the Air Force was pressing for an entirely new and more efficient rocket to compete with Energia. Such rockets would expedite construction of the planned space station, relieve pressure on shuttle schedules, and provide the capability to boost large solar system probes, including components for any missions that might be authorized for Moon outposts and Mars expeditions. The White House and Congress, however, had been unwilling to provide substantial funding. Beefing up the nation's launching capability is a necessary precondition for any expanded space program, but no substitute for the goals that were still lacking.

For the moment, in official Washington and much of the country, Mars was an option that no one seemed ready to exercise. No one sounded alarms over the Russians going to Mars. With the Soviet plans mainly in the talking stage and with the changing complexion—or, dare we hope, even the passing—of the Cold War, the Soviet threat in space no longer seemed as clear and present as it had in the 1960s—all in all, a healthy turn of events permitting a more rational approach to establishing space policy. Nor did anyone invoke the name of Lowell or the Martians. Old enchantments and fears die with knowledge. But Mars had not lost its allure. The idea of going to Mars was planted in the human consciousness. More than ever, going to Mars seemed inevitable, a matter of human destiny.

The Russians, as we shall see, may yet force the pace of destiny. Supporters of a major American commitment to Mars exploration hoped so. But at the end of the decade, the only encouraging words were contained in two presidential declarations. Neither came close to matching the rousing call to action of Kennedy's Apollo speech in 1961. Still, here was official recognition at least that Mars beckons and the United States should respond.

In a national space policy statement issued by the Reagan administration in January 1988, an American President for the first time declared it the long-range goal of the nation to "expand human presence and activity beyond Earth orbit into the solar system." Little of substance backed up the words. Specifically, the administration requested $100 million (about half of which was eventually appropriated) to begin developing and testing advanced technologies that would be necessary for establishing a human outpost on the Moon and dispatching astronauts to Mars.

Michael B. Duke, a NASA geologist who oversaw the new Moon and Mars studies, conceded that this cautious policy statement hardly ranked with the ringing Kennedy declaration to send men to the Moon. But it had a liberating influence, he said, on scientists and engineers throughout the agency and in universities. They were eagerly dusting off old blueprints for Mars vehicles and studying a wide range of mission concepts.

"Two years ago, you couldn't find anyone in authority who would talk about missions to Mars," Duke said in 1988. "That environment, a fear of ideas that might be considered too far-out, is definitely changing. After the Challenger accident, we got criticized for not being safe enough, but also for not being aggressive enough. We began to recognize that what we're doing is exploration, not simply transportation, and we ought to address ourselves to exploration goals."

The new administration of President Bush has shown a willingness to revitalize the civilian space program and establish more challenging goals. In contrast to Reagan's chief advisers, who had no interest in nonmilitary space activities, several key members of the Bush White House are ardent supporters. A National Space Council, chaired by Vice President Dan Quayle, has been created to coordinate the programs of various government agencies and examine options for new endeavors, notably the return to the Moon by astronauts and eventual missions to Mars.

By 1989, circumstances had reduced NASA to celebrating past glories, in the absence of much else to brag about, and so in July the three astronauts of Apollo 11 were paraded around the country to mark the twentieth anniversary of the first Moon landing. At ceremonies in Washington, President Bush delivered a long-awaited speech outlining his vision of the nation's future in space. He proposed a national commitment to "a sustained program of manned exploration of the solar system and, yes, the permanent settlement of space." He further instructed the National Space Council to determine the "money, manpower and materials, the feasibility of international cooperation," and make "concrete recommendations to chart a new and continuing course to the Moon and Mars and beyond."

The speech invited, and received, criticism for promising too little or too much. Advocates of a stronger program complained that Bush had set no timetables and pledged no money. Was this only empty rhetoric? Those who felt Mars would be a more inspiring goal were disappointed at the priority accorded lunar exploration. Where was the promised vision in going back to the Moon? Critics looked at cost estimates—at least $100 billion to return to the Moon and establish an outpost there and some $400 billion for a drive to the Moon and Mars—and shook their heads. "There is no such thing as a free launch," said Richard A. Gephardt, the Democratic majority leader of the House of Representatives. Where, indeed, was a nation mired in debt and suffering chronic trade imbalances with the rest of the world going to get the money?

In its first national budget, which was introduced in January 1990, the Bush administration seemed to signal that it intended to put

President Bush hands a pen to former astronaut Buzz Aldrin after signing a proclamation promoting space exploration, July 21, 1989. Behind the President, from left, are Michael Collins, former astronaut; Richard Truly, NASA administrator; Neil Armstrong, former astronaut; and Vice President Dan Quayle. (AP/Wide World Photos)

money behind the pledged commitment to an expanded civilian space program. A hefty 24 percent increase in spending, the biggest boost for any major agency, was proposed for NASA. The budget message was uncharacteristically lyrical in its affirmation that "no quantitative measure of any kind can capture the benefit of expanding human horizons, human dreams, and the human domain." The proposed NASA budget included, in particular, a new category called the "human exploration initiative"—a modest beginning toward developing the technologies and precursor missions for the return of humans to the Moon and for eventual human expeditions to Mars.

It is too early to tell if the Bush actions represent a true beginning of an American commitment to explore Mars with an eye to the "settlement of the solar system." Still, President Bush has put Mars on the national agenda. If he provides forceful leadership, decisions can be made soon to develop in measured steps the technological capabilities for such a grand venture. Then the United States would be in position to respond not only to the lure of Mars but also to opportunities to join other nations in possible international endeavors.

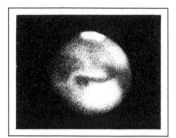

CHAPTER 10

TOGETHER
TO MARS

IN OCTOBER 1987, on the thirtieth anniversary of the launching of the first Sputnik, the Soviet Union held an impressive International Space Future Forum in Moscow. Some five hundred space leaders from around the world, Americans, Europeans, and Japanese, as well as Russians, accepted the invitation to join in celebrating past accomplishments and assaying the possibilities for greater international cooperation in space endeavors. Roald Sagdeyev, impresario of the celebration, used the occasion to renew more forcefully an appeal that, in all its technological, managerial, and geopolitical implications, amounted to a bold and imaginative challenge. To the scientists and space agency managers of the spacefaring nations, Sagdeyev proposed: "Let's go to Mars together."

There it was, simply put, an offer that could mark a dramatic turning point in the space age. The idea of American-Soviet cooperation in space, focusing on Mars as the goal, had emerged as a tantalizing possibility.

The timing seemed propitious. Soviet space officials had been talking informally of cooperative Mars ventures—unmanned at first, eventually manned—in their recent meetings with American scientists, who listened eagerly and hopefully and had begun to rally to the cause. A new American-Soviet agreement on space cooperation, signed in April of that year, had cleared the way officially for resumption of modest levels of collaboration after a period of strained relations. Both governments indicated that this could lead beyond the sharing of space flight data and the exchange of scientists and scientific instruments to arrangements for more intimate cooperative ventures. For the Russians in the time of *glasnost,* the invitation made sense because they had already set their sights on Mars, were looking for international partners in their entire interplanetary program, and must have felt that their chances for success—and the prestige this would bestow on them—would be improved by bringing Europeans, Americans, and others into the enterprise. For the Americans, Soviet officials figured, the timing might just be right. Americans were searching for new goals to focus and reenergize their space program. And Washington was testing the waters of warmer relations with the Kremlin.

The case for making Mars exploration an international undertaking also had merit on economic, technological, and possibly humanitarian grounds. At the Moscow celebration, Sagdeyev noted that cooperative efforts would help share the costs and take advantage of different technological expertise. Both sides would stand to benefit. The Russians would get access to the superior American deep-space tracking network and gain from the use of American and Western European technology in automated controls, telecommunications, and scientific and remote-sensing instrumentation. For their part, Americans and Western Europeans would benefit from the Soviet operational readiness in spacecraft production and powerful rockets and their more recent experience in developing robotic missions to the planets and in long-duration human flight in space. Moreover, working together, Sagdeyev said, would "create a better political climate."

Sagdeyev, in issuing the invitation to go to Mars together, seemed to have the weight of the Kremlin behind him. If there was any doubt about this—sometimes scientists get carried away in their enthusiasm for pet projects—it was dispelled less than a year later. During an interview with journalists from *The Washington Post* and *Newsweek* in May 1988, Gorbachev rose from his desk at the Kremlin and reached for the model of a Soviet rocket on a nearby shelf. At the summit meeting with President Reagan in a few days, he said, the United

States would be invited to join in a flight to Mars. He had advocated such a high-profile joint mission several times in recent months and now was prepared to put it on the diplomatic agenda. "Why shouldn't we try to work together?" Gorbachev said. "We have great experience, you have great experience—let us cooperate to master the cosmos, to fulfill big programs. . . . This is a field of cooperation that would be worthy of the Soviet and American peoples."

If the invitation was indeed proffered, President Reagan did not accept it, then or later. At the Moscow summit in May 1988, however, the two leaders did endorse the idea of exchanging scientific instruments on each nation's flights and agreed to explore opportunities for closer cooperation on future missions in the solar system. Although no commitments were made to undertake joint or even coordinated American-Soviet missions to Mars, much less to a joint human expedition, the Soviet invitation is on the table and someday could be the basis for embarking on a human adventure that could influence the course of history.

DESPITE THE early setbacks, it seems likely that Mars will be explored by one after another Soviet spacecraft, probably with the increasing participation of Europeans. The Phobos failures have already slowed the momentum, but they were not expected to derail Soviet plans. At least one American craft will return to Mars in the next decade and others might follow, although in the absence of any clear policy, American plans regarding Mars remain without form or direction at this crucial time. If Mars becomes the target of a concerted Soviet program of exploration leading to human landings, and other nations join in, what role will the United States play?

The question is rich in irony. The Russians, who unintentionally spurred the United States to its greatest accomplishments in space with the threat of competition posed by Sputnik, are now forcing the American hand with the lure of cooperation. American officials are again put in the position of having to make important decisions on space in response to a Soviet challenge, rather than on the merits of particular programs, and at a time of perceived weakness. Whether to concede Mars to the Russians, mount a competing program, or enter into extensive cooperation arrangements with them—these are the choices. The issue of whether or how to join the Russians in going to Mars, said Raymond Arvidson, a planetary geologist at Washington University in St. Louis, who is a consultant to NASA, is "our biggest challenge since the days of Sputnik."

At the Sputnik anniversary celebration in Moscow and, by and large, in the remaining years of the Reagan administration, the official American reaction to Soviet overtures about Mars cooperation was one of suspicion and a somewhat embarrassed indecision. The White House was wary of the motives behind the Soviet policy of *glasnost* and not sure the Russians could be trusted in any long-term venture such as Mars exploration. The Defense Department was watching NASA "like a hawk," as a congressional staff member put it, concerned that, in any cooperative undertaking, the Russians would benefit more in the exchange of data and technology than Americans. In the view of some Washington insiders, the Pentagon was also worried that cooperation with the Russians might lull us into a false sense of security and thus make it harder to win approval for more weapons systems. Throughout the government there was the feeling that, with the shuttles grounded and the lack of any clear-cut policy on Mars, this was no time to be negotiating with the Russians. "I don't think we have our act together in order to be responsive," remarked the space policy expert John Logsdon, who attended the Moscow meeting. "Rather than try to collaborate from a weakened position, the American decision is to duck the issue."

For these reasons, only relatively low-ranking NASA officials attended the conference; by contrast, the heads of the Japanese and the major European space programs all showed up. NASA knew the issue of cooperation would come up, and it was not authorized to enter into any formal discussions on the subject. Most American planetary scientists at the meeting, under no such constraints, reacted to the Soviet invitation with enthusiasm and impatience. Their interest was, of course, not entirely unselfish. Frustrated by the absence of any American flights to Mars since the Vikings, they welcomed the opportunity to fly their instruments on Soviet craft and hoped the offer of broader cooperation would put pressure on their government to reinvigorate its own program of planetary exploration. They were envious of the Soviet plans and dejected over their own country's lack of a Mars program. "The Russians have a program and we don't," said Bradford

A. Smith, an astronomer at the University of Arizona. "We're floundering around and don't understand what we should be doing."

The pressure to react to the Soviet initiative, however, made some scientists uncomfortable. Arvidson voiced concern—which he admitted was a "minority opinion among Mars aficionados"—that cooperative ventures with the emphasis on expensive human exploration could disrupt the balance of NASA's science programs. With Mars taking precedence, the exploration of other planets and the universe beyond might suffer sharp cutbacks.

Some government space specialists recommended a cautious approach, especially if cooperation involved any commitment to an eventual joint manned mission to Mars. "We would be committing ourselves to harmonious relations with the Russians over fifteen or twenty years," a congressional aide observed. "Is that realistic? Do we have that kind of confidence in the future?"

In time, though, assuming the Soviet offer stands and the Soviet commitment to an aggressive program of Mars exploration is not rescinded, the United States will be forced to choose a course of action. Gerald Wasserburg of Caltech said the issue will have to be faced when it comes time, in the early 1990s, to decide on the American posture regarding a proposed mission to bring back a soil sample from Mars. Judging by Soviet pronouncements and growing European interest, the mission is likely to be an international undertaking and could be mounted as early as 1998.

As Wasserburg described the choices in a 1986 article, the American decision could be (1) to assume a leading role with its own mission; (2) to work jointly in some fashion, and play a cooperative and substantial role; or (3) to defer to other powers in this area and not seek a substantial role. "Considering the historical significance of a major Mars venture," Wasserburg said, "it appears to me to be most unreasonable to follow alternative (3)." To exercise the first option, proceeding with an independent program and inviting the participation of other nations at our discretion, he said, was a possibility but was not recommended. It could drive other spacefaring nations into even closer ties with the Soviet Union, further excluding the United States from a leadership role in cooperative space endeavors. (At the Moscow meeting, Western European officials were courted by the Russians and said they could not wait much longer to see what, if anything, the Americans planned for Mars.) Choosing the second option, to work jointly on the project, was the preferred course, in Wasserburg's view.

If this policy is adopted, Americans would have to decide if they intended to be a leader in the international mission (at least equal to the Soviet Union) or only a strong participant. "We have previously played the leader in this area," Wasserburg said, "and I believe we should continue to lead but with the full recognition that the enterprise is a cooperative and multilateral one." But if the decision is not made soon, the Soviet Union may have already seized the leadership role.

In any event, American decisions about Mars—or space policy in general—must be based on a recognition that this is not 1961. When President Kennedy threw down the gauntlet and the race to the Moon ensued, it was feasible for the United States to pursue a goal of space preeminence across the board. Technology limited the scope of the contest mostly to simple, near-Earth opportunities. There were only two contestants, and one of them, the Soviet Union, was a remote and suspicious adversary. By the end of that decade, Americans held a clear advantage over the Russians in all areas of space flight. No such advantage is likely to be gained by any single nation again.

The difference between then and now is more profound than the greater distance of Mars, compared with the Moon. The world's political relationships are different. Western Europe and Japan have emerged as economic and technological giants and are making strong bids to be major spacefaring powers. The Soviet Union has suddenly and surprisingly come out of its isolation. After steadily improving its space capabilities, and announcing clear goals and showing an openness to the inclusion of other spacefaring nations in its expanding program, Logsdon has observed, the Soviet Union "has put itself in a better position to compete with the United States for space leadership."

This poses a problem for American policy, Logsdon said. Do we try to undercut Soviet cooperative initiatives? This could jeopardize the efforts of Gorbachev and Sagdeyev toward revoking the politics of confrontation, in space as well as with armaments, and possibly drive the Russians back into hostile isolation. A "better approach," he said, would be to support Soviet advocates of a more open and international space program. An attempt to reprise the competitive rivalry of the early space age is likely to end in wasteful futility, for world power is shifting away from the familiar bipolar struggle of the Cold War.

In an article, "Leading Through Cooperation," Logsdon wrote: "Given the realities in which the U.S. space program must operate—a very successful and much more open Soviet space program, Europe and Japan pursuing their independence of action through developing autonomous space capabilities, and similarity of goals and tight budget constraints for all space powers—a U.S. space strategy that emphasizes international collaboration makes better sense."

This is not to say that Mars should necessarily be the near-term or long-term goal of expanded cooperative efforts. Is Mars too demanding an objective? American advocates of going to Mars and joining with the Russians in the effort conceded that the Phobos setback might make it more difficult to win support. Although NASA is assessing the technical aspects of cooperative ventures to Mars, agency leaders have been notably cool to the idea of working closely with the Russians. Care would certainly have to be taken in assessing the technical as well as political realities.

Official American reluctance to try such a policy is based in part on residual distrust of the Russians, but also on a genuine concern over linking the American space program to the constantly changing character of American-Soviet relations. Political upheaval in the Soviet Union and the entire Soviet bloc points up the risk that the Russians might not be totally reliable partners. These concerns are legitimate and must be addressed before any decisions are reached.

But we can be too timid and negative. Through a rare conjunction of technology and politics we find ourselves with the opportunity to engage in a grand adventure to the beckoning Mars. Seizing the opportunity would be an act of optimism. Pessimists have it easier in influencing policy. They have the weight of human experience on their side; so many efforts to harmonize global relations founder. But theirs is a pinched view of the human potential that never gives hope a chance.

Of course, the Soviet proposals have to be examined critically. This means avoiding the reflexive responses conditioned by Cold War rigidities and not dismissing the proposals out of hand. This means acknowledging that cooperation, no matter how appealing, could

In 1987, American scientists and engineers in Boulder, Colorado, discussed plans for Mars with Soviet scientists in Moscow; the "Spacebridge" created by the Planetary Society was accomplished with a satellite linkup. (Rhoda Pollack)

come to naught and being prepared for that eventuality. Success would depend on political fortunes and the measure of confidence the participants bring to the undertaking—their optimism. People would have to believe that, for all their differences, they can still join in the pursuit of a common goal. They would have to believe that it is never too late to try to change their tormented history while in the bold act of moving the human drama out to a new and distant stage.

CARL SAGAN IS one of these optimists. As the Russians began talking of going to Mars and suggesting an international effort, Sagan transformed his long advocacy of Mars exploration into a crusade for a joint American-Soviet manned mission.

If the scientific exploration of Mars were the only objective, it is agreed, the job could be done effectively and at less cost with an assortment of robotic missions. The "chief reason to send humans is political," Sagan says. This was also the case in the Apollo program. Sending men to the Moon was fundamentally a political response to the orbital flight of Yuri Gagarin in 1961 and the growing impression of Soviet superiority in space flight and rocketry. Scientific investigations were a bonus. Apollo served the political purposes of mobilizing a vast space flight capability and demonstrating to the world the American capability to build and launch rockets that, not incidentally, could deliver nuclear payloads anywhere. In the era of threatening superpower confrontation, the Moon race served as the moral equivalent of war. A joint mission to Mars, Sagan says, would be a more reassuring demonstration of the potential political benefits of bringing Americans and Russians together in such a long-term, peaceful, and widely admired enterprise. This would demonstrate, he says, "that they can work together on behalf of the human species; that high technology need not be a gun aimed at our own heads." Going to the planet named for a god of war might reduce the risks of nuclear war on Earth.

Is this a naïve hope? "The notion that by doing things together in space we can somehow affect the political relationships on Earth in positive and productive ways," Logsdon cautioned, "is a very difficult idea to sustain in practice—looking at human history in the broad sweep, or even in the last 20 years." When the Russians and Americans conducted the simpler Apollo-Soyuz joint mission in 1975, this was a ratification of the prevailing American-Soviet détente—an effect, not a cause, of better relations. And the era of good feelings soon came to an abrupt end, the joint mission notwithstanding. Still, it is possible to argue—and hope—that the current improvement in relations is more firmly rooted in fundamental change (détente was only a recognition of stalemate) and, if properly nurtured, could have a long life.

Advocates like Sagan present a compelling case that should at least be given serious consideration. One immediate and practical benefit, they argue, is that the Mars goal would give a "crisp and unambiguous purpose" to the planned American space station, which would be needed for in-orbit assembly of the Mars vehicles. The entire American civilian space program, still reeling from the Challenger disaster and years of budgetary neglect, would be revitalized and given a much-needed sense of direction.

Such an undertaking is technologically feasible, the advocates say, requiring no major "breakthroughs." It would be expensive. Even so, Sagan argues, the cost would be "much less than deployment of Star Wars, no greater than a major strategic weapons system, and, if shared among two or more nations, still less." Indeed, Sagan contends that joint Mars missions would have the important "subsidiary advantage" of serving as an alternative use of technologies now applied on such a prodigious and alarming scale to arms. "It is foolish," he says, "to have powerful vested interests—jobs, careers, profits, dividends— mainly dependent upon a continuing arms race. Expeditions to the planets use the same high technology, and the traditional military values of organization and valor, in a humane and benign cause."

Perhaps the most pervasive concern is the fear that the Soviet Union would benefit more than the United States from the exchange of data and technology. "If we are to partially justify our space investments as a stimulus to advancement in the state of the art," said Christopher Kraft, the former NASA official, "then it just plain doesn't make sense to help our competitors."

Also, what if political relations deteriorated in the course of the mission preparations? Or if one nation or another suddenly withdrew for economic or other reasons?

Any agreement would have to take into account these concerns and include provisions protecting against "technological transfer" and the withdrawal of participants. Proponents of the Mars program recommend that, for these and other reasons, the nations should proceed by slow steps, with each developing technologies independently and operating separate but closely coordinated missions. The first steps would be limited to joint planning of early robotic missions to Mars and the exchange of scientists and perhaps some instruments; some progress has already been made along these lines for the American Mars Observer in 1992 and the Soviet mission in 1994. Fully cooperative international missions could then be attempted, perhaps beginning with the roving robotic vehicles and sample-return expedition. There would be plenty of time to learn to work together and build mutual confidence.

In their 1988 article "Let's Go to Mars Together," John L. McLucas and Burton I. Edelson wrote: "Each step in the process, from planning to doing, from coordination to cooperation, and from robotic to

manned operations, would be contingent on the success of its predecessor."

McLucas is an aerospace corporation executive and former Secretary of the Air Force, and Edelson is a former associate administrator
of NASA. So they were particularly sensitive to concerns about Russians "stealing our technology," but believed precautions could easily
be taken to control the flow of valuable information. "For example,"
they wrote, "since the Soviets have built and launched their Phobos
spacecraft and we are building our Mars Observer independently,
there should be no technology lost in coordinating scientific observations from the two programs. Similarly, if each builds a Mars lander,
and they operate cooperatively on the Martian surface, the technology of each side would be protected. Even if instrumentation is ex-
changed for flight on each other's spacecraft, this could be done on a
'black box' basis; the boxes could be sealed with their components
'potted' (encased in plastic) to prevent inspection and reverse engineering. Items for which there is too great a risk of loss can simply
be omitted from joint missions; there is no compelling need to use our
latest technology on every program, especially if its inclusion causes
deep concern."

Sagdeyev has made similar suggestions. Since the proposed sample-
return mission would require at least two separate systems, a roving
vehicle to collect the soil and another craft to rocket off the surface
and bring the sample to Earth, one nation could build and deploy the
rover and the other nation could build and operate the return vehicle.
Each nation, Sagdeyev said, would be mounting a distinct mission on
its own, would not have to share any technology, and would be protected against the failure or withdrawal from the project of the other
nation or nations.

When the ultimate steps are taken, the expeditions carrying people
to Mars, the participating nations could operate under a similar arrangement. The missions would require many rockets, supply ships
and fuel tankers, surface rovers, and a spaceship assembled in Earth
orbit out of many components. With careful planning and coordination, the United States, the Soviet Union, and other nations could
build and operate different vehicles. Astronauts from the major participants would be chosen for the journey. Who would be the first to
set foot on Mars? "If this really worries us," Sagan once wrote, "we

can arrange for the ankles of the American and Soviet commanders to be tied together as they alight in the gentle Martian gravity."

THE TIME FOR a decision is at hand. The changed political climate is conducive to adventurous new approaches in all things, space exploration included. For their own reasons, the Soviets have signaled their willingness—their urgent need—to end the era of hostile Cold War rivalry. This has triggered an explosive chain reaction that has rocked the postwar political foundations of Eastern Europe. The ultimate result may well be a Europe transformed, with a more autonomous Eastern Europe seeking closer ties with the West and with the Soviet Union itself knocking on the door of the "common European house" envisaged by Gorbachev. The Soviets want to join other nations in cooperative ventures, the most dramatic of which could be joint expeditions to Mars.

From all indications, their invitation to go to Mars together is genuine, and certainly their exploration of a more benign and "de-ideologized" approach to world affairs should be encouraged. A wait-and-see policy, the initial response of American officials, may not be as risk-free as it seems. We may wait and see an opportunity to influence history vanish. We may wait and see ourselves left on the ground. Soviet officials assert that they plan an expanded program of Mars exploration, with or without American participation. Western Europeans are receptive to Soviet overtures, which could lead to closer European-Soviet space ties and the disruption of the long-standing cooperative relationship in space science between the United States and its allies. If the United States is to seize the opportunity and have a major role in one of the most exciting and challenging undertakings of the twenty-first century, some decisions must be made soon.

Sentiment in favor of an expanded program of Mars exploration is rising among Americans—or at least it was in 1988, if the rhetoric of the presidential election campaign that year is a reflection of opinion. George Bush, the victor, urged a "long-term commitment to manned and unmanned exploration of the solar system" and added that this included "a mission to Mars." As President, he has reiterated this position. The Democrats seemed ready to enter into negotiations for a possible American-Soviet mission. Senator Albert Gore, Jr., declared: "The next logical target for exploration is Mars. I will challenge the other spacefaring nations of the world, including the Soviet Union, to join with us in planning a long-range international expedition to Mars." The Rev. Jesse Jackson said: "A joint U.S.–Soviet mission to Mars is an idea with great potential to bring our peoples together in both practical and symbolic ways." The Democratic Party nominee, Michael Dukakis, said: "We should explore with the Soviet Union and other nations the feasibility and practicality of joint space-engineering activities that might pave the way to a joint manned mission to Mars."

If these words are to be transformed into policy, the American government would need to initiate a new program of robotic flights to Mars in the 1990s and expand research in the technologies that would be necessary for a human expedition later. Americans must have something to offer in any eventual international endeavor. Then American scientists and space officials should be authorized to meet officially with their Soviet counterparts, and representatives of other spacefaring nations, to work out plans for a step-by-step international program. Care should be taken that the steps are measured so as to be affordable and also scientifically productive in their own right. A permanent international organization would have to be established to coordinate national plans, set schedules, and assign roles for each participating nation. The first fully international project could be the unmanned mission to return samples of Mars soil and rock for analysis.

At the earliest, the mission could be launched in 1998 and completed about three years later, with the return of the samples. Proponents propose that, if planning begins immediately, the announcement— that Americans and Russians and probably others will together launch spacecraft to Mars in 1998 and plan to send their astronauts there in another decade or two—might be made with appropriate fanfare in 1992. How fitting, they believe, to set in motion the international Mars venture on the 500th anniversary of Christopher Columbus' discovery of the way to the New World. For someday Mars could become humanity's new New World.

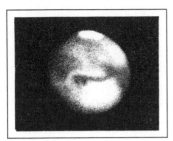

CHAPTER 11

PREPARING
TO GO

THE POSSIBLE future of Mars exploration can be glimpsed already in an arroyo at the edge of Pasadena, California. Running down from the Jet Propulsion Laboratory in the San Gabriel foothills toward the Rose Bowl, Arroyo Seco is a desolate, boulder-strewn wash. Here, in the 1930s, professors and students from the California Institute of Technology hunkered behind sandbags and fired experimental liquid-fueled rockets, which sometimes worked. Here they tested small rockets that in World War II were used to give a surge of extra power to assist aircraft on takeoff—the JATOS, for jet-assisted takeoffs—and in time called their enterprise the Jet Propulsion Laboratory. The name was not really apposite then, and ever since it has been a rather prosaic deception, an eccentricity the people at the lab have clung to defiantly while sending their craft far beyond the limits of jet engines, out to the planets. The dry and eroded arroyo is not unlike the surface of Mars, and this is its appeal to some people at JPL. Once a week in recent years, under the watchful eye of engineers, a vehicle comprising three two-wheel cabs, strung together by flexible joints, creeps across the landscape like an inchworm. Stopping and starting, it navigates the many hazards—dodging rocks, skirting ditches, and halting short of a precipice. This is an 8-foot-long test version of a robotic Mars rover.

Something like this driverless, computerized vehicle will be a key component in the mission to Mars. Going by the working designation of Mars Rover/Sample Return Mission, this project would probably involve two separate flights launched to arrive at Mars within a month of each other. One spacecraft would carry the rover to Mars orbit and act as an orbiting communications relay station while the rover is on the surface. The other spacecraft would haul the sample-return system to Mars orbit. After the sample-return system descended to the surface, the rover would follow, landing at the same site. The rover would traverse the landscape as far as 20 miles away from the landing site, inspecting diverse geological features, drilling into the surface, chipping rocks, and collecting an assortment of samples. Since, to be on the safe side, landings on Mars must occur on smooth plains, the only way to reach areas of greater geological interest, such as volcanic slopes or erosion channels, will be with these little runabouts.

After operating some 300 days, the rover would bring its samples, weighing no more than 20 or 30 pounds, back and transfer them to the return vehicle. This craft would rocket away from the surface and link up with the "mother" craft that had brought it to Mars. A small capsule containing the samples would then be launched for the journey to Earth. One current plan calls for the return capsule to rendezvous with an Earth-orbiting space station. There a preliminary analysis of the samples could be conducted under quarantine, just in case they are contaminated with dangerous Martian organisms. Eventually, the pieces of Mars would make their way to Earth aboard a space shuttle.

Such a mission has been under study by American engineers since the 1970s, when prospects for new Mars expeditions seemed vanishingly dim. Planetary scientists advising NASA put the return of a Mars sample at the top of their "wish list." In 1986, the Solar System Exploration Committee, a group of NASA advisers, affirmed the mission's importance, declaring: ". . . the return of unsterilized martian samples to Earth is the best and only way to make certain kinds of critical measurements that will determine: (a) the geologic history of martian rock units; (b) the evolution of the martian crust and mantle; (c) the interactions between the martian atmosphere and surface materials; (d) the presence of contemporary or fossil life."

Engineers designing the rover have been given specific requirements. The vehicle, including its payload of scientific instruments and cameras, has to weigh less than 1,500 pounds. Its size and configuration has to be such that it could be transported to Mars in a container approximately 19 feet long, 9 feet wide at the base, and 6 feet wide at the top. It has to be able to travel more than half a mile each day on the surface, surmount obstacles as high as 5 feet, and climb grades of up to 27 degrees on firm surfaces and 16 degrees on loose sand. In general, NASA planners have decided on a "conservative design philosophy." Instead of pushing the state of technology, engineers should use off-the-shelf systems to reduce development costs and help assure reliable operations.

Looking over engineering drawings in her office up the hill from the arroyo, Donna L. S. Pivirotto, who supervises the rover studies at JPL, said: "We're looking at all kinds of configurations, whether to

A rover to sample the Martian surface, shown here in an artist's rendering, is already being tested at the Jet Propulsion Laboratory. (NASA)

go with wheels or mechanical legs—we'll probably end up with some wheeled version. How much autonomy we can give the rover—that's the real challenge because there's so little technology inheritance for this. We have to do everything from scratch. And Mars is so far away, round-trip communications can take from twenty to forty minutes. Each time the rover has a problem there will not always be time to call home and talk to mother."

The only experience with operating unmanned roving vehicles on another world was gained by the Soviet Union in the early 1970s. Their Lunokhods, resembling wheeled bathtubs, made short surface excursions on the Moon and picked up soil samples, which were rocketed back to Earth. This was a relatively simple, unsophisticated rehearsal for Mars. For one thing, the Lunokhods were operated almost entirely by human controllers sitting at television consoles on Earth. Since radio signals travel between Earth and the Moon in only three seconds, the Soviet rovers could be guided around obstacles in an instant.

The Mars rover, however, would need the advanced robotic intelligence to be semi-autonomous—under remote control from Earth, but smart enough to follow elaborate instructions and to make many decisions on its own. According to current design concepts, the rover's stereo camera system would take and transmit to Earth controllers panoramic images of its surroundings. After reviewing these images, controllers would radio the course and planned activities for the next day's traverse. The rover's computer would be given instructions that say something like "Go to this point, then stop, and take more pictures" and so on for a total traverse of about half a mile. The rover would proceed at a glacially slow pace, using precise guidance instruments to get to each programmed point. As it moved, the rover would keep taking stereo pictures of the terrain and compare these with a computer-stored map based on photographs taken from orbit. The rover would rely on a laser range finder to measure the distance between it and any obstacles not previously considered or planned for. In these situations, its computer would command evasive actions.

A NASA preliminary study in 1987 concluded that the "necessary technology to accomplish a U.S. rover mission is either in hand or will be available in the near term." This assessment apparently reflects not only progress in technology but lower expectations of the amount of automation that can be realistically incorporated in the rover. Earlier studies, engineers now concede, were based on overly optimistic ideas. Engineering perceptions had been "infected" by the movie *Star Wars*, said James R. French, Jr., formerly of JPL and now a vice president of the American Rocket Company. "There was a feeling that if R2D2 and C-3PO could do all of those remarkable things," he said, "we certainly ought to be able to build a rover that could find its way around Mars. It didn't turn out to be quite so easy."

In the current test model, the rover's front cab is designed to contain the surface-sampling equipment—drills, mechanical arms with picks, rakes, and scoops, and also sensing instruments to test for water, analyze atmospheric gases, and identify the composition of objects it sees. The rover will have to be highly selective in what it picks up for the return to Earth. The middle cab will contain the computers, the communications antenna, and control and navigation systems. The stereo cameras for navigation will be mounted on a mast rising from this unit. The third of the three cabs will carry the radio-isotope thermoelectric generator, a type of nuclear-power system capable of producing an average of 280 watts.

No name, other than rover, has been bestowed on the vehicle, but Pivirotto has a suggestion for the one that actually goes to Mars. Call it Sacajawea, she says, after the resourceful Shoshone woman who served as guide and interpreter for Lewis and Clark on an earlier journey of exploration.

Soviet engineers are presumably conducting similar studies and tests, and the French, who increasingly collaborate with the Russians, are investigating rover technology. Soviet officials talk of sending a fairly simple roving vehicle to Mars in 1994 or 1996 for a broad surface reconnaissance. They also raise the possibility of testing a sample-return capability by bringing back photographic film from one of these landers. But a sample-return mission does not seem to be in their plans until the end of the decade. Likewise, American engineers base many of their studies on a three-year mission that would probably begin in 1998.

At first, their studies were predicated on the mission being an all-American affair, but now engineers at JPL and the Johnson Space Center in Houston have also explored the practical aspects of splitting the mission into separate, coordinated parts undertaken by two different nations. These were their guidelines: (1) One mission—either the rover or the sample-return system—will be performed by the United States and the other by an international partner, with each participant assuming the role that it perceives itself to be most capable of performing. (2) Roles should be defined such that technology transfer is minimized and the sharing of results is maximized. (3) Each mission role should be independently credible in the event that the cooperative effort is abandoned or that the other mission fails.

The 1988 NASA report on mission studies suggested that, in a cooperative arrangement, the United States might prefer to run the rover half of the project. Most American studies have concentrated on rover technology. Moreover, according to the report, present American rocket capabilities are not sufficient to handle the heavier sample-return payload in one launching. The Russians, with their Energia rocket, could. Other considerations are that the rover is estimated to cost less than the other half of the mission, its operations on the surface of Mars might have greater public appeal, and the technology would be more challenging and potentially rewarding in advancing the science of robotics.

These, of course, are the types of issues that would have to be negotiated, once an agreement was reached by the United States, the Soviet Union, and other nations to join in exploring Mars.

AMERICAN AND Soviet engineers agree on the critical importance of one particular technology in plans for the sample-return mission and subsequent human expeditions. This new and so far untested technology would make it possible to reduce the weight of the main spacecraft and thus increase the weight of payloads delivered to the surface of Mars. What the engineers have in mind is a technique known as aerocapture.

In all previous flights, spacecraft on approaching a planet have applied rocket power in a braking maneuver. By firing forward, the rocket slows down the craft, allowing it to be captured by the planet's gravity. The craft is thus pulled into an orbit of the planet. But the maneuver consumes an enormous amount of fuel. Having to haul so much fuel all the way to Mars puts severe weight constraints on the craft and its payload. If the requirement for this propulsive maneuver could be eliminated, there would be more capacity for the rover, scientific instruments, and the rocket and fuel needed to get a craft off the surface of Mars and back to Earth.

"Aerocapture is perhaps one of the most productive techniques we have studied," French said. "A Mars flyby trajectory is a hyperbolic approach trajectory that essentially targets the spacecraft to shoot past Mars and out into space. Aerocapture makes it possible to turn the spacecraft's trajectory into a closed orbit around the planet without the need for a major propulsive maneuver."

At planets with an atmosphere, even one as thin as Mars's, the spacecraft would dip into the upper fringes of the air. The spacecraft's airframe would have to be built along certain aerodynamic lines, with a large flat surface to maximize atmospheric drag. This enables air friction to slow down the descending craft. The American and Soviet space shuttles use their heavily insulated, flat underbellies and wings for the same purpose in returning to Earth. An alternative method for planetary craft is to deploy a saucer-shaped shell to produce the atmospheric drag. In either case, at Mars the craft would make a shallow plunge into the atmosphere and reemerge, traveling slower. After repeated dips into the atmosphere, controlled with small rocket firings, it would finally be moving slowly enough—from an arrival velocity of more than 20,000 miles per hour down to 12,100—to be captured in an orbit of the planet, above the atmosphere. Similarly, the craft, with the aerodynamic shell facing forward, would descend to the planet's surface, using air friction to slow it until its velocity is low enough for parachutes to ease it down the rest of the way.

The technology is not yet ready. The configuration and composition of the aerodynamic shell and other surfaces that would be exposed to the friction must be decided upon and tested. Computerized controls and guidance systems must be carefully developed. Even the slightest miscalculation, by more than one degree in the angle of attack, could be disastrous. If the craft descends too steeply into the atmosphere, frictional heating would burn it up. If its descent is too shallow, the craft would skip off the atmosphere and out into space, beyond recovery. Ron Kahl, a supervisor of Mars engineering studies at the Johnson Space Center, said that models of different aerodynamic shapes would be dropped from space shuttles flying in Earth orbit to study their performance entering Earth's atmosphere.

Much depends on the success of this technology. Engineering studies indicate that using aerocapture, rather than conventional propulsive orbital and descent techniques, would save about one ton in the weight of the rover–sample-return vehicles. One reason for the delay in fixing the payload for the planned Soviet Mars mission in 1994 is that officials are waiting to see if they can count on using aerocapture technology. The weight saving would be even more critical in developing the machinery for human landings.

SCIENTISTS DO not have to wait for the perfection of technology to be considering where on Mars they would like to land. Americans have joined Russians in a comprehensive study of photographs and maps from the Mariner and Viking programs.

The broad windswept plains would be the safest place for a landing. Near the poles would be the place to look for evidence of climate changes. In the basins below volcanic peaks ancient lava flows could tell of the planet's more dynamic past. Where the cratered highlands slope down to dry river channels it might be possible both to sample the oldest Martian rocks and to tackle the perplexing question of how a planet so dry now could have had such an apparently watery past. Any site where water once ran and could remain as permafrost might answer the question of whether Mars ever flirted with life itself.

"Is there any site that can address all the questions we're raising," asked Ronald Greeley, a geologist at Arizona State University and leader of an American project to map potential landing sites. "The answer is, probably, no."

More than twenty widely scattered sites are being mapped in detail, and the results will be shared with the Russians for planning their 1994 unmanned landing mission. The areas range from the north polar cap to the south pole, from the slopes of towering Olympus Mons to the valleys and water-eroded channels. A region called Alba Patera, for example, is covered with the remains of ancient lava that must have been extremely fluid. Greeley said: "We don't see features like these anywhere else in the solar system." There and at several other crater-pocked sites, notably the Argyre basin in the southern hemisphere, soil samples could give scientists a means of gauging geologic time on Mars. Another attractive site is Lunae Planum, a basin between Chryse Planitia and Valles Marineris. A roving vehicle could visit former riverbeds and dig into sediments of a delta where an ancient river must have flowed into the basin. Greeley said that the Mangala Valley comes close to having something for every geologist: lava from young volcanoes, dry river channels, crustal rock, old craters, and relatively fresh ones.

At a meeting with American scientists in 1988, Ruslan O. Kuzmin, a geologist at the Vernadsky Institute in Moscow, said that two sites had been singled out for detailed study in planning the 1994 Soviet mission. One is on the same northern plain, Chryse, where Viking 1 landed. The other is near the edge of the large southern basin, Hellas. If the mission to Hellas included a small rover, Kuzmin said, it could be sent out to explore volcanic deposits and also the nearby cratered highlands. Soviet officials said that the final landing places for their 1994 mission could be determined after the spacecraft reached Mars orbit and had a better look at conditions at several possible sites. There will be even more time for selecting the place where humans are to set foot.

HUMAN FLIGHT to Mars may not, as the advocates maintain, require any "breakthroughs," but it will push present technology well beyond proven capabilities. Both Soviet and American engineers recite long lists of critical areas for intensive research and testing. It may also be, as American planners say, that the years 2010 to 2020 are a reasonable working target for the first human expeditions. But even assuming an early political commitment, this is probably overly optimistic. We cannot be sure until the engineers, scientists, physicians, and psychologists have learned more about dealing with the extraordinary requirements and hazards of sending people to Mars and bringing them back. A mission lasting more than two years and reaching out millions of miles from Earth, beyond any thought of a quick return in an emergency, imposes new standards of performance and reliability on both crew and machinery.

Propulsion seems to cause the fewest worries. The large, chemical-powered rockets already in use or anticipated should provide the necessary muscle. The Soviets have a distinct edge. Their new Energia rockets are capable of boosting as much as 110 tons of payload into low Earth orbit and probably will be upgraded to a 170-ton, or possibly 230-ton, capacity. By contrast, the American shuttle can effectively lift little more than 25 tons; the Titan 4, the most powerful American expendable rocket now in use, can deliver slightly less than 20 tons into low Earth orbit. (The Saturn 5, decommissioned at the end of the Apollo program, had a 150-ton capacity.) If the United States is to send people to Mars—or set up bases on the Moon or, for that matter, engage in a more efficient and reliable program of Earth-orbit scientific, industrial, or military activity—it must develop modern, heavy-lift launching systems.

Even with rockets of the Energia class, a trip to Mars will not be a simple and direct operation. At best, an Energia could boost only a 30-ton payload on a direct trajectory to Mars, hardly sufficient even for the food, water, and oxygen for such a mission; Mars-bound craft carrying people would probably weigh as much as 1,000,000 pounds. Accordingly, Soviet officials have described preliminary plans calling for at least ten Energia launchings to haul into Earth orbit all the components for the expedition—the habitation modules, landing vehicle, tanks for fuel and water, propulsion units, and so forth. There, in the vicinity of a space station, the parts for one or more spaceships would be fitted together. (A single ship might be inadequate and would certainly be more risky, as Columbus understood. If it is an international expedition, each major participant might launch its own ship in the flotilla.) Taking off for Mars from Earth orbit would require much less rocket energy, because the assembled spaceships would not have to climb through the atmosphere or struggle to overcome the full restraining power of Earth's gravity.

Only time, clever designing, and years of practice will determine how feasible it is to assemble large structures in orbit—including "tank farms" storing rocket propellant—and then fuel up for the journey. Some engineers suspect that this is the most critical unknown, though the Russians are beginning to build up some rudimentary experience through putting together their orbiting Mir station. The planned American space station would be a similar test bed for orbital construction.

The Mir has also gone a long way toward answering questions about how well humans can stand up physiologically and psychologically to long flights in weightlessness. Even so, Michael Bungo, director of the Space Biomedical Research Institute at the Johnson Space Center, said: "We're nowhere near ready to send a human to Mars. We've got years more of basic research to do."

The human body evolved to respond to Earth's gravity, and in its absence the body grows slack. Much the same thing happens to sick people who are bedridden for months and suffer muscular atrophy and a loss of bone mass, leaving them weak and fragile. Astronauts on long-duration flights have lost as much as 15 percent of their bone tissue in six to seven months. The calcium is excreted mainly in the urine, which may lead to painful kidney stones that could disable a person at a critical moment in the mission. Floating free, with no gravity to work against, astronauts find that their muscles—including the most vital muscle, the heart—grow lazy and shrink. Yuri Romanenko, a cosmonaut who spent 326 days aboard Mir, ran on a treadmill daily to help reduce cardiovascular and muscular deconditioning and the loss of bone calcium. Although the results seemed to prove that exercise in weightlessness is beneficial, physicians are not sure this will apply equally to all people. And they worry that the exercises are so boring and time-consuming that crews will have trouble maintaining the regimen. Romanenko grew so weary and worked so much on conditioning exercises that he was down to only two hours of productive work a day toward the end of his orbital stay. Like Americans on the Skylab station in the 1970s, he also showed the psychological strain in occasional outbursts of temper.

"We need proof that the human organism can function very superbly after months in zero gravity," said James D. Burke, an advanced-planning engineer at JPL. "A crew has to live in that can for seven or eight months and then get out on Mars and work up to human potential. We may find out we'll have to provide some artificial gravity by spinning the spaceship slowly all through the journey. Artificial gravity is not easy or inexpensive. We don't know how that'll be resolved."

To create the effect of gravity, in the form of centrifugal force, the spaceship must be rotated on its central axis. It need not be the equivalent of Earth's full gravity, only enough to make the body work more and thus reduce or eliminate the deleterious consequences of weightlessness. Producing artificial gravity, however, would mean using fuel to initiate and terminate the spinning. This would add weight and complexity to the spaceship. With its antennas always moving, communications would become more difficult to maintain.

As long as astronauts remain in orbits close to Earth, they enjoy a great degree of protection from solar and cosmic radiation. Earth's magnetic fields deflect most of the charged particles before they can get dangerously close. Only when the Sun is especially turbulent and produces bursts of radiation in the form of solar flares are astronauts close to Earth in any potential danger. On a Mars trajectory radiation will be a more constant menace, which poses a serious design problem. If the walls of the spaceship are shielded against the radiation, the weight would be prohibitive. So engineers are studying ideas for "storm cellars." Instead of shielding the entire vehicle, only one compartment would be protected. At the first sign of intense solar flares, observers on Earth would alert the astronauts to take cover. The cellar, moreover, would not have to be shielded with heavy metal. The spaceship could be designed so that hollow walls around the compartment could be filled with water or liquid propellants—all effective energy absorbers.

Every possible effort will have to be made to keep the crew happy as well as healthy. With psychological needs in mind, NASA engineers are designing "private space" for occupants of their space station, which has been named Freedom. Their plans call for private sleeping cubicles, each equipped with a television set, sound systems, and a personal computer. Similar arrangements will be required for the Mars spaceship.

Psychologists and mission planners are only beginning to ponder questions about the qualities to look for in selecting a crew and about "group dynamics" in the confinement and isolation of such a long journey. How many should be in the crew—five, six, or eight? an even number or odd? an equal number of men and women? Would they be married couples? How should sexual relations on board be viewed— as a healthy outlet or a potential cause of conflict and jealousy? Would there be a hierarchical order, with a commander in full control? Or a family arrangement? Perhaps there should be a commander with power to make the critical decisions about operating the spaceship, but with the crew acting more democratically in handling housekeeping decisions and other social issues. For the shorter missions to date, these were not paramount concerns, and only one astronaut, a member of a Soviet space station crew, has become "mentally unstable" while on a mission. Even so, there have been numerous instances of astronauts on long flights showing very human responses to boredom, tiredness, and frustration. They became testy and irritable, with each other and in their conversations with ground controllers. Mild depression and lethargy have overcome some men on marathon flights. Toward the end of one long flight, Soviet cosmonauts began sleeping twelve hours a day in what was apparently a subconscious attempt to escape their situation.

Reviewing the experiences of early astronauts and Arctic explorers, Robert Helmreich, a psychologist at the University of Texas and expert on small groups in stressful environments, has noted that people react more positively to confinement and danger if the psychic rewards are great. They would accept and adjust to just about anything to be the first to the Moon or in some other endeavor. This may well apply to the first people who travel to Mars. But no one has ever ventured so far from Earth, which they will see as only a point of light in the sky, and stayed away so long. And what about psychological considerations for the crews on the missions that will follow?

Providing the necessities of life on such a prolonged journey will also be challenging. A crew of eight on a two-and-a-half-year mission could need more than 75,000 pounds of food, water, and oxygen. The daily requirement for a person is three pounds of food, five pounds of water, and two pounds of oxygen. On the American space shuttles fuel cells that generate electricity also supply as a by-product all the necessary water. But the proven lifetime of fuel cells may be too short for a Mars mission. Solar cells will probably be deployed as the main source of electric energy. So a large supply of water will have to be hauled along in the spaceship, and it must be recycled carefully, employing systems for reclaiming potable water from cabin humidity, urine, and wash water. Oxygen, to some extent, may also be reclaimed with chemical processes that separate oxygen out of the carbon dioxide that accumulates in the cabin. Or by growing plants on board it could be possible to remove carbon dioxide from the air and expel oxygen. On early missions, however, this may be done only on an experimental basis, looking toward the day when flights to Mars would be conducted with a more or less completely closed life-support system.

Remnants of the spacecraft could serve as initial building blocks in constructing living and growing areas. (NASA)

ON THE EARLY missions, astronauts would probably not stay on the surface of Mars more than a few weeks at a time. Their landing craft would be their primary shelter against the cold and wind and radiation. Or they could put up an inflatable structure, complete with a small nuclear power plant, for working and living—and simply for stretching their travel-weary limbs. Engineers will also have to provide the landing party with comfortable pressure suits, jet-powered backpacks, and a small wheeled vehicle for excursions beyond the base. They must develop portable gear for geological studies and for erecting a permanent science station to be left there. And, of course, there must be an ascent rocket system designed to fire without fail after more than a year in space.

For later missions, when the objective will be to establish a permanent outpost, the astronauts will be staying longer and assigned more rigorous tasks. They must set up cylindrical habitat modules, buried under a layer of dirt for shielding against radiation; install nuclear power plants; erect greenhouses for growing some of their food; and begin experiments in extracting oxygen and water from the rocks and permafrost.

"If we 'plan' to go to Mars only one time—essentially to plant the flag, stick out our chests, take a few pictures, and then come home—it probably doesn't matter how that mission is done," French of the American Rocket Company said at a NASA conference on Mars in 1986. "But if we want to go, return, and then establish a continuing presence, reflecting the kind of continuity most of us want to see, then we'd better figure out how to do it efficiently and well—and as early as possible."

The Ride task force, in its report, concluded: "A significant, long-term commitment to developing several critical technologies and to establishing the substantial transportation capabilities and orbital facilities is essential to the success of the Mars initiative. The Mars expeditions require the development of a number of technologies, including aerobraking . . . , efficient interplanetary propulsion, automation and robotics, storage and transfer of cryogenics [super-cold liquid fuels] in space, fault-tolerant systems, and advanced medical technology."

Work must begin immediately, the task force said, to support a goal of sending humans to Mars in the first decade of the twenty-first century. The Congressional Budget Office estimated that a concerted program of Mars exploration with human expeditions, while also continuing other space activities, would require more than a threefold increase in NASA spending over the next decade, from the $9 billion expenditure in 1988 to $33 billion in the year 2000. Such spending levels would be twice what it would take to maintain a moderately expanding NASA operation that includes little more than a continuation of present programs and goals. They would be only 50 percent above the $22 billion (in 1988 dollars) that NASA spent in 1965, the peak year of Apollo preparations.

Even if no firm commitment is made now—if the American decision is only to accelerate unmanned Mars exploration and leave to a later time the choice of sending humans—development of some of the necessary technologies should begin soon. This would give the engineers and mission planners ample time to understand the requirements and problems of sending people to another world. The propulsion systems, robotics, and many other technologies would have applications elsewhere in space and on Earth. And we would be getting ready for the twenty-first century, which almost assuredly will see people going off on expeditions to Mars.

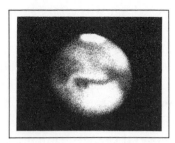

CHAPTER 12

WAYS TO GO

EVEN THOUGH no commitment to a human expedition to Mars has been made, the wheels of planning are turning. For years engineers have been quietly developing scenarios of possible missions. These are more than exercises in fantasy. One purpose is to determine technological requirements. Another purpose is to give policy makers a sense of probable costs and timetables and also, more recently, an understanding of the opportunities for participation by a number of nations. Through such studies space agency planners are examining the many ways of going to Mars, depending on the strategy that is finally adopted for human exploration of the planet. Do we wish to pursue a strategy that is geared to getting to Mars fast and first? Or do we wish to adopt a more evolutionary approach?

The following are some of the scenarios that have emerged from recent studies. These are not predictions. They are meant, instead, as suggestions of the possible options.

If the strategy is to strive for early, relatively simple voyages to Mars, one way to go is with piloted round-trip "sprints" that could possibly be accomplished in the first decade of the twenty-first century. Such flights were identified as an option by Sally Ride's task force in 1987 and were described in further detail the next year in a report by NASA's Office of Exploration, which was established at the recommendation of the task force.

Each sprint mission would be conducted in two separate parts, one involving a cargo vehicle and the other the crew transport. The unmanned cargo ship would depart first. Assembled in low Earth orbit, it would be launched toward Mars on a slow, low-energy Hohmann trajectory, carrying everything to be delivered to the planet's surface. That would include the landing vehicle and surface habitat, exploration gear, and the ascent vehicle. In addition, the cargo ship would hold the fuel that the crew transport would need for its return to Earth. Only after the cargo ship is safely in orbit of Mars, checked out and waiting, would the astronauts embark on their journey.

The crew transport, also assembled and fueled in Earth orbit, would take off with perhaps eight astronauts on board. They would travel a more direct trajectory, which could cost them more fuel but would considerably reduce flight time. After an 8-month journey, the piloted craft would rendezvous with the cargo ship in Mars orbit. Four crew members would transfer to the landing craft and descend to the surface for a stay of at least 20 days. The other four astronauts would remain in orbit, tending to the transfer of fuel from the cargo ship to the piloted craft and conducting their own scientific explorations. As soon as the surface explorers returned to the orbiting craft, the entire crew would depart for Earth, arriving 6 months later. (Travel times between Mars and Earth change because the distance changes as the planets orbit the Sun at different speeds.) The total time of the first human expedition to Mars would be little more than 14 or 15 months.

Two similar missions could be mounted during the subsequent four years. They would visit different landing sites and perhaps include an excursion to Phobos and Deimos.

The advantages of the sprint scenario are the significant reduction in the amount and weight of equipment that would have to be launched from Earth to low Earth orbit. And by keeping flight time to about 15 months, there would be fewer concerns about the physical effects on the astronauts; occupants of the Soviet space station have already lived for 12 months in weightlessness. Moreover, as NASA planners pointed out, sprint missions would be more likely to enable the United States to be the first to reach Mars with people. The first such flight could come as early as 2005.

A space station in Earth orbit will be an essential stepping-off place for the journey to Mars; here, the shuttle is shown bringing people and parts for the trip. (NASA)

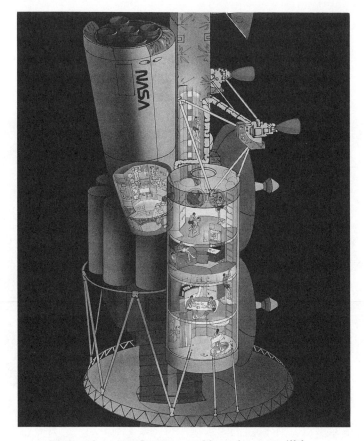

During the 9-month voyage to Mars, the crew will have plenty of opportunity for rest and recreation. (NASA)

As an alternative sprint mission, the first human expedition might aim for a landing instead on the Martian moon Phobos. "Going to Phobos would allow initially simpler, earlier human exploration of the Mars system," the Office of Exploration said.

The mission would employ the same two-part transportation system. The cargo ship would carry the Phobos exploration equipment, Mars rovers, and the crew's return fuel. This would be followed by a second spaceship carrying perhaps four astronauts. After their rendezvous with the cargo ship in Mars orbit, two of the astronauts would move into a small vehicle and depart to explore the surface of Phobos and gather samples for analysis of their potential for producing fuel and other resources. The other two crew members would remain in the orbiter, where they would operate the rover as it explored Mars and gathered samples. These pieces of Mars would be launched for return to the orbiter. After some 30 days, the entire crew, rejoined, would head back to Earth. This mission also would require no more than 15 months. It could be launched as early as 2003.

THE FOREGOING scenarios have met with sharp criticism as being narrow, possibly dead-end approaches to Mars exploration. They are said to put too much emphasis on the nationalistic goal of getting to Mars first, with little thought to building capabilities for the long run of establishing bases for more enduring human operations on the planet. Even the most ardent Mars advocates caution against any strategy that does not lay a foundation for a long-term exploration of Mars. They warn against an Apollo-like drive, the triumph being followed by letdown and no sustained program of follow-up exploration. The Ride task force expressed other concerns. It questioned whether the sprint missions could be launched in the first decade of the next century without such a concentrated effort that it would risk crippling the rest of the American space program. "We must pursue a more deliberate program," the task force concluded in its report, which generally favored strategies involving the Moon as a stepping-stone to Mars.

Many scientists want to go back to the Moon anyway. They recommend establishing a "science outpost" on the Moon where people could practice extraterrestrial living, learn mining and materials processing on another world, and conduct astronomical observations. Radio telescopes on the far side, for example, would be shielded from all electronic noise of Earth and thus would be more sensitive than similar observatories on Earth or in Earth orbit. Looking ahead, NASA planners—and apparently the Bush administration—conceive of expanded lunar operations as an important precursor to Mars exploration.

Studies exploring this option envisage chemically propelled rockets sending people to the Moon as early as 2004 and a fleet of cargo ships, possibly powered by a new kind of rocket using nuclear-electric propulsion, arriving with supplies for setting up a lunar base. Construction crews would spend several years building a facility that could be home for shifts of scientists and workers, much as bases in Antarctica are operated today. Experiments would be carried out in all aspects of long-duration human planetary habitation: life sciences, psychological effects and group dynamics, exploitation of natural resources, and scientific exploration. One objective would be to produce, from the lunar soil, the liquid oxygen needed as rocket propellant for subsequent flights to Mars.

After some years—no earlier than 2010—people would be ready to take the greater stride, to Mars. An electric-powered cargo ship, assembled in Earth orbit, would head out with all the Mars surface equipment, as well as excursion modules for transportation between Mars and Phobos. As the cargo ship approached Mars, it would drop off communications satellites to orbit the planet, send robot probes to Deimos, and deposit on Phobos the equipment for a factory to produce rocket fuel out of the little moon's soil. Later, if all had gone well, a crew of astronauts would embark from the Moon.

Their transport ship would have been towed from Earth to lunar orbit by another electric cargo vehicle. There the transport would be fueled with propellants produced on the Moon. Getting the fuel off the Moon, with its gravity one-sixth that of Earth's, would require less power than if it had to be shipped from the Earth's surface into low Earth orbit. Launching the expedition from lunar orbit would mean having to overcome less gravitational restraint than would be the case in low Earth orbit.

The journey from lunar orbit to Mars would take the astronauts about 8 months, in time to plant the first human footprints on Martian soil as early as 2014. The basic plan is for the crew to stay on Mars about 1 year, their total mission time spanning nearly 3 years. Other flights of cargo ships could follow to supply future crews and to deliver equipment for constructing a base on Mars.

In its 1988 report, NASA's Office of Exploration said this "evolutionary" approach to Mars flight "shows considerable promise for scientific and exploration benefits and opportunities, as well as having the budgetary and policy advantages of a reduced and essentially constant annual requirement of resources." The concept will require a much more thorough analysis.

ANOTHER WAY to go to Mars could be, believe it or not, via Venus. No astronauts would be landing there or producing fuel on its cloud-veiled surface, of course. Venus is much too hot for human occupation. But Venusian gravity could be used to give the spaceship a big boost in velocity, thereby shortening flight time by a little while conserving fuel. Such a mission would take more time than the "sprint" flights, but somewhat less than if the usual fuel-efficient Hohmann trajectory were to be followed. Preliminary studies of a Venus "gravity-assist" mission caught the attention of Michael Collins, who amplified on it in developing his own concept for a human journey to Mars.

Writing in the November 1988 issue of *National Geographic,* Collins, the former astronaut, who is now a writer and occasional adviser to NASA, presented a scenario for a 22-month international mission. From Wernher von Braun, the great German-born rocket engineer, whose book *Mars Project* in 1953 was a seminal work in mission planning, Collins borrowed the idea of having two separate ships, each carrying people. In this case, Collins proposed that one be built by the Soviet Union and the other one by the United States. The craft would be similar, virtual duplicates in capability, but would be launched separately by each nation and the components assembled at their own space stations in low Earth orbit. When all was ready, Soviet and American shuttles would deliver the crews to their respective ships. There would be four people, two men and two women, in each crew. After the two ships depart from their space stations, they would rendezvous and link up for the rest of the outbound journey. If something should happen to one craft, there would be enough room— barely—for all the people to occupy the remaining craft.

Five and a half months out from Earth, the joined ships would swing by Venus. The planet's gravity would pull the ships in at increasing velocity and then sling them out on a new, faster trajectory to Mars. It is sometimes called the "slingshot" effect—pull in and let fly. Once at Mars, in another 4 months, the Soviet and American craft would separate to go into Mars orbit and then link up again. Four people, two Americans and two Russians, would climb into the one landing craft and descend to the surface for 6 weeks of exploration.

Afterward, they would return to the two mother ships in orbit and head home.

SOVIET PLANNING for human expeditions, despite a widely proclaimed desire, has apparently advanced no further than the stage of conceptual studies similar to those of the United States. From what Soviet engineers have said and Western experts have inferred, a minimum Soviet mission to Mars might be possible with the use of current technology. Here is one possible scenario.

The first of four Energia rockets would boost the Mars lander, plus rocket stages, into Earth orbit. The second Energia would follow by sending a large, fully fueled rocket stage into orbit, where it would automatically dock with the Mars lander. With these two Energia launchings, the unmanned elements of the mission would be in orbit and ready to head for Mars. Once these are on the way, the Russians would move ahead with the second step, employing two more Energias.

The next Energia would carry the main spaceship and an attached rocket system into orbit. The spaceship would probably be derived from the Mir space station technology. This would be followed shortly by another Energia launching, this time sending up additional rocket stages to be attached to the spaceship. Some of the rocket stages would be used to get out of Earth orbit, others would be used to slow down to get into Mars orbit. Finally, when all this has been accomplished, Soviet astronauts would be dispatched from Earth to their waiting spaceship in orbit. The new Soviet shuttle Buran could carry a crew of four or more cosmonauts. In addition, the Russians might send out one or two unmanned cargo vehicles with supplies for the cosmonauts when they arrive in Mars orbit.

After a journey of 9 months, following the fuel-efficient trajectory, the Soviet cosmonauts would reach Mars and use one of the attached rockets to slow down into orbit. There they would rendezvous with the lander. At least two of the cosmonauts would transfer into the lander and proceed to the surface of Mars. They might stay there a month or a year. If it is the latter, this would assume that a cargo ship had preceded the crew with supplies. If it is to be only a month's visit, the entire mission would take less than 20 months.

This type of Soviet mission makes sense because it adheres to the Soviet conservative principles of space flight. Keep flying that which works. Improve it a little. Introduce some new variations, building all the time on the tried-and-true, never striking out too boldly into new technologies. But always, as the aviation people say, extending the envelope—pressing the technology slowly but resolutely and bravely to its limits.

Soviet officials have also talked of grander plans for a mission carrying a crew of ten to twelve people. At least ten launchings of the Energia would be required to assemble the main spaceship, module by module, which would probably resemble the Mir, but on a much larger scale. A combination of chemical rockets and nuclear propulsion might be employed for the escape from Earth orbit and the maneuvers into and out of Mars orbit. After a flight of 9 months, the crew would land and roam the surface in a wheeled vehicle and perhaps reconnoiter greater distances in a Martian airplane.

SOME AMERICAN engineers are looking beyond the first missions to Mars. They are trying to imagine and plan for what could be, if we choose to make travel to Mars a regular thing. One of their proposals, reflecting this kind of thinking, concerns cycling spaceships. The idea is to have spaceships always flying an orbital course between Mars and Earth, taking advantage of the gravity of each planet to stay on course and to accelerate at each planetary encounter. All you would have to do is wait for the proper moment and "taxi" to the arriving ship and hop aboard for a trip from Earth to Mars, or back again from Mars to Earth.

The National Commission on Space, headed by Thomas Paine, cited this cycling concept in its study of future travel to Mars. Conceived by John C. Niehoff, an engineer at Science Applications International Corporation, a consulting firm in Chicago, the idea is to put Mars–Earth travel on a regular basis by having several spaceships always in an elliptical orbit around the Sun that would keep them passing near the two planets. Some liken it to an escalator or a cosmic ski lift. Niehoff figured out that if four or five interplanetary vehicles were placed into such an orbit, it would be fairly easy to hitch a ride each time one of them came close to Earth or to Mars. Niehoff calls this a Versatile Station for Interplanetary Transport, or VISIT. Each vehicle would be a habitat capable of carrying several people to and from Mars. Crews that hopped a ride would, of course, have to bring along their own food and other supplies.

Enlarging on the concept, the Paine Commission concluded that the cycling spaceships could contain all the necessities for extended journeys. "They will be sufficiently spacious," the report said, "to provide passengers with comfortable quarters for long voyages through space, and would include substantial research facilities. They will have food production and . . . 'artificial biosphere' closed-ecology life support."

Buzz Aldrin, the former Apollo 11 astronaut, has become an evangelist of the cycling Mars spaceships that, in his words, would sail the "gravitational 'trade winds' of the next great age of exploration." "Traditional, Apollo-type modular spacecraft that shed their components along the way will be impractical for regular travel between the Earth-Moon system and Mars and its moons," he wrote in 1989. Instead, he said, a cycling spaceship could accelerate away from Earth, loop outward, and then swing close to Mars about 5 months later. At the same time, a similar spaceship could be returning toward Earth, also a 5-month trip. When a cycling ship reaches the vicinity of Mars, Aldrin explained, it would discharge several manned taxi vehicles, equipped with shieldlike aerobrakes for the short trip to a station in Mars orbit, where the crews would transfer for an eventual landing on the surface of Mars or of Phobos or Deimos. Later, the taxis would be used to transport crews back to the next cycling spaceship, and again used to shuttle people from the ship to a station back in Earth orbit.

As Niehoff said: "These are orbits that are designed to repeatedly re-encounter both Earth and Mars, such that their application is relevant to a potential Mars base which must be supported continuously with both supplies and people." In other words, he is thinking about the future when people have already reached Mars and are settling down to make it a place to live.

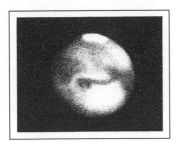

CHAPTER 13

BECOMING MARTIANS

ANALOGIES BETWEEN Columbus and explorers of the solar system, though tempting, should be invoked with care. One cautionary example should suffice. Columbus and those who followed in his wake found a new world that was ready and waiting as a place to live and work and prosper. America already abounded in life, including humans. Seeing the warm and verdant islands, hearing the song of birds, Columbus was reminded of Andalusia in spring. He thought of home. In making this favorable comparison, to be sure, the Admiral was intent on justifying the royal investment in his enterprise and promoting colonization, by which, pursuant to the terms of his agreement with Ferdinand and Isabella, he stood to gain immense wealth. But not even an exuberant Columbus could possibly see in Mars a likeness to springtime anywhere on Earth. The early explorers of Mars will not find a new world ready for human expansion; they will have to create it.

This, more than distance, frames the qualitative difference between the Age of Discovery set in motion by Columbus and any similar period of expansion into the solar system that might follow in the generations after the first landings on Mars. It is the difference between finding and creating.

The Red Planet may be the most clement place in the solar system, outside Earth. As it is, though, Mars is cold and dry and apparently lifeless. Its thin atmosphere is mostly carbon dioxide. A likely place to visit, no doubt, but you would be hard put to live there. Transforming Mars into a livable planet, inviting human colonization, thus would call for technological efforts of a magnitude that even the visionaries have trouble grasping, much less quantifying.

By contrast, America did not have to be significantly altered before it could be settled by Europeans. The Europeans who settled America did not find a pristine wilderness or a true virgin land, as it has so often been characterized in our histories. If it had been a true wilderness, argues Francis Jennings, a historian of the American Indians, America "would possibly be so today, for neither the technology nor the social organization of Europe in the sixteenth and seventeenth centuries had the capacity to maintain, of its own resources, outpost colonies thousands of miles from home." As it turned out, America had ample resources waiting to be exploited. The technology that got the Spaniards there in the first place, the sailing ships, was sufficient for the subsequent task of settlement.

In the case of America, as soon as travel there became possible, Europeans were eager to make the uncomfortable and perilous crossing for reasons succinctly and frankly expressed by Bernal Díaz. This soldier who rode with Cortez and chronicled the conquest of Mexico in 1519 wrote that he and his fellow conquerors went to the New World "to serve God and His Majesty, to give light to those who were in darkness, and to grow rich, as all men desire to do." Not everyone, of course, lived to cash in. Columbus himself died in relative poverty and obscurity, and only after lengthy litigation did his descendants receive a token of the wealth the explorer had expected. But for others the rewards were ample and immediate. They searched out the gold and began a lucrative traffic back to Europe. They cultivated and harvested the land, introduced cattle and pigs and sugarcane, and wiped out most of the indigenous people (through cruelty, in part, but more often inadvertently through disease), replacing them with African slaves. In time the settlers transformed America into New Europes. The transformation came as the result of settlement, not as a prerequisite.

No political and economic inducements can be readily envisaged that would hasten the settlement of Mars—no known military advantage to one nation or another, no gold worth the hauling charge, no heathen to convert. In the next few centuries, some people may feel the need to flee an overcrowded Earth. If the technologies become available and the need is extreme, they might mine the asteroids for resources and make their home on Mars. Thomas Paine, who headed the National Commission on Space, suggested that the "driving forces" behind Mars settlement might not be only economic. He listed national pride and leadership, which often is one but not necessarily the most enduring incentive to expansion. He also imagined "ideological and humanistic" motives: "The basic desire to preserve life and to expand and transmit deeply treasured human beliefs and cultural heritage to an expanding posterity." A related motive Paine classified as the desire for a "fresh start." Mars may draw settlers, he said, because of "an advanced, intellectually-based civilization working toward a limitless future for mankind free of many of the old world's diseases, ignorance, fears and outworn prejudices."

Obviously, we can only speculate on the imperatives that could lead humans to colonize Mars. The first people who land on Mars will probably have no clearer idea of what will ultimately follow their achievement than did Columbus. So, in this sense, the Columbus analogy may be apt—to a point. The first visitors to Mars will be constrained in their imagination by the technology at their command and the immediate motives that brought them there. Columbus' vision was similarly limited. If anything, he was sorely disappointed by what he did not find. He had not arrived at the fabled court of the Grand Khan. The vision that took him across the sea into the unknown could not make him see that he had found a new world and understand where this would lead in a hundred years or five hundred years. We should be excused, therefore, for not being able to imagine where Mars exploration will lead, especially since we, far more than the European settlers of America, will be confronted with the task of making the planet habitable before we can truly inhabit it.

THE FIRST explorers to Mars can make a start. A goal of every mission, manned or unmanned, should be to leave behind selected materials, equipment, and supplies for use by subsequent visitors. At several widely scattered sites, semi-permanent outposts could be established, complete with roving vehicles, nuclear reactors, greenhouses for growing food, habitats buried in the dirt for protection against ultraviolet rays, and experimental processes for producing water, oxygen, fuel, and other essential resources. This is where people will learn to live and work on Mars, but scientists are already outlining what it will take.

A decade ago, when it was still officially taboo in NASA to contemplate ambitious plans for Mars travel, much less settlement, a number of graduate students at the University of Colorado formed what they called the Mars Underground. They quietly conducted studies of propulsion, psychology, medicine, finance, life-support systems, materials processing, spaceship design, and mission concepts—everything it would take to make Mars habitable. At public symposia at Boulder in 1981 and 1984, titled "The Case for Mars," they shared their ideas and increasingly attracted others interested in the planet, including some NASA scientists and engineers, who participated in an unofficial capacity. Several of the Underground leaders eventually "infiltrated" NASA, notably Christopher P. McKay.

At the NASA Mars Conference in 1986, McKay described the results of Underground studies, evoking the image of a time when people would be working on the surface of Mars on a routine basis—comparable perhaps, he said, "to living and working in California!" But, first, people must learn to use Martian resources. Of vital importance, McKay said, would be the development of gas-extraction technology at early Mars bases. As conceived in preliminary studies, such a facility would suck in Martian atmosphere, compress it, extract the carbon dioxide, and then send it off to be thermally decomposed into oxygen and carbon monoxide. Since these gases burn together, they could be used as engine fuel, for the roving vehicles and other machinery, as well as for rockets. Much of the oxygen would also be stored in balloon tanks and used to create a breathable atmosphere for the human habitats. The same gas-extraction facility could also compress and cool Martian air to condense out the small amount of water vapor. This could be a supplement to the water supply from permafrost and the recycling of human wastes.

Experiments on other colonization technologies could begin even sooner. Paine, drawing on ideas presented to the National Commission on Space, outlined several steps to be taken. One is the development of advanced robotic mining and metallurgical and ceramic processing. If the initial outposts are to expand into colonies, indigenous materials must be used for the brick and mortar. Factories on Mars would also need to take advantage of robotic systems that can replicate themselves using local materials. Another step will depend on advances in genetic engineering to create a Martian agriculture that converts carbon dioxide and water into food and fiber in a low-gravity, cold environment.

Paine recommended that research on robotic factories and genetic-engineered agriculture for Mars should be started now "because of their long lead-times and the great promise for valuable terrestrial spin-offs." Some other essential technologies, such as automated cargo rocket ships, could be developed later when the work could benefit from engineering advances for the next generation of propulsion systems and heavy-lift rockets.

At some point, people will want to go back to the Moon and use it as a test bed for future Mars settlement technologies. Not for tests of atmospheric extraction techniques, of course; the Moon is airless. But, in Paine's view, lunar research stations could serve as prototypes for the agricultural and manufacturing processes using other indigenous resources and for closed-ecology life-support systems. For someday people on Mars will outgrow the cramped and limited outposts and will want to spread out under vast glass domes where plants grow, water flows, and the air is warm and sustaining.

WHEN THAT DAY comes, a colony on Mars may look something like a large-scale version of a futuristic glass-and-steel bubble that already stands in the desert near Tucson, Arizona. Called Biosphere II, this capacious greenhouse, with 5 million cubic feet of interior space, is a privately financed experiment in the environmental problems of Earth and in the design of space colonies. If current plans are realized, eight people will soon enter the airtight facility and live for two years like Mars colonists.

The volunteers will be cut off from everything in the outside environment, except sunlight. They will live in a domed house, complete with apartments, library, and gymnasium, under the larger glass can-

A Biosphere test module outside Tucson, Arizona, for experiments in sustaining life independent of air, water, and nutrients from Earth. (Associated Press)

opy. They will become part of an intricate ecosystem that includes miniature oceans, rain forests, marshlands, savannas, and deserts. Everything in the man-made world will be recycled. Carbon dioxide exhaled by humans will be used by the plants, while oxygen given off by the plants will revitalize the air for human breathing. Human wastes will provide fertilizer for land crops and feed algae, bacteria, and water plants, which in turn will feed fish. Sharing this environment will be about 300 land vertebrates, including bats, frogs, and songbirds; some 4,000 plant species; and a host of microbes in the soil to break down organic matter and convert nitrogen gas in the air into compounds that can be used by plants. The trick, which has never been accomplished before on such a grand scale, will be to keep all the life cycles balanced well enough to avoid an ecological disaster.

In its 1986 report, the National Commission on Space pointed out that "to explore and settle the inner solar system, we must develop biospheres." The Commission added: "The builders of Biosphere II have several goals: to enhance greatly our understanding of Earth's biosphere; to develop pilot versions of biospheres, which could serve as refuges for endangered species; to prepare for the building of biospheres in space and on planetary surfaces, which would become the settlements on the space frontier."

The $30 million project was begun in 1984 by a private company, Space Biospheres Ventures, and financed primarily by Edward P. Bass, an oil multimillionaire from Texas. The investors are hoping the project will lead to patents on a variety of new technologies in agriculture and for the monitoring and treatment of air and water.

Despite its somewhat eccentric origins, Biosphere II has enlisted the expertise of biologists and ecologists from the Smithsonian Institution, the New York Botanical Garden, and the University of Arizona's Environmental Research Laboratory. The results so far have been generally praised by scientists familiar with the difficulties of closed life-support systems. "They're being bold enough to take that first step," said B. C. Wolverton, a NASA authority on the biological support systems for spaceships. The space agency itself has begun a modest program of similar research, called Controlled Environmental Life Support System, but its focus is on the more immediate goal of developing technologies for the space station. Speaking of Biosphere II, James H. Bredt, former chief of biological systems research at NASA

A Space Biosphere Ventures worker raises fish in an aquaculture system that one day may be used to feed humans on Mars. (Peter Menzel)

headquarters, said: "There will be many lessons for us in this kind of thing."

Bredt, like other space scientists, expressed skepticism about Biosphere II's application to planetary settlements. The system may not be big enough to be a true experiment in life's complexities. "It may turn out that the environment [in Biosphere II] will not have enough diversity," Bredt said. "It may turn out they have to do a lot of engineering and mechanical intervention to make it work." Moreover, he questioned the feasibility of transporting the components for such large structures on a place like Mars. Joseph P. Allen, a former astronaut who is a business executive, praised the experiment, but added: "Many, many attempts like this are going to be essential before it's possible to really consider, not just dream about, a colony on the Moon or Mars or someplace else."

HERE WE ARE clearly moving into a twilight zone of speculation. Robot-operated factories, genetically engineered agriculture, and domed biospheres may come to Mars sooner than we might imagine, in a few decades or at least sometime in the twenty-first century. No one can really say when. But for a frame of reference—of what might be possible, not of what is necessarily predicted—here is Thomas Paine's optimistic exercise in futurology.

Assuming that Soviet and American efforts lead soon to human travel to Mars, Paine said, the 2015–25 decade could see the first extraterrestrial community of robotic mining and closed-cycle agriculture in experimental operation on the Moon. Oxygen is being separated from lunar rocks to refuel lunar surface-to-orbit shuttles. A space station is docked to the Martian moon Phobos, serving as a refueling station using Phobos resources and as Mission Control for operations on the surface of Mars.

In the 2025–35 decade, people in the mining and agriculture community on the Moon are becoming increasingly self-sufficient. Several hundred people now live on Mars, experimenting with resource development and the construction of airstrips, shelters, and larger facilities.

The 2035–45 decade brings at least 1,000 people to Mars, where the emphasis is on installing the Moon-tested robotic technologies for mining, industry, and agriculture. Fuels produced on Mars sharply reduce Mars–Earth transportation costs. The first baby is born on Mars.

In the decade between 2045 and 2055, the robotic factories on Mars have direct software links to identical factories on Earth, achieving an effective "teleportation." Equipment like hydrogen-oxygen-fueled roving vehicles with artificial intelligence guidance produced on Earth can be simultaneously duplicated on Mars, and vice versa.

In succeeding decades of the twenty-first century, the population of Mars settlements reaches 100,000 people and close to 1,000,000 robots. Life on Mars is no longer dependent on imports from Earth, though a lively trade exists between the two planets. Zoos and museums on Mars boast extensive collections of terrestrial life.

As we said, such a future is conceivable and may be achievable, perhaps as early as in the next century. But this is nothing compared with the grand plans that some serious scientists have for transforming Mars into a place much like Earth. The word for this is "terraforming."

VISIONS OF terraforming Mars have appeared repeatedly in science fiction. In his 1952 novel, *Sands of Mars*, Arthur C. Clarke imagined human settlers on the planet creating a warmer climate by setting off a nuclear fusion reaction on one of the Martian moons, turning it into a glowing mini-Sun. They generated their oxygen with the help of specially designed vegetables. In the sequel, *Fountains of Paradise*, written two decades later, Clarke has a character describe the terraforming principle: "If we could thaw out all that water and carbon dioxide ice, several things would happen. The atmospheric density would increase, until men could work in the open without spacesuits. There would be running water, small seas, and, above all, vegetation—the beginnings of a carefully planned biota. In a couple of centuries, Mars could be another garden of Eden. It's the only planet in the Solar System we can transform with known technology."

Mars settlers in Isaac Asimov's 1953 story "The Martian Way" sent pilots to Saturn and diverted an iceberg from the rings. Towed back to Mars, the iceberg became the colony's main source of water. A more classic example of terraforming was described by Jerry Pournelle in his 1976 novel, *Birth of Fire*. His settlers used atomic bombs to trigger dormant Mars volcanoes into releasing pent-up gases, thus creating a denser, warmer atmosphere over the entire planet and melting the frozen water. Science fiction had entered a decidedly post-Lowellian phase, and scientists were beginning to think along similar lines.

In the summer of 1975, shortly before the launchings of the Viking spacecraft, a group of scientists met at NASA's Ames Research Center to consider the habitability of Mars. They looked far beyond the familiar concepts of colonists sequestered in domed cities. The approach they examined was to make the entire planet fit for human life by altering the Martian environment to provide the oxygen, water, moderate temperature, and protection from ultraviolet radiation that terrestrial life forms have grown accustomed to. Their basic conclusion: "No fundamental, insuperable limitation to the ability of Mars to support terrestrial life has been unequivocally identified."

A report of the study, *On the Habitability of Mars: An Approach to Planetary Ecosynthesis,* has inspired a cottage industry of terraforming, or planetary engineering, research over the years, especially by members of the Mars Underground. The researchers agree on the broad outlines of what must be done. First, Mars must be heated up by about 100 degrees to liberate water frozen in the polar caps and in the permafrost. Then microorganisms should be introduced on Mars to cycle atmospheric carbon dioxide into oxygen so that humans could breathe the planet's air.

One way to warm up Mars would be to increase the amount of sunlight absorbed by the surface. The ideas for accomplishing this are nothing if not innovative. Giant mirrors, thinner than aluminum foil, could be placed in space near Mars to focus sunlight and aim the more intense rays on the Martian polar caps. Or the dark surface material of Phobos and Deimos could be transported by electromagnetic cannon and spread over the Martian landscape, increasing its absorption of incoming sunlight. The higher temperatures and the increase of water vapor and atmospheric carbon dioxide, from the melting polar caps, should produce a "greenhouse effect," trapping heat and further modifying the entire Martian environment.

A more recent variation on this theme has been proposed by Christopher McKay. His idea is to warm Mars by spraying tons of Freon and other chlorofluorocarbons into the planet's atmosphere. Although on Earth these gases destroy ozone in the upper atmosphere, exposing us to increased ultraviolet radiation, on Mars there is no ozone, and the gases would act as a "greenhouse" lid, allowing sunlight to reach the surface but preventing much of the heat from escaping back out into space. The gases could be produced from indigenous materials at a factory on Mars.

"Temperature manipulation particularly seems the key to unlocking the potential of Mars for human habitation," the report of the Ames conference said.

Is it not ironic? What we contemplate doing on Mars, drastically altering the global climate through the greenhouse effect to make it habitable, is what we have been doing unwittingly to our home planet, rendering it potentially less habitable.

Terraformers also look to microbes as essential agents of change on Mars, repeating their revolutionary work on Earth more than 3.5 billion years ago. In the beginning, Earth's atmosphere was poisonous to life as we know it now. But once algae emerged and began proliferating, these hardy organisms generated the oxygen that is the vital ingredient of Earth's present atmosphere. They made the world habitable for the more advanced plants and animals that began to evolve. If blue-green algae, lichen, and other organisms were introduced on the surface of Mars, at a time when the atmosphere has been engineered to a warmer and denser state, a similar transformation might take place there.

Mars presents some difficulties, though. Could the organisms survive the deadly ultraviolet radiation? Robert D. MacElroy and Melvin M. Averner, the Ames scientists who led the 1975 study, have recommended that the vast mats of algae and lichen might be protected with a covering of Martian dust. Beyond that, most scientists believe genetic engineering will be an indispensable tool. They suggest that organisms introduced on Mars should be genetically modified to produce oxygen more efficiently, to thrive in the dry climate, and to resist radiation.

In his provocative book *Infinite in All Directions,* Freeman J. Dyson, a theoretical scientist at the Institute for Advanced Study in Princeton, pondered the possibilities of "cosmic biology." He was writing of the spread of life throughout space, but his ideas also apply to Mars—perhaps as a starting point. "Now that genetic engineering is rapidly becoming a practical proposition," Dyson wrote, "it is not absurd to think of redesigning terrestrial creatures so as to make them viable in space or on other celestial bodies. Once we have successfully planted a variety of species in space and provided appropriate mechanisms of dispersal for their spores, we can safely rely on the ancient processes of mutation and natural selection to take care of their subsequent evolution. The mistakes which we shall inevitably make in our initial plantings will in time be rectified as their offspring diversify and spread through the cosmos."

No one knows how long it would take to complete the climate transformation of Mars—3,000 years or 100,000 years. Long before this comes to pass, however, people will be living on Mars and becoming Martians. Their histories may record that it all began in the final years of the twentieth century.

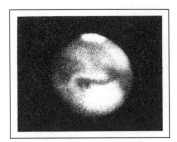

CHAPTER 14

DESTINY

HUMANS WILL GO forth to Mars. Of this we may be as sure as we can be of anything. In the next two or three decades perhaps, in the twenty-first century almost certainly, astronauts will make the long journey. They may be Americans or Russians, traveling separately or together, and they may be Europeans, Chinese, and Japanese as well. Their journeys should be only the beginning of human expansion out into the solar system.

At this point in any discourse on future space travel, the custom is to cite the prophecy of Konstantin E. Tsiolkovsky, the Russian schoolteacher who pioneered the principles of space flight. A century ago, working alone on concepts of rocket propulsion, Tsiolkovsky foresaw travel beyond Earth and proclaimed this in words evoking the image of an elemental step in every human's development. His words bear repeating: "Earth is the cradle of the mind, but one does not live in the cradle forever." On the obelisk over his grave at Kaluga is inscribed another expression of Tsiolkovsky's vision: "Man will not stay on earth forever, but in the pursuit of light and space will emerge timidly from the bounds of the atmosphere and then advance until he has conquered the whole of circumsolar space."

The implication is that travel to other worlds is human destiny. And so it probably is, at least in one sense of the idea of destiny.

True to Tsiolkovsky, we are spacefarers now and can reasonably contemplate people going to Mars and people living there someday. Visionaries are not embarrassed to speak of this, and more. Freeman Dyson styles himself a preacher of the "manifest destiny" of expansion into the universe. "The destiny which I am preaching," he writes, "is not the expansion of a single nation or of a single species, but the spreading out of life in all its multifarious forms from its confinement on the surface of our small planet to the freedom of a boundless universe. This unimaginably great and diverse universe, in which we occupy one fragile bubble of air, is not destined to remain forever silent. It will one day be buzzing with the murmur of innumerable bees, rustling with the flurry of feathered wings, throbbing with the patter of little human feet. The expansion of life, moving out from Earth into its inheritance, is an even greater theme than the expansion of England across the Atlantic."

Loren Eiseley, the anthropologist and essayist, took a more melancholic view of this human urge to explore and colonize space. In his 1970 book, *The Invisible Pyramid,* he drew an invidious comparison between humans and a slime mold colony. A slime mold, to reproduce, must scatter its spores from atop a "spore tower," the erection of which has consumed the collective energies of the entire colony. For all this effort few of the spores survive their dispersion. Humans have reached the point in their history when they can contemplate space travel, Eiseley contends, by consuming "the resources of a world" in constructing their own spore towers as the means for leaving it. "Perhaps," he speculates, "man has evolved as a creature whose centrifugal tendencies are intended to drive it as a blight is lifted and driven outward across the night."

Eiseley felt there may be no turning back. The destiny he gloomily foresaw is inevitable, and deplorable. "Man," he concludes, "is part of that torrential living river, which, since the beginning, has instinctively known the value of dispersion. He will yearn therefore to spread beyond the planet he now threatens to devour. This thought persists and is growing. It is rooted in the psychology of man."

No one would argue that it is worth going to Mars if to do so means the destruction of our home planet. No one would condone any evasion of our responsibilities on Earth. No one would deny that our technologies are taking a toll on Earth's habitability, or that much needs to be done to reduce our profligate use of natural resources and to husband our precious air, water, and land. But Eiseley's view is bereft of hope. He seems to have given up on humans. Despair can breed self-fulfilling consequences, reason enough to adopt a more optimistic outlook and strive to justify the wisdom of the choice.

Dyson sees humans not as a blight but as the potential bearers of life far and wide. We have arrived at a point where we can make choices that could lead to such a destiny.

But "destiny" is a word to be used carefully. It does not mean, in this context, a predetermined state or some end foreordained by divine will. Insofar as destiny connotes inevitability, the whole idea can be deflating to the human spirit, for it implies a certain powerlessness to affect our fate. Where is the motivation in fatalism? Destiny, instead, should be taken to mean the culminating condition if certain trends persist and certain courses are pursued. There is ample room here for humans to affect their destiny.

Barring human actions of catastrophic consequence (through malevolence or folly), choices already made have put us on a course that could carry people to Mars in the foreseeable future. Early astronomers chose to study Mars and the other heavenly objects, which led in time to an understanding of the laws governing the cosmos and underlying the principles of space flight. Succeeding generations chose to encourage scientific inquiry as a valued part of our culture. Out of this emerged the technologies that in the twentieth century gave people the choice of realizing an old dream of flying in space. We took those first steps out of fear, Soviets and Americans alike, neither powerful rival wishing the other to gain a commanding advantage in this new arena. But we also elected to employ this new capability to satisfy our curiosity about the solar system at large and, in particular, to explore the planet that Lowell had implanted in our imagination. We had chosen to become spacefarers. Only in retrospect does it seem to have been inevitable.

The phenomenon of exploration itself illustrates the role of choice in what is called destiny. Curiosity may be an innate human characteristic, but not so the planned and concerted exercise of curiosity, which goes by the name of exploration. As Stephen J. Pyne, a historian of exploration at Arizona State University, has said: "Exploration is a specific invention of specific civilizations conducted at specific historical times. We explore not because it is in our genetic makeup but because it is within our cultural heritage."

Americans are, by and large, products of the European culture that fostered exploration. For a variety of economic, political, and religious reasons, Europeans were the first global explorers. They sought new trade routes to the wealth of the East, circumventing Islam. Their rediscovery of the learning of classical Greece and Rome awakened in them the imagination and curiosity that produced the Renaissance. Slowly turning away from their feudal past, they began to consolidate political and military power in nascent nation-states. They also felt compelled to convert others to their God. Inspired and audacious as he was, Columbus was not a singular figure in history. He was a European Christian at a time of expansionary historical forces. Even if he had failed to win Isabella's support or had been blown off course, America would have been reached in not too many more years—and by other Europeans, because they were the explorers. The indigenous Americans themselves lacked the sailing technology to reach Europe or Asia. The Arabs, despite their seafaring tradition and knowledge of geography, were satisfied to keep to the Indian Ocean and their caravan routes. A century before Columbus, China, the other advanced civilization, had sent fleets of ships as far west in the Indian Ocean as Africa and had the capability to reach America. But when a new emperor came to the throne in 1435, China withdrew from exploration into self-imposed isolation and, in a policy mistake often cited by defenders of a more vibrant American space program, redirected the money for repairs of the Great Wall and for wars with the Mongols. Today, the Wall is a magnificent relic and the Mongol threat a distant memory; the European discoveries, by contrast, changed the world. In *The Discoverers,* Daniel Boorstin writes: "Fully equipped with the technology, the intelligence, and the national resources to become discoverers, the Chinese doomed themselves to be the discovered."

In the solar system Western culture has found a new dimension for its exploratory drive, promising a new age of discovery. As defined by historians, the first age, beginning in the fifteenth century with the Portuguese and then Columbus and the Spanish, saw the exploration of the ocean. The second age, centered in the nineteenth century, focused on exploration of the continental interiors. The "geographic domain" of the third age, Pyne contends, is the solar system, including Earth as a whole planet, whose study is being facilitated by observations from the perspective of space. "Discovery among the planets is qualitatively different from the discovery of continents and seas," Pyne says, and the prospect "forces us to rethink our expectations of exploration."

The most obvious difference is that there are no people to be encountered elsewhere in the solar system. There will be no new "moral universes," Pyne points out, to challenge and enrich the exploring culture. Explorers will be out there talking to themselves and looking at these new worlds only as reflections in the mirrors of their own experience. An honest look in the mirror can be at once humbling and revealing of the nature, warts and all, that got us this far. But neither will there be people to be victims of exploration's corollary in earlier ages: imperialism. So discovery in the new age, Pyne believes, is not as likely to corrupt the discoverer and make him cry out, "The horror! The horror!"—as the dying Kurtz does in Conrad's *Heart of Darkness*.

Wherever this new age leads us, Mars is the immediate destination.

The call of Mars echoes through centuries of history. The response, once limited to the imagination, is now to send our machines to get a sense of the place and report back. The report is of a world without apparent life, but not inhospitable to visiting life or, with major alterations, to permanent settlement. We—Americans and Russians and, increasingly, others—will no doubt keep alive Mars exploration by automated means. The accumulating knowledge and technological capability will build momentum that will eventually lead, with the enabling political commitment, to flights of humans bound for the planet. But it is not predestined that Americans will be among the first explorers to visit Mars. They must choose to go.

Decisions made in the coming years will dictate the timing and character of human exploration of the solar system. Will the United States assume a leading role? Will it sit back and let others take the lead? Can the United States ignore the challenge and remain a major force in the next century? What would be the verdict of history if the United States did not earnestly pursue the opportunities to go for Mars and do so in collaboration with the other heirs to the Western culture of exploration? It would mean establishing a grand strategy of space exploration, something the United States has failed to do so far in the more than three decades of spacefaring. If Mars is not a central component of that strategy, Americans may forfeit their place in the vanguard of the human future that will be lived outside the cradle of Earth.

For Mars is not only a destination; it can be the beginning of the irreversible expansion of humans into the cosmos.

Think of it the way Freeman Dyson does. "When life spreads out and diversifies in the universe, adapting itself to a spectrum of environments far wider than any one planet can encompass," he writes in *Infinite in All Directions*, "the human species will one day find itself faced with the most momentous choice that we have had to make since the days when our ancestors came down from the trees in Africa and left their cousins the chimpanzees behind. We will have to choose, either to remain one species united by a common bodily shape as well as by a common history or to let ourselves diversify as the other species of plants and animals will diversify. Shall we be forever one people, or shall we be a million intelligent species exploring diverse ways of living in a million different places across the galaxy?"

Thinking of it this way sharpens the focus, clarifying the import of choices before us. But this is really getting ahead of the story. The immediate destiny we can choose, to expand exploration of Mars and deliver life there in the twenty-first century, is sufficiently daunting and exciting.

APPENDIXES
BIBLIOGRAPHY
ACKNOWLEDGMENTS
INDEX

MISSIONS TO MARS, 1960–89

SPACECRAFT	DATE LAUNCHED	OBJECTIVE	RESULTS
Unannounced (U.S.S.R.)	10 Oct. 1960	Flyby	Failed to achieve Earth orbit
Unannounced (U.S.S.R.)	14 Oct. 1960	Flyby	Failed to achieve Earth orbit
Unannounced (U.S.S.R.)	24 Oct. 1962	Flyby	Failed to leave Earth orbit
Mars 1 (U.S.S.R.)	1 Nov. 1962	Flyby	Communications failed 21 Mar. 1963 at distance of 66 million miles
Unannounced (U.S.S.R.)	4 Nov. 1962	Flyby	Failed to leave Earth orbit
Mariner 3 (U.S.)	5 Nov. 1964	Flyby	Failed when aerodynamic shroud did not eject after launching
Mariner 4 (U.S.)	28 Nov. 1964	Flyby	Success. On 14 July 1965 flew 6,118 miles above surface of Mars, transmitting 22 close-up photographs
Zond 2 (U.S.S.R.)	30 Nov. 1964	Flyby	Communications failed 4–5 May 1965
Zond 3 (U.S.S.R.)	18 July 1965	Test	Photographed far side of Moon. Passed Mars orbit to test communications at Mars distance
Unannounced (U.S.S.R.)	27 Mar. 1967	Possibly landing mission	Rumored launching failure
Mariner 6 (U.S.)	24 Feb. 1969	Flyby	Success. On 30 July 1969 flew by Mars and transmitted 75 photographs
Mariner 7 (U.S.)	27 Mar. 1969	Flyby	Success. On 4 Aug. 1969 flew by Mars and transmitted 126 photographs
Mariner 8 (U.S.)	8 May 1971	Orbit	Failed when second stage of Atlas-Centaur rocket malfunctioned 5 minutes after lift-off
Cosmos 419 (U.S.S.R.)	10 May 1971	Orbit/Landing	Failed to leave Earth orbit
Mars 2 (U.S.S.R.)	19 May 1971	Orbit/Landing	Orbiter successful on 27 Nov. 1971. Lander crashed

SPACECRAFT	DATE LAUNCHED	OBJECTIVE	RESULTS
Mars 3 (U.S.S.R.)	28 May 1971	Orbit/Landing	Orbiter successful on 2 Dec. 1971. Lander reached surface on same day, survived 110 seconds; no photographs or science results
Mariner 9 (U.S.)	30 May 1971	Orbit	Success. Entered Mars orbit 13 Nov. 1971 and operated until 27 Oct. 1972—698 orbits and 7,329 photographs of surface and moons
Mars 4 (U.S.S.R.)	21 July 1973	Orbit	Engine malfunction prevented craft from entering Mars orbit. Flew by 10 Feb. 1974
Mars 5 (U.S.S.R.)	25 July 1973	Orbit	Apparent success. Entered Mars orbit 12 Feb. 1974
Mars 6 (U.S.S.R.)	5 Aug. 1973	Landing	Radio signals from craft stopped seconds before landing, 12 May 1974
Mars 7 (U.S.S.R.)	9 Aug. 1973	Landing	Engine malfunction caused craft to miss planet 9 Mar. 1974
Viking 1 (U.S.)	20 Aug. 1975	Orbit/Landing	Success. Entered Mars orbit 19 June 1976. Lander reached surface 20 July 1976 on Chryse Planitia. Lander ceased operations Nov. 1982. Orbiter ceased 4 July 1980. Lander photographs: 2,450
Viking 2 (U.S.)	9 Sept. 1975	Orbit/Landing	Success. Entered Mars orbit 7 Aug. 1976. Lander reached surface 3 Sept. 1976 on Utopia Planitia. Lander ceased operations Mar. 1980. Orbiter ceased 24 July 1978. Lander photographs: 2,170. Total photographs from both Viking 1 and 2 orbiters: 51,500

SPACECRAFT	DATE LAUNCHED	OBJECTIVE	RESULTS
Phobos 1 (U.S.S.R.)	7 July 1988	Orbit Mars/Place instruments on Phobos	Failure. Loss of radio contact 1 Sept. 1988. Erroneous command from flight controllers caused craft to become disoriented, losing power from the Sun
Phobos 2 (U.S.S.R.)	12 July 1988	Orbit Mars/Place instruments on Phobos	Partly successful. Craft entered Mars orbit 29 Jan. 1989. Photography and scientific survey of Mars and the moon Phobos. On 27 Mar., prior to placement of instruments on Phobos, radio contact lost. On-board computer malfunction caused failure in orientation control, leading to energy exhaustion

Sources: Jet Propulsion Laboratory.
   Nicholas L. Johnson, *Handbook of Soviet Lunar and Planetary Exploration*. San
      Diego: American Astronautical Society, 1979.
   R. Z. Sagdeyev and A. V. Zakharov, "Brief History of the Phobos Mission." In
      Nature, 341, Oct. 19, 1989, pp. 581–85.

	MERCURY	VENUS	EARTH	MARS
Mean Distance from Sun (*Millions of Miles*)	36	67.1	92.9	141.5
Surface Gravity (*Earth = 1*)	.37	.88	1	.38
Equatorial Diameter (*Miles*)	3,031	7,521	7,926	4,221
Mass (*Earth = 1*)	0.055	0.814	1.000	0.107
Density (*Water = 1*)	5.43	5.24	5.52	3.93
Volume (*Earth = 1*)	0.06	0.86	1.00	0.15
Revolution around Sun	88 days	224.7 days	365.26 days	687 days
Rotation Period	58.65 days	243 days	23 hr 37 min 4 sec	24 hr 37 min 23 sec
Inclination of Orbit to Earth's Orbital Plane	7°	3.4°	0.0°	1.8°
Atmosphere	*Virtually none*	*Carbon dioxide*	*Nitrogen, oxygen*	*Carbon dioxide*
Number of Satellites	0	0	1	2

APPENDIX 2

THE SUN'S FAMILY

JUPITER	SATURN	URANUS	NEPTUNE	PLUTO
483.4	886.7	1,782.7	2,794.3	3,666.1
2.64	1.15	1.17	1.18	Undetermined
88,734	74,734	31,816	30,199	1,417
317.8	95.16	14.53	17.23	0.00216
1.33	0.71	0.233	0.297	0.368
1,323	752	62.4	57	0.0059
11.86 yr	29.46 yr	84.01 yr	164.8 yr	247.7 yr
9 hr 55 min 30 sec	10 hr 39 min 24 sec	17 hr 14 min	16 hr 3 min	6 days 9 hr 16.8 min
1.3°	2.5°	0.8°	1.8°	17.2°
Hydrogen, helium	*Hydrogen, helium*	*Hydrogen, helium, methane*	*Hydrogen, helium, methane, nitrogen*	*Methane*
15	17+	15	6	1

BIBLIOGRAPHY

The literature on Mars is vast. Numerous reports of recent scientific findings are buried in journals and special publications of the National Aeronautics and Space Administration. Much of the debate over space policy and goals, especially as it relates to Mars, is scattered in the pages of newspapers, magazines, and various government documents. But for an introduction to, and elaboration on, the many subjects and issues raised here, a few books can be recommended:

Beatty, J. Kelly, Brian O'Leary, and Andrew Chaikin, eds. *The New Solar System.* 2d ed. New York: Cambridge University Press, 1982. Chapters on Mars.

Boston, Penelope J., ed. *The Case for Mars.* San Diego: American Astronautical Society, 1984. Science and Technology Series, 57. Proceedings of a conference of the Mars Underground at Boulder, Colo., in 1981.

Bradbury, Ray, et al. *Mars and the Mind of Man.* New York: Harper & Row, 1973. From a symposium in November 1971 which was a forum for the contrasting views of Carl Sagan and Bruce C. Murray on the possibility of finding life on Mars, with the romantic excursions of Bradbury intermingled.

Burgess, Eric. *To the Red Planet.* New York: Columbia University Press, 1978. Account of the Viking spacecraft and missions.

Carr, Michael H. *The Surface of Mars.* New Haven: Yale University Press, 1981. Excellent summary of the geological findings of Viking, by a member of the mission science team.

Cooper, Henry S. F., Jr. *The Search for Life on Mars.* New York: Holt, Rinehart and Winston, 1980. Most of the book originally appeared in *The New Yorker.*

Ezell, Edward C., and Linda N. Ezell. *On Mars: Exploration of the Red Planet, 1958–1978.* Washington, D.C.: U.S. Government Printing Office, 1984. NASA SP-4212. A product of the NASA History Series, which is a thorough document of the Mariner and Viking missions to Mars.

Glasstone, Samuel. *The Book of Mars.* Washington, D.C.: U.S. Government Printing Office, 1968. NASA SP-179. Somewhat dated, but Chapter 2 is a good review of Mars in history.

Hartmann, William K., and Odell Raper. *The New Mars: The Discoveries of Mariner 9.* Washington, D.C.: U.S. Government Printing Office, 1974. NASA SP-337.

Horowitz, Norman H. *To Utopia and Back: The Search for Life in the Solar System.* New York: W. H. Freeman, 1986. The best book on the Viking search for life on Mars, by a leader of the biology research team.

Miles, Frank, and Nicholas Booth. *Race to Mars: The Harper & Row Mars Flight Atlas.* New York: Harper & Row, 1988. Concise, illustrated review of recent missions to Mars and future plans and possibilities.

McKay, Christopher P., ed. *The Case for Mars II.* San Diego: American Astronautical Society, 1985. Science and Technology Series, 62. Proceedings of another conference on Mars, in 1984, emphasizing technological requirements for human expeditions.

National Commission on Space. *Pioneering the Space Frontier.* New York: Bantam Books, 1986. Report of the commission headed by Thomas O. Paine. Profusely illustrated.

Reiber, Duke B., ed. *The NASA Mars Conference.* San Diego: American Astronautical Society, 1988. Science and Technology Series, 71. Proceedings of a conference in 1986. Includes summaries of previous mission results, plans for future unmanned flights, and scenarios for possible human expeditions.

Stoker, Carol, ed. *The Case for Mars III.* San Diego: American Astronautical Society, 1989. Science and Technology Series, 75. Proceedings of conference on Mars, 1987.

Washburn, Mark. *Mars at Last!* New York: Putnam, 1977.

I. THE ALLURE OF ANOTHER WORLD

Crowe, Michael J. *The Extraterrestrial Life Debate, 1750–1900: The Idea of a Plurality of Worlds from Kant to Lowell.* Cambridge, Eng.: Cambridge University Press, 1986. For history of the idea of life on other planets.

Ferris, Timothy. *Coming of Age in the Milky Way.* New York: Morrow, 1988. Early astronomy.

Glasstone, Samuel. *The Book of Mars.* Chapter 2.

Ley, Willy. *Mariner IV to Mars.* New York: Signet, 1966. Chapters 1 and 4 on Mars lore.

———— and Wernher von Braun. *The Exploration of Mars.* New York: Viking Press, 1956.

Sagan, Carl. *Broca's Brain.* New York: Random House, 1979. Chapter 16 on the "golden age" of planetary exploration.

———. *The Cosmic Connection: An Extraterrestrial Perspective.* Garden City, N.Y.: Doubleday, 1973. Chapter 9.

Wilford, John Noble. "Destination: Mars." In *The New York Times Magazine,* March 12, 1988.

2. LOWELL'S MARS

Anderson, John. "Planet X: Fact or Fiction?" In *Planetary Report,* 8, July–Aug. 1988.

Crowe, Michael J. *The Extraterrestrial Life Debate.*

Greenslet, Ferris. *The Lowells and Their Seven Worlds.* Boston: Houghton Mifflin, 1946.

Hoyt, William Graves. *Lowell and Mars.* Tucson: University of Arizona Press, 1976. Most thorough biography.

Lowell, Percival. *Mars.* Boston: Houghton Mifflin, 1895.

———. *Mars and Its Canals.* New York: Macmillan, 1906.

———. *Mars as the Abode of Life.* New York: Macmillan, 1908.

Malone, Dumas, ed. *Dictionary of American Biography.* New York: Scribners, 1933. Vol. 11, for biography of Lowell.

Sagan, Carl. *Broca's Brain.* For Lowell's influence on Goddard and planetary science.

Sinnott, Roger W. "Mars Mania of Oppositions Past." In *Sky and Telescope,* 76, Sept. 1988.

Trefil, James. "Phenomena, Comment and Notes." In *Smithsonian,* 18, Jan. 1988. A modern physicist's thoughts, inspired by Lowell, of how well modern ideas will survive.

Wallace, Alfred Russel. *Is Mars Habitable?* London: Macmillan, 1907.

3. THE MARTIANS ARE COMING!

Barron, James. "Celebrating the Day the Martians Came." In *The New York Times,* Sept. 16, 1988.

Bradbury, Ray. *The Martian Chronicles.* Garden City, N.Y.: Doubleday, 1950.

——— et al. *Mars and the Mind of Man.*

Cantril, Hadley. *The Invasion from Mars: A Study of the Psychology of Panic.* Princeton: Princeton University Press, 1940. Complete script of the broadcast, as well as the reaction.

Dunning, John. *Tune in Yesterday: The Ultimate Encyclopedia of Old-Time Radio, 1925–1976.* Englewood Cliffs, N.J.: Prentice-Hall, 1976.

Higham, Charles. *Orson Welles: The Rise and Fall of an American Genius.* New York: St. Martin's Press, 1985.

Jackson, Charles. "The Night the Martians Came." In Isabel Leighton, ed., *The Aspirin Age*. New York: Simon & Schuster, 1949.

Klass, Philip. "Wells, Welles, and the Martians." In *The New York Times Book Review*, Oct. 30, 1988.

Washburn, Mark. *Mars at Last!*

West, Anthony. *H. G. Wells: Aspects of a Life*. New York: Random House, 1984.

4 . FIRST ENCOUNTERS

Bradbury, Ray, et al. *Mars and the Mind of Man*. Especially for the views of Bruce Murray.

Carr, Michael H. "Mars: The Red Planet." In Byron Preiss, ed. *The Planets*. New York: Bantam Books, 1985.

Chapman, Clark. *Planets of Rock and Ice*. New York: Scribners, 1982. Good chapter on new discoveries of Mars.

Ezell, Edward C., and Linda N. Ezell. *On Mars*.

Hartmann, William K., and Odell Raper. *The New Mars*.

Horowitz, Norman H. *To Utopia and Back*.

Kellogg, W. W., and Carl Sagan. *The Atmospheres of Mars and Venus*. Washington, D.C.: National Academy of Sciences–National Research Council, 1961. Space Science Board report.

Murray, Bruce C. "Mars from Mariner 9." In *Scientific American*, 228, Jan. 1973.

Mutch, Thomas A., et al. *The Geology of Mars*. Princeton: Princeton University Press, 1976.

National Aeronautics and Space Administration. *Mars as Viewed by Mariner 9*. Washington, D.C.: U.S. Government Printing Office, 1974. NASA SP-329.

Sinnott, Roger W. "Mars Mania of Oppositions Past."

5 . THE MOONS OF MARS

Ashbrook, Joseph. *The Astronomical Scrapbook: Skywatchers, Pioneers, and Seekers in Astronomy*. Cambridge, Mass.: Sky Publishing Co., 1986. Section 57 on Asaph Hall.

Dick, Steven J. "Discovering the Moons of Mars." In *Sky and Telescope*, 76, Sept. 1988.

Hall, Asaph. "The Discovery of the Satellites of Mars." Royal Astronomical Society *Monthly Notes*, 3, Feb. 1878.

Ley, Willy, *Mariner IV to Mars*. Chapter 6 on the moons.

Moore, Patrick. *Guide to Mars*. New York: Norton, 1977. Chapter 13 on Phobos and Deimos.

Oberg, James. "Phobos and Deimos." In *Astronomy*, 5, March 1977.

Sagan, Carl. *The Cosmic Connection*. Chapter 15.

Saint-Exupéry, Antoine de. *The Little Prince.* New York: Harcourt, Brace & World, 1943.
Whipple, Fred L. *Orbiting the Sun.* Cambridge, Mass.: Harvard University Press, 1981. For theories of the Moon's origin.

6. VIKING AND THE SEARCH FOR LIFE

Beatty, J. Kelly, et al., eds. *The New Solar System.* Chapter 9 on "Life on Mars?" by Gerald A. Soffen.
Chandler, David L. "Life on Mars." In *Atlantic,* 242, June 1977.
Cooper, Henry S. F., Jr. *The Search for Life on Mars.*
Ezell, Edward C., and Linda N. Ezell. *On Mars.*
French, Bevan M. *Mars: The Viking Discoveries.* Washington, D.C.: U.S. Government Printing Office, 1977. NASA SP-146.
Goldsmith, Donald, and Tobias Owen. *The Search for Life in the Universe.* Menlo Park, Calif.: Benjamin-Cummings, 1980. Chapters 14 and 16.
Gore, Rick. "Sifting for Life in the Sands of Mars." In *National Geographic,* 151, Jan. 1977.
Horowitz, Norman H. *To Utopia and Back.*
Metz, William D. "Viking: End of the First Phase of 70's Space Spectacular." In *Science,* 194, Nov. 19, 1976.
Mutch, Thomas A. *The Martian Landscape.* Washington, D.C.: U.S. Government Printing Office, 1978. NASA SP-425. Excellent Viking landing photography, with commentary.
National Aeronautics and Space Administration. *Viking 1 Early Results.* Washington, D.C.: U.S. Government Printing Office, 1976. NASA SP-408.
Whipple, Fred L. *Orbiting the Sun.* Chapter 11.

7. AN INVENTORY OF KNOWLEDGE — AND QUESTIONS

Arvidson, Raymond E., A. B. Binder, and K. C. Jones. "The Surface of Mars." In *Scientific American,* 238, May 1978.
Baker, Victor R. *The Channels of Mars.* Austin: University of Texas Press, 1982.
Carr, Michael H. "Mars: The Red Planet."
———. *The Surface of Mars.*
Carroll, Michael. "Digging Deeper for Life on Mars." In *Astronomy,* 16, April 1988.
Horowitz, Norman. "The Search for Life on Mars." In *Scientific American,* 237, Nov. 1977.
Leovy, Conway. "The Atmosphere of Mars." In *Scientific American,* 237, July 1977.
Mutch, Thomas A. *The Martian Landscape.*
Reiber, Duke B., ed. *The NASA Mars Conference.* Several good summary papers on Mariner and Viking results.

Snyder, Conway W. "The Planet Mars as Seen at the End of the Viking Mission." In *Journal of Geophysical Research*, 84, Dec. 30, 1979. Issue includes other reports on Viking results.

8. THE RUSSIANS ARE GOING

Banks, Peter M., and Sally K. Ride. "Soviets in Space." In *Scientific American*, 260, Feb. 1989.

Chernyshov, Mikhail. "Post-Mortem on Failure." In *Nature*, 339, May 4, 1989. Aftermath of Phobos mission failures.

Clarke, Phillip. *The Soviet Manned Space Program.* New York: Orion, 1988.

Connor, Steve. "Perestroika and the Phobos Factor." In *New Scientist*, 122, April 22, 1989.

Covault, Craig. "Perestroika in Space, Science Commitment by Soviet Officials." In *Aviation Week & Space Technology*, 129, Dec. 12, 1988.

———. "Soviets Study Mars Return Vehicles, Mission to Saturn." In *Aviation Week & Space Technology*, 129, Feb. 29, 1988.

Johnson, Nicholas L. *The Soviet Year in Space: 1988.* Colorado Springs: Teledyne Brown Engineering Co., 1989.

Lenorowitz, Jeffrey M. "Launch of Two Phobos Spacecraft Begins Ambitious Mission to Mars." In *Aviation Week & Space Technology*, 129, July 18, 1988.

———. "Soviets Plan Medium-Duration Missions on Board Mir This Year." In *Aviation Week & Space Technology*, 130, Jan. 9, 1989.

Murray, Bruce C. "Members' Dialogue." In *Planetary Report*, 9, July–Aug. 1989. Weaknesses of Soviet space management exposed by Phobos failures.

Sagdeyev, Roald Z. "Science and Perestroika: A Long Way to Go." In *Issues in Science and Technology*, 4, Summer 1988.

Sawyer, Kathy. "The Soviet Union's Paradoxical Space Program." In *The Washington Post*, Jan. 1, 1988.

Zakharov, Aleksandr V. "Close Encounters with Phobos." In *Sky and Telescope*, 76, July 1988.

Soviet scientists and officials were much in evidence at two international meetings in 1987. Transcripts of the "Spacebridge Meeting," on July 18, 1987, were made by the Planetary Society, Pasadena, Calif., sponsor of the American-Soviet teleconference that included Valery Barsukov. Another dialogue occurred at the American Institute of Aeronautics and Astronautics/Jet Propulsion Laboratory International Solar System Exploration Conference, Pasadena, May 1987.

9. AMERICAN INDECISION

Chaikin, Andrew. "Why Haven't We Gone Back?" In *Air and Space*, 4, June–July 1989. Entire issue devoted to articles related to 20th anniversary of the Apollo 11 landing on the Moon.

Kraft, Christopher C. "Space Flight: One of Man's Most Challenging Adventures." In *Earth '88: Changing Geographic Perspectives*. Washington, D.C.: National Geographic Society, 1988.

Logsdon, John M. "Resist the Pull of Mars." In *Air and Space*, 3, April–May 1988.

——— and Ray A. Williamson. "U.S. Access to Space." In *Scientific American*, 260, March 1989.

Matsunaga, Spark M. *The Mars Project: Journeys Beyond the Cold War*. New York: Hill and Wang, 1986.

McDougall, Walter A. *The Heavens and the Earth: A Political History of the Space Age*. New York: Basic Books, 1985.

Murray, Bruce C. *Journey into Space: The First Thirty Years of Space Exploration*. New York: Norton, 1989.

———. "Whither America in Space?" In *Issues in Science and Technology*, 2, Spring 1986.

National Commission on Space. *Pioneering the Space Frontier*.

Ride, Sally K. *Leadership and America's Future in Space*. Task force report to NASA administrator, Aug. 1987.

Wasserburg, Gerald J. "Exploring the Planets: A Strategic but Practical Proposal." In *Issues in Science and Technology*, 2, Fall 1986.

Wilford, John Noble. "America's Future after the Challenger." In *The New York Times Magazine*, March 16, 1986.

———. "Budget for the Space Agency Sets a Broader Course in Exploration." In *The New York Times*, Feb. 2, 1990.

———. "The Allure of Mars Grows as U.S. Searches for New National Goal." In *The New York Times*, March 24, 1987.

10. TOGETHER TO MARS

"The Gorbachev Interview: Transcript of the Face-to-Face Meeting." In *The Washington Post*, May 22, 1988.

Logsdon, John M. "Leading Through Cooperation." In *Issues in Science and Technology*, 4, Summer 1988.

McLucas, John L., and Burton I. Edelson. "Let's Go to Mars Together." In *Issues in Science and Technology*, 4, Fall 1988.

Murray, Bruce C. *Journey into Space*.

Sagan, Carl. "It's Time to Go to Mars." In *The New York Times*, Jan. 23, 1987.

———. "Let's Go to Mars Together." In *Planetary Report*, 6, July–Aug. 1986.

Excerpted from an article that appeared in the Feb. 2, 1986, issue of *Parade* magazine.

Wasserburg, Gerald J. "Exploring the Planets: A Strategic but Practical Proposal."

Wilford, John Noble. "As Mars Beckons, U.S. Is Wary and Indecisive." In *The New York Times,* Oct. 13, 1987.

II. PREPARING TO GO

Collins, Michael. "Mission to Mars." In *National Geographic,* 174, Nov. 1988.

French, J. R., "Aerobraking and Aerocapture for Mars Missions." In Penelope J. Boston, ed., *The Case for Mars.*

Koppes, Clayton R. *JPL and the American Space Program.* New Haven: Yale University Press, 1982.

McKay, Christopher P., ed. *The Case for Mars II.*

National Aeronautics and Space Administration. "A Preliminary Study of Mars Rover/Sample Return Missions." Jan. 1987 Report by Mars Study Team of NASA's Solar System Exploration Division, Washington, D.C.

Reiber, Duke B., ed. *The NASA Mars Conference.*

Ride, Sally K. *Leadership and America's Future in Space.*

Shipman, Harry L. *Humans in Space: 21st Century Frontier.* New York: Plenum, 1989.

Wilford, John Noble. "Soviet and U.S. Scientists Join in Quest to Select Sites for Mars Landing." In *The New York Times,* April 5, 1988.

12. WAYS TO GO

Aldrin, Buzz, and Malcolm McConnell. *Men from Earth.* New York: Bantam Books, 1989.

Collins, Michael. "Mission to Mars."

Covault, Craig. "NASA Accelerates Lunar Base, Mars Studies for Input to New Administration." In *Aviation Week & Space Technology,* 129, Nov. 28, 1988.

Miles, Frank, and Nicholas Booth. *Race to Mars: The Harper & Row Mars Flight Atlas.*

National Aeronautics and Space Administration. *Beyond Earth's Boundaries: Human Exploration of the Solar System in the 21st Century.* 1988 report of the NASA Office of Exploration, including case studies of various Moon and Mars exploration scenarios.

National Commission on Space. *Pioneering the Space Frontier.*

Niehoff, John C. "Pathways to Mars: New Opportunities." In Duke B. Reiber, ed., *The NASA Mars Conference.*

O'Leary, Brian. *Mars 1999.* Harrisburg, Pa.: Stackpole Books, 1987.

Ride, Sally K. *Leadership and America's Future in Space.*

13. BECOMING MARTIANS

Averner, Melvin M., and Robert D. MacElroy, eds. *On the Habitability of Mars: An Approach to Planetary Ecosynthesis.* Springfield, Va.: National Technical Information Service, 1976. NASA SP-414.

Boston, Penelope J., ed. *The Case for Mars.*

Broad, William J. "Ultimate Survival: Desert Dreamers Build a Man-made World." In *The New York Times,* May 27, 1986.

Davis, Bob. "Mars Could Become the Place to Live, But It Needs Work." In *The Wall Street Journal,* Jan. 5, 1989.

Dyson, Freeman J. *Infinite in All Directions.* New York: Harper & Row, 1988.

McKay, Christopher P. "Living and Working on Mars." In Duke B. Reiber, ed. *The NASA Mars Conference.*

National Commission on Space. *Pioneering the Space Frontier.*

Oberg, James E. *Mission to Mars.* New York: New American Library, 1982. Chapter 13 on terraforming.

———. *New Earths: Restructuring Earth and Other Planets.* Harrisburg, Pa.: Stackpole Books, 1981.

Paine, Thomas O. "A Timeline for Martian Pioneers." In Christopher P. McKay, ed. *The Case for Mars II.* Also several reports on utilizing Martian resources.

Pennisi, Elizabeth. "The Making of Biosphere II." In *Science Year 1989.* Chicago: World Book, 1988.

Robinson, Arthur L. "Colonizing Mars: The Age of Planetary Engineering Begins." In *Science,* 195, Feb. 18, 1977.

14. DESTINY

Boorstin, Daniel J. *The Discoverers.* New York: Random House, 1983. Chapter 26.

Dyson, Freeman J. *Infinite in All Directions.* Chapters 7 and 16.

Eiseley, Loren. *The Invisible Pyramid.* New York: Scribners, 1970.

Goetzmann, William. *New Lands, New Men.* New York: Viking, 1986.

Pyne, Stephen J. "A Third Great Age of Discovery." Unpublished lecture, delivered at George Washington University, Dec. 1987. His ideas are also developed in Pyne, *The Ice: A Journey to Antarctica.* Iowa City: University of Iowa Press, 1986.

Tsiolkovsky, Konstantin E. *Dreams of Earth and Sky.* Ed. B. N. Vorobyeva. Moscow: U.S.S.R. Academy of Sciences, 1959. For summary of Tsiolkovsky's contributions to space flight, see Wernher von Braun and Frederick I. Ordway III, *History of Rocketry and Space Travel.* New York: Crowell, 1966. Chapter 3.

ACKNOWLEDGMENTS

An idea has been orbiting the neurons of my mind since that long night in the summer of 1965 that I spent writing a cover story for *Time* magazine. The subject was Mariner 4's flyby of Mars. By dawn, the manuscript completed, I tried to get some sleep on an office couch. But my thoughts left me wide-eyed with excitement. I had come to a realization: Seeing Mars up close, going to the planets, this is the exploration of our time. The thought has been with me ever since, a perspective inspiring and guiding much of my career as a journalist.

More specifically, the idea for this book took root when, many years later, I wrote another article on Mars, this time for *The New York Times Magazine*. The magazine's editor, James Greenfield, was enthusiastic and encouraging (we had conspired on a Loch Ness caper years before). I began to see before me the outline for a book—and the need for it. Much has been written about Mars, but no single book has fully addressed all aspects presented here: the history of human fascination with Mars, past and present attempts to explore the planet, and the prospects and arguments for future human ventures to Mars.

In writing this book and reporting on the exploration of all the planets, my debt is great to many people at the California Institute of Technology and the Jet Propulsion Laboratory. Pasadena has become one of my professional hometowns. It was there that I got to know Thomas A. Mutch, of Brown University, who was the chief geologist on the Viking missions. We shared an enthusiasm for exploration and its latest manifestation, which centered on Mars. We all miss Tim.

This book is informed by the writings of many people who have been involved in Mars exploration and by interviews with many of them: Bruce Murray, Carl Sagan, Norman Horowitz, Harold Klein, Gerald Soffen, Arden Albee, Michael Duke, Michael Carr, James W. Head III, Gerald Wasserburg, David Pieri, Christopher McKay, Donna Pivirotto, Donald Rea, Roger Bourke, James Burke, Ronald Greeley, Roald Z. Sagdeyev, Valery L. Barsukov, Sam W. Keller, Sally K. Ride, James C. Fletcher, Noel E. Hinners, Bradford Smith, Raymond Arvidson, John M. Logsdon, Lew Allen, and Thomas O. Paine.

At the Jet Propulsion Laboratory, I was assisted in many ways by Frank Colella, Frank Bristow, George Alexander, Robert MacMillin, Mary Beth Murrill, Don Bane, Alan Wood, Jim Doyle, Jim Wilson, Franklin O'Donnell, and Jurrie van der Woude. They are special people.

Richard Flaste, an editor at *The New York Times*, has been especially helpful, encouraging me to undertake the book, reviewing many of the chapters, and handling arrangements for most of the illustrations.

My wife, Nancy, has seen me through journeys to the Moon, the mapping of Earth, and investigations of the late great dinosaurs. Now she has freely given her invaluable support as I responded to the beckoning Mars. I could not wish for a better companion.

INDEX

Note: Page numbers in *italics* refer to illustrations.

Index

A NOTE ABOUT THE AUTHOR

John Noble Wilford is a science correspondent for *The New York Times*. He won the 1983 American Association for the Advancement of Science/Westinghouse science-writing award and two Pulitzer Prizes—one in 1984 for his reporting of space and science and the other in 1987 as a member of the *Times* team reporting on the aftermath of the Challenger accident. He was a Visiting Journalist at Duke University in 1984, the McGraw Lecturer at Princeton University in 1985, and Professor of Science Journalism at the University of Tennessee in 1989–90. He has worked for *The Wall Street Journal*, *Time* magazine, and, since 1965, the *Times*. He is the author of *We Reach the Moon* (1969), *The Mapmakers* (1981), and *The Riddle of the Dinosaur* (1985), co-author of *Spaceliner* (1981) and *The New York Times Guide to the Return of Halley's Comet* (1985), and editor of *Scientists at Work* (1979).

A NOTE ON THE TYPE

This book was set in Janson. The hot-metal version of Janson
was a recutting made direct from type cast from matrices long
thought to have been made by the Dutchman Anton Janson,
who was a practicing type founder in Leipzig during the years
1668–1687. However, it has been conclusively demonstrated that
these types are actually the work of Nicholas Kis (1650–1702), a
Hungarian, who most probably learned his trade from the
master Dutch type founder Dirk Voskens. The type is an
excellent example of the influential and sturdy Dutch types
that prevailed in England up to the time William Caslon
(1692–1766) developed his own incomparable designs from them.

Composed by ComCom, a division of The Haddon Craftsmen,
Inc., Allentown, Pennsylvania
Printed and bound by Courier Companies, Inc.,
Westford, Massachusetts
Designed by Valarie J. Astor

	DATE DUE	